# Middle Office
# Managing Financial Institutions in Turbulent Times

2nd Edition

Essays by Philip Lawton

Art by John Rubino

ISBN:
978-1983934438

ISBN-10:
1983934437

To my grandchildren, Fin and Annabelle

# Table of Contents

# Preface to the Second Edition

Why, after all, publish in January 2018 a second edition of a book about managing financial institutions in turbulent times? The global financial crisis ended in 2009, and, while the first few years were mighty hard, the U.S. economy has surely recovered. Inflation remains moderate. Interest rates are low, and even under new leadership the Fed is almost certain to raise them judiciously and at a measured pace. Corporate profitability has been robust, and last month Congress passed a new tax regime that is highly favorable to corporations and partnerships. The price level of the domestic stock market, as measured by the S&P 500 Index, has risen from 700.82 on March 2, 2009, to 2,684.57 as of year-end 2017, a bull market that has already lasted almost a decade. The 10-year total return is a very respectable 8.5%, and the total return for the year just ended was, incredibly, 21.83%. The Shiller PE ratio stands at 36.25, far above its 137-year average of 16.81 but still below the historical high of 44.19 recorded on the eve of the dot-com bust. Turbulent times? Not at all, not, at least, for the economy and the capital markets. They're just humming along. These are the good times. Never mind that, at this valuation level, expected returns are modest....

Knock wood.

The global financial system is exposed to exogenous shocks of a nature that we have not seriously contemplated since the end of the Cold War. Under the current president, the United States has abandoned its progressive diplomatic leadership of the postwar international order, encouraging Russian belligerence and Chinese expansion. North Korea openly threatens to cry havoc and launch nuclear-tipped missiles at the U.S., its possessions, and its ally, Japan, whose people will never forget their experience of fire and fury in August 1945. Iran is, at this writing, beset by a populist uprising which may induce the ayatollah to seek internal unity by initiating hostilities with Israel as a proxy war against the great Satan. Inflamed by third-world and Latin American immigration, right-wing nationalist and white supremacist movements have cropped up across the West, even in my beloved city of Charlottesville, Virginia. The left, historically the champion of labor, has long since defaulted to identity politics holding that we cannot even discuss our differences, let alone empathize with one another. Later this year, evidently none the wiser, we will pause to celebrate the centenary of the armistice. And, while the aging American leisure class somnambulates through antique shops and dozes through symphonies, the administration resolutely undoes financial regulations designed to reduce systemic risk.

Going on 10 years, this bull market has been running so long that bank managers may once again have been lulled into thinking that model risk is merely academic.[1] And yet another generation of up-and-coming investment professionals has experienced volatility as nothing more than interesting variability around a smartly rising trend line. Let me suggest that, although it's smooth sailing now, financial turbulence is not behind us for good.

New to the second edition is Part One, Investment Thinking, which opens with a previously unpublished essay ("Do Premises Produce Profits?"). The same section additionally includes five pieces I wrote while employed from 2013 through 2015 by Research Affiliates, LLC, a quantitatively oriented firm headquartered in southern California that revolutionized the financial services industry as a leader in smart beta investing.[2] The following four essays are reprinted here by kind permission of Research Affiliates: "Calling the Turns: Why Market Timing Is So Hard;" "Pricing Fine Wines and Common Stocks;" "The Psychology of Contrarian Investing;" and "Searching for a New Investment Paradigm." The fifth, "The Valuation Puzzle," was written in the same happy period (and admittedly presents some of the same ideas, albeit from a different angle). I also moved "Back to the Basics: Value and Growth Investing" from the back of this volume to Part One. I think it deserves to be kept, but I acknowledge that it does not reflect the well-established research on factor investing that I came to appreciate while on the West coast, and I must avow that I would qualify its anodyne conclusion today.

---

[1] See Philip Lawton and Jonathan Leonardelli, "Managing Model Risk," Financial Risk Group (April 2017). Accessed January 6, 2018 at https://www.frgrisk.com/managing-model-risk/.

[2] In brief, smart beta may be described as a third approach beyond the previous alternatives of active investing, with its high fees and generally disappointing results, and capitalization-weighted passive investing, with its ineluctable exposure to herd behavior. Inherently contrarian, rules-based smart beta strategies break the link between security prices and portfolio weights. They offer the potential outperformance of active management while preserving desirable qualities of conventional indexing, such as transparency, liquidity, and relatively low implementation costs.

The first edition rested upon a fairly expansive concept of the middle office, including regulatory compliance as well as risk management, performance evaluation, and client reporting. Even by this liberal definition, however, the addition of a section on investment thinking takes this work into a somewhat wider field of inquiry. Nonetheless, I wrote in the Introduction that the middle office is staffed by professionals who support the firm's internal decision-making processes, and it seems obvious that they can be fully effective only if they understand investment as well as business strategies.

Also new to this edition are six pieces that I wrote after *Middle Office* first appeared but before I joined Research Affiliates. Four of them are presented at the head of Part Two: "The Motivation to Work," "Smarts," "Speed Bumps," and "The Sociology of Morality." One, called "Assessing the Cost of Basel III," opens Part Three, and the other, "Real Risk," is at the top of Part Four. With a few minor exceptions, these essays are published as written. In "The Motivation to Work," for instance, I have added to an existing footnote some new remarks on the likely employment impact of artificial intelligence.

I have excised a few pieces that were too slight to retain in this edition.

Thanks largely to my colleagues at Research Affiliates, the past five years have been a period of intense intellectual growth for me. Rob Arnott is a world-class thinker and a model of conscious leadership. Michael Aked, Tzee Chow, Jason Hsu, Vitali Kalesnik, Engin Kose, Feifei Li, Michele Mazzoleni, Katy Sherrerd, Jonathan Treussard, and others challenged me every day; in semi-retirement I continue to work with some of them. And, in that heady environment, Jaynee Dudley's gentle forbearance and sound priorities kept my feet on the ground. It was one of the most rewarding experiences of my career, matched for personal development only by my apprenticeship with Tom Messmore at The Travelers way back in the 1980s and my partnership with Holly Miller at Stone House Consulting during the great recession.

All that being said, the opinions expressed in these pages are entirely my own, just as I alone am responsible for any factual errors or editorial lapses.

Philip Lawton
Keswick, Virginia
January 16, 2018

## Introduction

Every age has its problems, but managing banks, investment firms, and broker-dealers may never have been more challenging. The short essays collected here represent an unsystematic attempt to clarify some of the issues and, occasionally, to indicate lines of thought that seem promising.

The present volume contains most of the posts on leadership, regulatory compliance, risk management, and investment performance measurement that have appeared to date in a WordPress blog called, simply, *Middle Office*. Over the period in which these pieces were composed, we witnessed a series of untoward and rather unnerving events at well-known financial institutions: MF Global failed and clients' funds went missing; a rogue trader was found out at UBS; JPMorgan Chase sustained huge losses in derivatives; Barclays and others were accused of falsifying LIBOR; Peregrine Financial entered bankruptcy amid charges of fraud; HSBC allegedly laundered money for drug cartels and dealt with firms linked to terrorism; and Knight Capital lost control of a high-frequency trading algorithm.[1]

Such occurrences—for the most part ethical lapses and operational breakdowns—raise pressing questions for regulators, boards, and senior management. Directors and officers are primarily concerned about their own organization's culture and internal controls, while regulatory authorities are additionally worried about resultant threats to the complex, fragile, jerrybuilt financial system. Work in the financial services industry can still be exhilarating, especially for individual contributors who don't have managerial or supervisory responsibilities, but there is an abiding disquiet in what one political scientist calls "these days of late capitalism."[2]

Given the complexity of large organizations, their entanglement with financial market utilities and one another, the sophistication of investment strategies, and the sheer volume and velocity of transactions, the managers of financial institutions find themselves under unremitting pressure. Tolstoy's description of a military commander's situation in wartime is apposite: "Moment by moment the event is imperceptibly shaping itself, and at every moment of this continuous, uninterrupted

---

[1] On the Knight Capital fiasco, see "Friendly Fire," below.
[2] Thomas L. Dumm, *Loneliness as a Way of Life* (Harvard University Press, 2008), 70.

shaping of events the commander in chief is in the midst of a most complex play of intrigues, worries, contingencies, authorities, projects, counsels, threats, and deceptions and is continually obliged to reply to innumerable questions addressed to him, which constantly conflict with one another."[3] Many executives at financial institutions are similarly beleaguered.

Tolstoy rejected the idea that exceptional leaders initiate and direct historical movements; he even repudiated the retrospective simplification that outcomes are traceable to commanders' battlefield orders. The "great illusion" his work attempts to debunk is "that individuals can, by the use of their own resources, understand and control the course of events."[4]

For my part, I don't think the C-suite is powerless to anticipate events, develop contingency plans, and execute them swiftly when necessary. But the nature of effective leadership in knowledge-based organizations is indubitably changing. In times like these, managing financial institutions means achieving genuine cooperation and probing the insights of people throughout the organization. I would like to suggest that the middle office is especially well-positioned to frame the issues, ferret out and analyze whatever information is available, and engage internal problem-solving resources wherever they are to be found.

A few words about the nebulous term "middle office" are in order. Some companies have placed risk management and investment performance measurement in the same chain of command, but to my knowledge none has a division or a department called the middle office. It is a concept, not an organizational reality, and an ill-defined concept at that. One might simply say that the middle office includes those functions that belong neither to the client-facing front office nor to the purely operational back office, but "front office" and "back office" are also rather imprecise designations that don't appear on organization charts. It seems more fruitful to suggest that the middle office is staffed by professionals whose responsibilities importantly include supporting the firm's internal decision-making processes.

---

[3] Leo Tolstoy, *War and Peace*, 2nd edition, edited by George Gibian (W.W. Norton, 1996), Book XI, Chapter 2, 735.
[4] Isaiah Berlin, *The Hedgehog and the Fox: An Essay on Tolstoy's View of History* (Elephant Paperbacks, 1993), Kindle edition.

Of course, this approach is also problematic. For example, decisions on portfolio construction and capital structure are supported, respectively, by security analysts and financial accountants, but the former would generally be considered front office employees, and the latter conventionally belong to the back office. Nonetheless, the suggested angle does, I think, capture a significant dimension of the value added by the middle office.

Risk managers and performance analysts are habitués, but compliance officers may be surprised to see themselves assigned to the middle office. Largely due to the worldwide wave of regulatory reform, however, both the pace and the nature of their work are changing. Staying abreast of developments, planning for new requirements, and monitoring compliance have acquired new urgency; in fact, these relentless demands have made the compliance officer's job exceedingly stressful. (In the U.S., compliance officers also face the possibility of being deemed supervisors personally subject to legal liability.)[5] In addition, it's progressively insufficient "merely" to know the many intricate laws, rules, and regulations pertaining to diverse businesses in multiple jurisdictions. If compliance officers are to certify the firm's compliance with applicable legal and regulatory requirements,[6] they may also have to extend their knowledge of the capital markets, investment strategies and instruments, quantitative methods, payment and settlement systems, custody, and investment operations.

Compliance officers add value by helping the firm maintain internal controls, uphold its reputation, and make sound decisions about business

---

[5] Bruce Carton, "Stressed-Out Compliance Officers May Soon Feel Even More Heat From SEC," *Compliance Week*, February 8, 2012. Accessed August 9, 2012. http://www.complianceweek.com/stressed-out-compliance-officers-may-soon-feel-even-more-heat-from-sec/article/226976/

[6] For example, The U.S. Commodity Futures Trading Commission (CFTC) notes, "The Dodd-Frank Act requires that the chief compliance officer of a swap dealer or major swap participant annually prepare, sign, and certify a report containing a description of the registrant's compliance with the CEA [Commodity Exchange Act] and regulations promulgated under the CEA....The report would include a certification by the chief compliance officer that, under penalty of law, the annual report is accurate and complete." CFTC, "Designation of a Chief Compliance Officer; Required Compliance Policies; and Annual Report of a Futures Commission Merchant, Swap Dealer, or Major Swap Participant," 75 FR 70881 (2010). Accessed August 9, 2012. http://www.cftc.gov/LawRegulation/FederalRegister/ProposedRules/2010-29021

strategies such as entering a new market or designing a new product. With due regard to potential conflicts of interest, compliance officers should not be kept in isolation and consulted at the last minute; rather, they should be viewed as a specialized resource for decision-makers at the holding company, subsidiary, and business line levels. Compliance officers arguably belong to the theoretical middle office. Far from demoting them,[7] this view accentuates their potential contribution to effective management.

Risk management is everybody's responsibility, as Thomas S. Coleman compellingly argues,[8] but the professional risk managers in the middle office have a distinctive role, one that calls upon them to engage both sides of the brain. Monitoring actual risk exposures in view of established limits requires systematic thinking and, as a rule, the application of advanced quantitative modeling techniques to derive key measures from rivers of white-water data. But looking ahead, sensing change, visualizing extreme developments, and perceiving remote dependencies—all those activities that fall under scenario forecasting and enable the organization to plan for contingencies—require imagination, intuition, and creativity, as well as continually refreshed awareness that assumptions are doubtful, models imperfect, data incomplete, and events, at the limit, unpredictable. Risk management is an artful discipline.

Investment performance measurement and client reporting sometimes seem to be regarded as little more than a necessary cost of doing business.[9] This view, however, discounts their potential contributions to effective firm management. Performance analysts are uniquely situated, trained, and equipped to present portfolio characteristics, *ex post* risk metrics, and attribution analyses that differentiate the effects of market conditions and portfolio decisions. They can, accordingly, help the organization evaluate the execution of investment strategies and judiciously refine the managerial process. Superior client reporting does

---

[7] As a matter of corporate governance, the Chief Compliance Officer should report directly to the board of directors or the Chief Executive Officer.
[8] "In the financial industry probably more than any other, risk management must be a central responsibility for line managers from the board and CEO down through individual trading units and portfolio managers." Thomas S. Coleman, *A Practical Guide to Risk Management*, The Research Foundation of CFA Institute, 2011, 1.
[9] Philip Lawton, "On the Road: Performance Measurement Today," Investment Performance Measurement Newsletter (CFA Institute, 2010). Accessed August 18, 2012. http://www.cfapubs.org/doi/full/10.2469/ipmn.v2010.n2.4

not support internal decision-making in the same way, but it contributes to sound client relations by enabling the front office to explain investment results clearly, accurately, and insightfully. Leading firms recognize that excellence in performance measurement and client reporting is a competitive advantage.

It is a privilege to show John Rubino's photographs of the sculptures in his five-piece series, *Anatomy of a Calamity*, on the cover (which he also designed) and at the start of each section. At each stage—complacency, calamity, reaction, recovery, and serenity—John powerfully communicates the experience of a trauma victim. His premise is, "Most catastrophic events, whether they be severe illness, accident, natural disaster, personal assault, or other traumatic event all follow a similar path as the survivor passes through life from before the incident, through the calamity, recovery, and a final re-definition of self." This extraordinary work of art may speak to all those who have lived through a takeover, a bankruptcy, or a financial, operational, or reputational risk event that threatened their firm's viability.

The lightly-edited short essays presented in this book are the product of my experience, reading, and interaction with far too many fine minds to name individually. I would, however, like to mention Stephen Campisi, Alex Dali, Jean Eaglesham, Russ Glisker, Stefan J. Illmer, Andre Mirabelli, Wes Morgan, Yogesh Ranganath, Ioannis Segounis, John D. Simpson, David Spaulding, Andreas Steiner, and Seth Wood, all of whom commented thoughtfully on various *Middle Office* blog pieces. I am especially indebted to Lee Buttles for stimulating conversations touching a wide range of topics over meals and on the road between Charlottesville and Richmond. Steve Shisko gave me solid legal advice; he is a serious advocate with a ready wit. As she always has done, my wife, Dena, sustained the conditions in which reading, thinking, and writing are possible, and she put up with my working all hours. I am solely responsible for any errors that survived the editorial process.

Finally, it makes me smile that the final piece in this collection ends with the word "but." There's always more that needs to be said.

Philip Lawton
Keswick, Virginia
September 3, 2012

# Part One: Investment Thinking

## Anatomy of a Calamity, Stage 1: "Complacency"

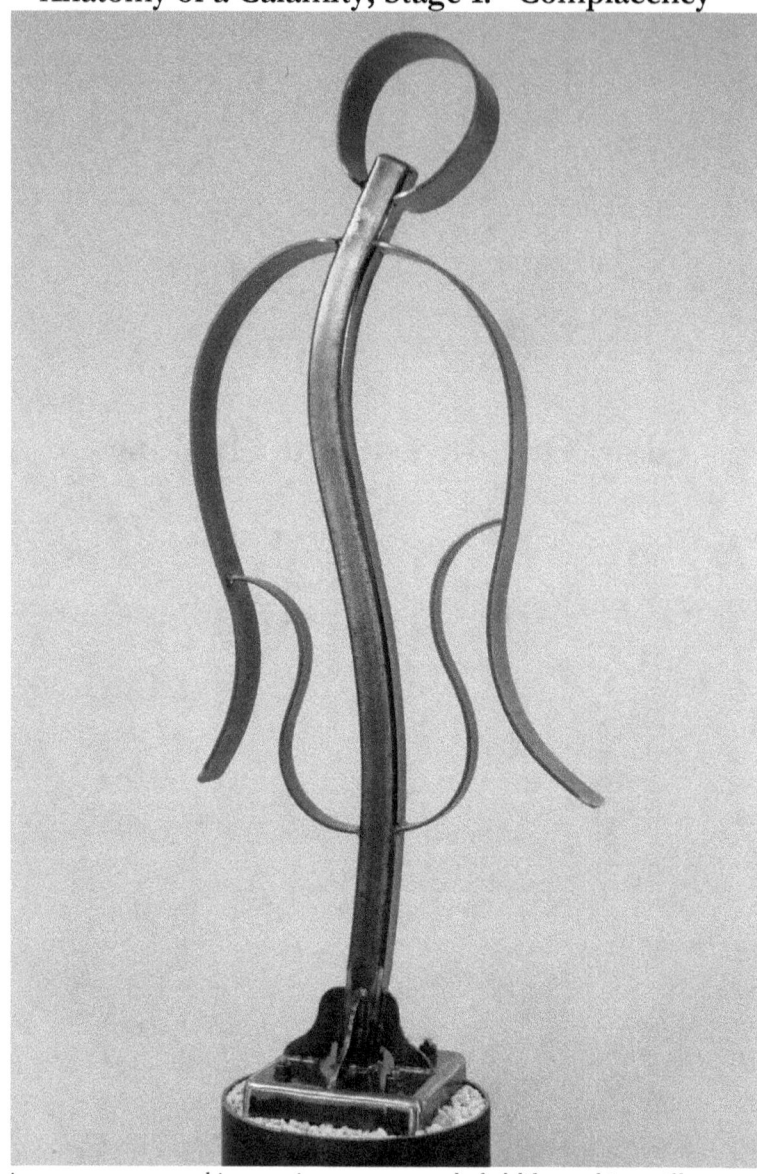

*Prior to any catastrophic experience most people feel like nothing will ever happen to them. They live a carefree life, often thinking that bad things only happen to other people.*

# Do Premises Produce Profits?
January 16, 2018

The consultants who conduct manager searches are unlikely to recommend firms lacking a cogent statement of investment philosophy that goes beyond marketing mantras and competitive positioning. Moreover, they expect managers to articulate the investment thesis underlying a particular strategy, explaining confidently and credibly how securities in a given market are sometimes mispriced and how the strategy aims to exploit that mispricing. As John R. Minahan puts it, the "investment philosophy test" helps consultants distinguish between "alpha-generators," who can reasonably be expected to produce excess returns in the future, and "alpha-pretenders," who are merely selling noise.[1] As a general rule, managers who cannot set forth a sound investment philosophy may be lucky, at least for a while, but they probably aren't skillful.[2]

This faith in the self-evident importance of investment philosophy is so ingrained in the investment profession that the question may sound foolish: do asset managers' beliefs actually have anything to do with their performance relative to cap-weighted indices? Yet the answer is…not necessarily.

In an award-winning paper, Arnott, Hsu, Kalesnik, and Tindall found that, with annual rebalancing, hypothetical U.S. portfolios constructed in accordance with a wide range of arguably sensible investment beliefs (such as high risk/high reward) outperformed a cap-weighted benchmark over the 49-year period from 1964 to 2012. But they found, too, that portfolios constructed with the inverse weighting algorithms[3] (favoring,

---

[1] John R. Minahan, "The Role of Investment Philosophy in Evaluating Investment Managers," *Journal of Investing*, vol. 15, no. 2 (Summer 2006), 6-11. Building on this now-classic framework, Minahan and Thusith I. Mahanama extend the analysis by examining the place of investment philosophy in an investment organization's culture, in "Investment Philosophy and Manager Evaluation, Again," *Journal of Investing*, vol. 26, no. 1 (Spring 2017), 26-32.

[2] Minahan (who doesn't use the adjectives "lucky" and "skillful") says he may sometimes make exceptions for inarticulate managers who show in other ways that they have a sound philosophy behind their investment process (*e.g.*, managers who recognize that their every strategy is potentially subject to being arbitraged away). "The Role of Investment Philosophy in Evaluating Investment Managers," *op. cit.*, 10.

[3] For each standard strategy, Arnott *et al.* tested two kinds of upside-down

for instance, low-risk stocks) also outperformed the benchmark, often by a greater margin. This outcome was not limited to the well-known low-volatility anomaly;[4] high-growth and low-growth portfolios that were not cap-weighted produced the same results, as, indeed, did the right-side-up and upside-down implementations of many other simulated strategies—11 in all, as well as an equal-weight reference portfolio containing all 1,000 stocks in the universe. In addition, the authors determined that an equal-weight portfolio whose holdings were randomly selected beat the cap-weighted index.[5]

The authors stated, "Our findings suggest that the investment beliefs upon which many investment strategies are ostensibly based play little or no role in their outperformance."[6]

Performance attribution analysis using the Fama-French four-factor model[7] (henceforth FF4) revealed that, in all but one of the strategy groups, the non-cap-weighted portfolios had meaningful value and/or small cap biases with no statistically significant net FF4 alpha.[8] Whatever the managers' investment beliefs, the real sources of returns in excess of those earned by the cap-weighted benchmark were the portfolios' value and small cap tilts.

If the investment thesis is likely to prove irrelevant, how should institutional investors and their consultants react when managers expound their philosophy? Wait politely for them to finish the yada-yada-yada, thank them for their logical coherence, and then inquire about the real sources of return?

Arnott and his coauthors offered two suggestions. First, they said, "It may behoove investors to emphasize more the FF4 factor-based analysis

---

portfolios: inverse ratio portfolios constructed by normalizing the inverse weights $(1/w)$, and inverse complement portfolios constructed by normalizing the original portfolios' complementary weight $(\max(w)-w)$.

[4] See Feifei Li and Philip Lawton, "True Grit: The Durable Low Volatility Effect," Research Affiliates (September 2014).

[5] Robert D. Arnott, Jason Hsu, Vitali Kalesnik, and Phil Tindall, "The Surprising Alpha from Malkiel's Monkey and Upside-Down Strategies," *Journal of Portfolio Management*, vol. 39, no. 4 (Summer 2013), 91-105.

[6] *Ibid.*, 91.

[7] The factors are market beta, size (SMB), value (HML), and momentum (UMD).

[8] The exception was that a few of the inverted fundamentals-based strategies delivered statistically significant alpha after taking the factor effects into account.

when analyzing investment philosophies." I would go further. Investment consultants should make it standard practice to include regression-based FF4 attribution analysis in their due-diligence examination of managers' historical results. Second, the authors said, "Given that both sensible and senseless strategies outperform for the same reasons (value and small-cap tilts), potential investors would do well to base much of their decisions on a comparison of implementation costs associated with turnover and market-price impact."[9] Empirical research into factor-based strategies confirms that those with inherently lower turnover sustain less return erosion due to trading costs.[10]

More basically, how should managers themselves respond to the message that their narrative may be nothing more than a selection ritual or a form of investment committee theatre?

In finance, as in science, research begins with a hypothesis.[11] We know, in principle, that our theories are always provisional. Nonetheless, in practice we accept the null hypothesis once we judge that the story makes sense, the assumptions are tolerably realistic, and out-of-sample tests are corroborative.[12] We suspend the search for alternate explanations and go on to find fault with others' published work. It is, after all, a matter of competitive urgency. We cannot successfully gather assets without a distinctive investment thesis, one that our organization is uniquely qualified to exploit.

Writing about the social sciences, Albert O. Hirschman acknowledged that we cannot even start to think without models and similar abstractions. "But," he said, "cognitive style, that is, the kind of paradigms we search out, the way we put them together, and the

---

[9] *Ibid.*, 99.

[10] See Jason Hsu, Vitali Kalesnik, Noah Beck, and Helge Kostka, "Will Your Factor Deliver? An Examination of Factor Robustness and Implementation Costs," *Financial Analysts Journal*, vol. 72, no. 5 (September/October 2016), 58-82.

[11] Karl Popper remarks, "It is quite true that any particular hypothesis we choose will have been preceded by observations—the observations, for example, which it is designed to explain. But these observations, in their turn, presupposed the adoption of a frame of reference: a frame of expectations: a frame of theories." "Science: Conjectures and Refutations," in *Conjectures and Refutations: The Growth of Scientific Knowledge*, Harper & Row (1963), 47.

[12] Note that the tendency under discussion here is distinct from datamining, the more or less conscious and deliberate selection of data series or time periods that directly support a researcher's or asset manager's hypothesis.

ambitions we nurture for their powers—all this can make a great deal of difference."[13] Although Hirschman's specific field of expertise was Latin American development, his discussion of "the compulsion to theorize"[14] is pertinent because capital market theorists are also prone to discover *a priori* patterns in the historical record and to manage complexity with a "quick theoretical fix." Hirschman preferred the cognitive style of one who "draws conclusions with the utmost diffidence and circumspection."[15]

For evolutionary reasons that account for the confirmation bias, most people are not very good at criticizing their own positions.[16] All the same, it is imperative that investment managers foster a culture of critical thinking. It is not enough to have one person whose traditional role it is to raise doubts, because over time that position grows stale and the debate becomes ritualized. ("Before we proceed, let's hear from the devil's advocate.") Everyone has to ask questions—naïve as well as sophisticated ones—from the start. The most productive meetings are the open, contentious ones whose participants are trying in good faith not to score points but to find the truth.

To my mind, despite the typical asset management firm's intellectual hierarchy, this means inviting the middle office staff to participate in research initiatives.[17] The performance analysts might reveal unexpected information about simulated or historical results. The risk managers might identify a flaw in the model or detect a structural change in the market. Because they are not already invested in the thesis, they may also be more alert to theoretical shortcomings and more open to alternate explanations of the data.

---

[13] Albert O. Hirschman, "The Search for Paradigms as a Hindrance to Understanding," *World Politics*, vol. 22, no. 3 (April 1970), 338

[14] Ibid., 329. Hirschman (*ibid.*, 335) presents « the compulsion to theorize » as his free rendering of Flaubert's phrase, "*la rage de vouloir conclure,*" which the latter called "one of humanity's most dreadful and sterile obsessions." Gustave Flaubert, Letter of October 23, 1865 to Mlle. Leroyer de Chantepie, *Correspondance,* Éditions Louis Conard (1929), vol. 5, 111.

[15] *Loc. cit.*

[16] Hugo Mercier and Dan Sperber, "Why Do Humans Reason? Arguments for an Argumentative Theory," *Behavioral and Brain Sciences*, vol. 34 (2011), 60. See "For the Sake of Argument," pages 110-112 below.

[17] See "Adding Value," pages 97-99 below.

Of course, when a firm has publicly put its name behind an investment theory, it is not only painful but also costly, disruptive, and potentially embarrassing to revisit the premises and the logic. It may even strike employees as disloyal to raise questions about the firm's understanding of its own strategy. But it's never too late to revise an interpretation of the facts. How did our beliefs shape our view of the pricing mechanism and frame the questions we asked? Can we formulate a better explanation today? Coming forward with new insights into the firm's investment thesis, portfolio construction methodology, and performance record does not betray weakness. Quite the contrary. At any point in a company's history, looking at the data again, with fresh eyes, and learning something new is a clear sign of intellectual vitality and organizational strength. Existing and prospective clients deserve to hear about it.

## Calling the Turns: Why Market Timing Is So Hard
April 2015

The stock market is cyclical, and any investor who could call the turns—buying when prices are lowest and selling when they are highest—would make a fortune. But only a fortuneteller would say, "The peak will arrive next Tuesday morning," and like the rest of us, she'd be guessing (and almost certainly guessing wrong). The facts are clear—most actively managed equity mutual funds underperform the market.[1] Even worse, most individual investors underperform the funds they invest in: their money-weighted returns—the rates of return they actually earn—are preponderantly lower than the time-weighted returns that the funds report.[2]

Investment managers' underperformance relative to their benchmark generally results from unfortunate decisions in one or more of three areas: market timing, sector weighting or factor exposures, and stock selection.[3] The practical reality is that timing is integral to all aspects of investment decision making. Allocating funds across sectors, setting factor exposure targets, and identifying attractively priced stocks all have an element of market timing. Mutual fund investors' underperformance relative to the active funds they hold is simply the result of their own inopportune purchases and redemptions.

If it's all in the timing, why is it so hard to get the timing right?

---

[1] According to the SPIVA Scorecard compiled by S&P Dow Jones Indices, for periods ended December 31, 2014, 76.25% of actively managed U.S. large-cap equity funds underperformed the S&P 500 for 3 years, 8.65% for 5 years, and 82.07% for 10 years.

[2] Jason Hsu and Viswanathan Vivek, "Woe Betide the Value Investor." Research Affiliates (February 2015).

[3] For an approach to performance attribution analysis that isolates the impact of tactical asset allocation in factor investing (i.e., timing the cyclicality of risk premiums), see Jason C. Hsu, Vitali Kalesnik, and Brett W. Myers, "Performance Attribution: Measuring Dynamic Asset Allocation Skill," *Financial Analysts Journal*, vol. 66, no. 6 (2010), 17–26, and Jason C. Hsu and Omid Shakernia, "A Framework for Examining Asset Allocation Alpha," *Journal of Index Investing*, vol. 3, no. 4 (2013), 64–72.

Copyright © 2013-2015 Research Affiliates, LLC. Reprinted by permission.

The standard model of investment management equips portfolio managers and traders reasonably well to determine if an individual stock is fairly valued. Most investment professionals use discounted cash flow (DCF) analysis to estimate a stock's inherent worth,[4] and so to judge whether it is mispriced. With a handle on a stock's true value, an investment professional can also observe the extent to which the market may have mispriced it. Similarly, by comparing the market's current cap-weighted price/earnings to the long-term average, analysts can judge whether, and by how much, the market as a whole is misvalued.

But DCF analysis, P/E multiples, and other theoretically sound valuation measures cannot tell us how much *more* misvalued the market will get, nor can they explain the wild swings we've experienced in the two equity market cycles in the last 15 years.[5] The stock market seems to go too far in both directions—up and down—and the amplitude of these movements cannot be satisfactorily explained within the cool analytical framework of the standard model.

Empirical research has established that sooner or later stock prices revert toward their long-term averages. There is also strong evidence that the value premium is mean reverting.[6] If the market rises or falls to an extreme level despite a natural tendency to self-correct, then countervailing forces must be at work.

One hypothesis is that many market participants view mental effort as an avoidable transaction cost. Disinclined to gather and analyze solid information about the stocks that interest them, they are carried along by the crowd, trading on momentum and noise.

In addition to this kind of indolence or inertia, Daniel Kahneman[7] and others have described a number of cognitive biases and patterns of

---

[4] Cornell and Hsu hold that the investment professionals to whom end investors delegate decision-making authority use DCF analysis so prevalently that their discount models are likely both to drive prices and determine the cross-section of expected returns. See Bradford Cornell and Jason Hsu, "The Self-Fulfilling Prophecy of Popular Asset Pricing Models," *Journal of Investment Management*, vol. 14, no. 1 (2016), 65-74.

[5] Nor does the standard model account for the sheer volume of non-algorithmic stock market trades.

[6] Jason Hsu, "Value Investing: Smart Beta versus Style Indexes," *Journal of Index Investing*, vol. 5, no. 1 (2014), 127-135.

emotionally charged behavior that affect individuals' choices under uncertainty—the selling and buying of securities being an excellent example of such an activity. They include overconfidence and the illusion of control,[8] mental accounts, availability cascades, loss aversion, overreacting to news, and herding, among others.

The field of neuroeconomics has also contributed much to our understanding of the autonomous brain, the old lizard brain, which leaps to conclusions while our conscious minds are still deliberating. The process of reasoning, it appears, is often rationalizing choices we may not know we've already made.[9] The insights into decision making that we've gained from behavioral finance and neuroeconomics go a long way toward explaining investors' actions and reactions when the outcome is in doubt.

Given the behavioral view of investors' practical decision-making processes, two promising ways of thinking about how markets really work are Vernon Smith's concept of ecological rationality and Andrew Lo's adaptive markets hypothesis.

Smith, the experimental economist who shared the 2002 Nobel Prize in Economic Science with Kahneman, distinguishes between constructivist and ecological rationality. The former involves the intentional use of reason to analyze the given and to advocate a course of action. (The standard model of investment management is a sterling product of constructivist rationality.) Ecological rationality, in contrast, emerges in institutions, such as markets, through human interaction rather than by human design.

---

[7] Daniel Kahneman, *Thinking, Fast and Slow*. New York: Farrar, Strauss, and Giroux (2011)..

[8] The novelist Italo Svevo satirized the illusion of control when he described a fictional character's apparently successful effort to regulate the stock exchange on behalf of a late friend's family: "I don't know anyone who has ever been able to tolerate similar exertion for fifty hours. Every shift in price I recorded, brooded over, and then (why not say it?) mentally urged shares forward, or held them back, as best suited me, or rather my poor friend. Even my nights were sleepless." *Zeno's Conscience*. Translated by William Weaver. New York: Vintage Books (2003).

[9] Jason Zweig, *Your Money and Your Brain: How the New Science of Neuroeconomics Can Help Make You Rich*. New York: Simon & Schuster (2009).

"Predominantly," Smith writes, "both economists and psychologists are reluctant to allow that naïve and unsophisticated agents can achieve socially optimal ends without a comprehensive understanding of the whole, as well as their individual parts, implemented by deliberate action."[10] But in Smith's account, personal exchanges gave rise to impersonal markets which serve to facilitate the specialization that creates wealth. Smith demonstrates that in a diverse set of circumstances, such as the airlines' response to deregulation, FCC spectrum auctions, and a variety of trust games, the interaction of individuals with partial knowledge leads in due time to near-equilibrium solutions.

Lo invokes pertinent findings of behavioral finance and neuroeconomics in his effort to develop a more realistic framework than the standard model.[11] He also introduces key concepts from evolutionary psychology—competition, adaptation, and natural selection—and reintroduces the classic notion of bounded or approximate rationality proposed by Herbert Simon. Remember that Simon's idea crucially takes into account "the simplifications the choosing organism may deliberately introduce into its model of the situation in order to bring the model within the range of its computing capacity."[12] For example, attempting to maximize the expected payoff from an action is a computationally intensive exercise. One of the simplifications Simon describes is "satisficing," more modestly requiring only that the benefit exceed some threshold.

Thanks to Kahneman, Smith, Lo, and many others, our understanding of the ways investors think and markets function is richer and more sensible than it was when the best minds of the time constructed the standard investment model. But these theoretical advances still don't solve the active investor's conundrum: when to buy and sell in strongly trending markets.

So, where will the solution come from? Let's think blue sky.

---

[10] Vernon L. Smith, *Rationality in Economics: Constructivist and Ecological Forms*. Cambridge: Cambridge University Press (2009), 157.

[11] Andrew Lo, "The Adaptive Markets Hypothesis: Market Efficiency from an Evolutionary Perspective," *Journal of Portfolio Management*, vol. 30, no. 5 (2004), 15–29, and "Reconciling Efficient Markets with Behavioral Finance: The Adaptive Markets Hypothesis." *Journal of Investment Consulting*, vol. 7, no. 2 (2005), 21–44.

[12] Herbert Simon, "A Behavioral Model of Rational Choice." *Quarterly Journal of Economics*, vol. 69, no. 1 (1955), 100.

Among the unfettered solutions that come to mind, one approach might be modeling the actions and reactions of distinct groups (Lo's "species," such as pension funds, retail investors, market makers, and hedge fund managers) whose members generally employ specifiable decision rules, but are subject to social influences and cognitive biases. Alternately, the industry might train its immense technological firepower on the markets themselves in a search for deep structures or path-dependent vectors that signal a change in direction: technical analysis with Cray supercomputers.

In either case, the analytical techniques that ultimately crack the code of market timing may originate in fields far removed from finance and economics—information theory, for example, or the study of complex networks. Recall that "Brownian Motion in the Stock Market," an article written by the physicist M.F.M. Osborne and published in a nonfinancial journal, contributed to the random walk theory of prices.[13]

The stock market's turning points, as well as the valuation peaks and troughs of individual stocks, increasingly appear to be driven more by mass psychology than by sober professional judgment based on disciplined valuation techniques. In fact, the active investor's conundrum is such a challenge that many investors have chosen passive investing—simply removing timing decisions from their purview. But there is strong evidence that the popularity of passive investing tied to prominent cap-weighted indices is actually associated with higher return correlations among stocks and, therefore, higher systematic equity market risk.[14]

At this juncture, we must acknowledge that financial theory does not provide clear and timely trading signals. Calling the turns is hard because we don't have a mechanics of mean reversion. Our best theories—including behavioral finance, neuroeconomics, experimental economics, and evolutionary psychology—do not enable us to foresee the sudden exogenous shock that will trigger a reversal, or to sense when a gradual change in investors' attitudes will reach the tipping point. Not even the

[13] M.F.M. Osborne, "Brownian Motion in the Stock Market," *Operations Research*, vol. 7, no. 2 (1959), 145–173. See Peter L. Bernstein, *Capital Ideas: The Improbable Origins of Modern Wall Street*, Hoboken, NJ: John Wiley & Sons (2005), 103, and Justin Fox, *The Myth of the Rational Market: A History of Risk, Reward, and Delusion on Wall Street*, New York: HarperCollins (2009), 64-67.
[14] Rodney N. Sullivan and James X. Xiong, "How Index Trading Increases Market Vulnerability," *Financial Analysts Journal*, vol. 68, no. 2 (2012), 70–84.

most skilled and experienced asset allocators can pinpoint in advance the onset of a reversal.

Most of us are well advised not to attempt market timing. The soundest plan is to choose a strategy that suits our investment objectives and risk tolerance—potentially including a disciplined smart beta strategy that systematically rebalances over time—and to stick with that choice for the long term.

## Pricing Fine Wines and Common Stocks
July 2014

Old wines, works of fine art, first editions, and rare stamps are sometimes called emotional assets. Owning them confers non-pecuniary benefits that might be described as psychic returns. This is not merely a metaphor; in the special case of wine, the psychic return can be quantified. Behavioral finance tells us that investing in financial assets also engages human emotions. But does behavioral theory reflect the way stocks are *actually* priced in the organizationally complex world of modern investing? Is our knowledge of capital market dynamics truly enhanced by studying individual investors' cognitive errors and psychological motivations?

The pricing of old wines and common stocks were among many topics explored at Research Affiliates' 2014 Advisory Panel meeting.[1] Elroy Dimson spoke about "Wine as an Investment"[2] and Bradford Cornell discussed "The Machinery of Asset Pricing."[3] Their perspectives on pricing are as different as the markets they study. My goal in this short article is not merely to juxtapose Dimson and Cornell's analyses, but to probe the implications of their findings for a behavioral approach to the valuation puzzle.

Looking at paintings doesn't wear them out, reading books doesn't deplete their store of language, and cataloguing stamps doesn't detract from their distinctiveness. But wine can be consumed. Accordingly, in modeling the price dynamics of wine, Dimson and his fellow researchers took into account its dual nature as a consumer product—indeed, in the case of high-quality wines, a luxury item—and a collectible. (It is the dichotomy between wine's consumption and ownership values that makes it possible to estimate the psychic return.) Their model postulates that the fundamental value of a wine is the highest of its immediate consumption value; the present value of consumption at maturity plus

---

[1] See Chris Brightman's account of the conference, "What We Know That Ain't So" (Research Affiliates, June 2014).
[2] Elroy Dimson, Peter L. Rousseau, and Christophe Spaenjers, "The Price of Wine," *Journal of Financial Economics*, vol. 118, no. 2 (2015), 431-449.
[3] Bradford Cornell and Jason Hsu, "The Self-Fulfilling Prophecy of Popular Asset Pricing Models," *Journal of Investment Management*, vol. 14, no. 1 (2016), 65-74.

the non-financial dividends received up to consumption; and the present value of lifelong ownership.

Dimson and his colleagues' research objective was to model the effect of aging on wine prices. In pursuing that objective, they did exemplary work in the economic history of wine. From first-hand documents, they meticulously assembled a unique database of historical prices from the end of 1899 to the end of 2012 for five first-growth Bordeaux wines by chateau, vintage year, sale year, and transaction type (dealer or auction). They also used records of annual production yield to estimate the effect of supply on prices, and records of temperature during the growing season and rainfall during the harvest season to distinguish high- from low-quality vintages.

In aggregate, the Dimson team estimated that the hypothetical annualized real return, net of insurance and storage costs, from 1900 to 2012 was 4.1%. They also found that the prices of low- and high-quality wines follow different paths. The price of a low-quality wine initially falls until the present value of ownership exceeds the value of consumption; then the price starts rising with age. The price of a high-quality wine rises strongly until the wine matures, then stabilizes, and rises again when the wine's value as a collectible becomes dominant. The psychic return on wines that are well past maturity is approximately equal to their underperformance vis-à-vis high-quality wines that are still maturing. In other words, the pleasure of ownership lowers the investor's required financial return. The researchers estimate that, over the prolonged measurement period, the psychic return was about 0.7% *per annum*.

Wine investors are likely to be wealthy individuals who personally select the wines they want, decide what price they're willing to pay, and store their acquisitions in a private wine cellar. In the language of neoclassical finance theory, individual investors strive to make intertemporal utility-maximizing choices using a discount rate that balances immediate and deferred consumption. In the standard model, prices are set by final consumers or investors. This theory eminently applies to the market for collectible wines.

Cornell argues, however, that the standard model does *not* fit the modern securities investment environment. On the basis of high-level research, he and his co-author, Jason Hsu, state that final investors do not set the prices of financial assets. Instead, acknowledging (whether openly or tacitly) that they have neither the information nor the training to identify

[Type text]

mispriced stocks, asset owners delegate decision-making to investment professionals, either by buying managed funds or by engaging financial advisors. *Investment professionals are the marginal price-setters.*

Moreover, investment professionals don't use a utility-maximizing model for asset pricing; they overwhelmingly use simpler discounted cash flow techniques to estimate fundamental values. There is evidence that, in an attempt to set themselves apart, advisors expend considerably greater effort developing cash flow projections than selecting the proper discount rate. Nonetheless, the cross-section of expected returns is determined by the marginal investors' discount rates; and those discount rates, in turn, are determined by the marginal investors' models. There is, consequently, a feedback loop, via discount rates, between asset pricing theory and the prices of financial assets. Cornell says that the implications of this feedback loop remain to be explored.

Delegating discretionary authority does not lead to a clear-cut principal-agent relationship; investment committees, consultants, regulators, and, in some cases, layers of distributors have roles to play. Investment committees, which are prone to small-group politicking, retain consultants to share the liability for their decisions, and the consultants have their own business objectives. Regulators, always playing catch-up, attempt to protect the investing public and their own bureaucracy by enforcing an ever-expanding set of detailed requirements. Distributors may be concerned as much about a product's fee structure as its suitability for individual clients. In short, the modern financial services industry is a complex ecosystem. The volume (in both senses: quantity and loudness) of hot financial information is a further complication; media personalities don't understand investing, and they are driven by the very-short-term news cycle to focus on what's trending.

If the asset owners are dissatisfied with the professionals' performance, they terminate the relationship, typically after three years. In consequence, investment professionals' recommendations and actions may not be fully aligned with their clients' true long-term interests. In order to maintain a steady (or, better yet, steadily growing) stream of advisory fees, investment professionals are financially incentivized to focus on short-term performance relative to a benchmark. This compensation structure does not make it easier to manage clients' portfolios in view of rational long-term objectives.

Grounded in psychology and experimental economics, behavioral finance purports to shed light on investors' actual decision-making processes, which are susceptible to cognitive error and influenced by non-financial needs and desires. Thus, like neoclassical finance, behavioral finance crucially assumes that investment decisions are made by the ultimate consumers—individual investors. This presupposition does not reflect the reality of asset pricing in the complex investment ecosystem.

What are we to make of these studies?

Clearly, Dimson's findings offer us a realistic idea of the very-long-term rate of return earned by wine collectors in the past, and, to that extent, it helps us situate wine among other investible assets. In addition, by translating the pleasure of owning fine wines into concrete financial terms, it gives objective economic support to the psychological notion that investors—or at least collectors—are motivated in part by non-financial considerations. At the turn of the 20th century, Thorstein Veblen described the symbolic rewards of conspicuous consumption: asserting one's social standing, belonging to a community of connoisseurs, exhibiting refined tastes, and demonstrating expertise in an inessential, unproductive, time-consuming activity.[4] For the present purpose, we only have to acknowledge that wine is an emotional asset and that wine investors implicitly seek to maximize their intertemporal utility by deciding if and when to open a bottle.

Cornell's conclusions are more disconcerting. There is no doubt that stock prices exhibit short-term momentum and long-term mean reversion. Behavioral finance seemed to have given a reasonable account of these phenomena in psychological terms. For instance, overconfidence, optimism, and social validation make sense of the herding by which individuals become collectives—sometimes, indeed, flash mobs—and create bubbles. But Cornell's description of the modern institutional arrangements under which financial assets are actually priced throws into question both the applicability of individual psychology and any facile transition to aggregate behavior. The market might be a construct, like "the law," or an institution, like "a court of law," but it is not a person, and we can ascribe intentionality, rationality,

---

[4] Thorstein Veblen, *The Theory of the Leisure Class*. Oxford, U.K.: Oxford University Press (2009). Full disclosure: I spend a great deal of time on the archetype of unproductive activity, reading philosophy, often while sipping wine.
[Type text]

and feeling to the market only by analogy, as though it were a quasi-person.

It would be a step in the right direction to suggest that, because discount rates vary over time, those who use discount rate models to set prices must be susceptible to mood swings. This observation re-centers the study of emotion in investment decision-making on the behavior of investment professionals, where John Coates, David Tuckett, and Richard J. Taffler have led the way.[5] Portfolio managers and traders buy, hold, and sell securities not only under conditions of uncertainty and rapid change but also under pressure from all sides—regulators, employers, competitors, and their peers within the same organization, as well as their clients, the final investors. From now on, any behavioral theory of finance that does not take into account the institutional setting will be interesting, no doubt, but pretty much irrelevant. We can do better than armchair psychology.

---

[5] See John Coates, *The Hour Between Dog and Wolf: Risk Taking, Gut Feelings, and the Biology of Boom and Bust.* New York: Penguin Press (2012); and David Tuckett and Richard J. Taffler. *Fund Management: An Emotional Finance Perspective.* Charlottesville, VA: Research Foundation of CFA Institute (2012).

# The Psychology of Contrarian Investing
December 2013

Behavioral finance, broadly defined, has given us a fairly comprehensive understanding of investors' real decision processes. It has taught us to set aside the timeworn fiction of "economic man"—the well-informed, utility-maximizing homunculus with stable preferences and superb computational skills—in favor of more realistic models of choice under risk.[1] Investors, we now see, are prone to cognitive errors, reluctant to realize losses, and overconfident in their own ability but nonetheless fearful that other market participants know something they don't. Moreover, investors seek not only utilitarian rewards but expressive and emotional benefits as well, such as status and a sense of belonging to a community.[2] Thanks to Herbert Simon, Daniel Kahneman, Richard Thaler, Meir Statman, and many others, we have a general psychology that illuminates the cognitive and affective recesses of investment decision-making.

Contrarian investors can be situated within the framework of the general psychology; there is no need for an abnormal psychology to make sense of their behavior. A contrarian stance is not a symptom of a personality disorder. If some contrarians are antisocial or apathetic, that is because, just like other investors, they are people. Nonetheless, contrarians may reasonably be expected to share some abiding personality traits, such as a spirit of self-reliance, a penchant for critical thinking, and a strong future time orientation.

---

[1] Simon wrote, "Broadly stated, the task is to replace the global rationality of economic man with a kind of rational behavior that is compatible with the access to information and the computational capacities that are *actually* possessed by organisms, including man, in the kinds of environments in which such organisms exist." Herbert A. Simon, "A Behavioral Model of Rational Choice," *Quarterly Journal of Economics*, vol. 69, no. 1 (1955), 99 (emphasis added). Joan Robinson debunked the "metaphysical concept" of utility in her classic work, *Economic Philosophy*. New Brunswick, NJ: Transaction Publishers (1962). Daniel Kahneman and Amos Tversky roundly demonstrated the inadequacy of utility theory in "Prospect Theory: An Analysis of Decision Under Risk," *Econometrica*, vol. 47, no. 2 (1979), 263-292.

[2] Meir Statman, *What Investors Really Want: Discover What Drives Investor Behavior and Make Smarter Financial Decisions*. New York: McGraw-Hill (2011), Introduction.

My limited objective in this short piece is to suggest some possible directions for experimental research on the psychology of contrarian investors. C. Howard Thomas provides a useful frame of reference in his important 2013 paper on behavioral portfolio management (BPM).[3] His trenchant description of emotional crowds focuses on certain characteristics that may help differentiate the hypothetical attributes of a lifelike contrarian.

In Howard's account, the first principle of BPM is that security prices are predominately set by emotional crowds comprising investors whose purchase and sale decisions are based on heuristic shortcuts, anecdotal evidence, and visceral reactions to unfolding events.[4] In terms Kahneman made familiar, emotional investors operate primarily at the level of System 1: their thinking is fast and automatic.[5] Emotional crowds, Howard says, are propelled by two forces: a deep-seated aversion to short-term losses and a compulsive need for social validation.[6]

BPM assumes, as others have established, that markets are not very efficient. Nor are emotional crowds wise in the sense that the averages of individual market participants' valuations would tend to approximate securities' true, fundamental, or inherent values.[7] James Surowiecki identified four conditions that characterize wise crowds: diversity of opinion, independence, decentralization, and aggregation.[8] Emotional crowds in the financial markets satisfy the last two conditions; participants can draw on their own resources, and there is a mechanism—the pricing mechanism itself—for reducing many individual judgments to a collective decision. But emotional crowds are unlikely to exhibit a strong diversity of opinion, and their members are

---

[3] C. Howard Thomas, "Behavioral Portfolio Management." 2013. Available at SSRN: http://ssrn.com/abstract=2210032 or http://dx.doi.org/10.2139/ssrn.2210032.

[4] Howard, *op. cit.*, 5-7.

[5] Daniel Kahneman, *Thinking, Fast and Slow*. New York: Farrar, Straus and Giroux (2011), 20-22. Kahneman attributes the terms "System 1" and "System 2" to psychologists Keith Stanovich and Richard West.

[6] Howard, *op. cit.*, 3.

[7] In principle, a security's true value is the present value of projected cash flows discounted at a rate that properly reflects the uncertainty of receiving them in full and on time. Nonetheless, the true value is unobservable, and estimating it is quite unlike guessing the number of marbles in a jar.

[8] James Surowiecki, *The Wisdom of Crowds: Why the Many Are Smarter Than the Few and How Collective Wisdom Shapes Business, Economies, Societies, and Nations*. New York: Doubleday (2004), 7-8.

certainly not independent in Surowiecki's sense. It cannot be said that "people's opinions are not determined by the opinions of those around them;" on the contrary, in emotional crowds, people take their cues from one another. They think what they think others think.

For the present purpose, it is enough to treat the emotional crowd as an assembly of undifferentiated investors. Indeed, from one perspective, it seems entirely fitting; the self can be submerged and carried along in a mass movement. Nonetheless, a more granular description of the crowd's composition (along the lines, for instance, of Andrew Lo's species of investors)[9] might facilitate empirical research and lead to further insights. Traditional index investing is a trend-following strategy—constituent weights rise and fall with prices—and it contributes to stock market volatility,[10] but passive investors do not necessarily belong to the emotional crowd. The decision to invest passively does not, in itself, indicate anything about an individual's cognitive style.

Howard's view of the price-setting mechanism does not rule out the possibility of rational investing. It does, however, call for a new kind of rationality in investment decision-making. In this view, rational investors are continually aware of other market participants' tendencies to overpay and overreact. (Rational investors also recognize that their own emotions are at work, but they try to bring them to the surface and subject them to cognitive control.)[11] Because market prices are not primarily based upon economic forecasting or security analysis, rational investors today are at least as much concerned with others' behavioral signals as they are with asset class correlations or discounted cash flows. Howard calls them behavioral-data investors (BDIs) and characterizes their cognitive style as System 2 thinking—"effortful, high-concentration, and complex."[12]

---

[9] "By *species*, I mean distinct groups of market participants, each behaving in a common manner. For example, pension funds may be considered one species; retail investors another; market makers a third; and hedge-fund managers a fourth." Lo (2004), 23. Andrew W. Lo, "The Adaptive Markets Hypothesis: Market Efficiency from an Evolutionary Perspective," *Journal of Portfolio Management*, vol. 30, no. 5 (2004), 15-29.

[10] Rodney N. Sullivan and James X. Xiong, "How Index Trading Increases Market Vulnerability," *Financial Analysts Journal*, vol. 68, no. 2 (March/April 2012), 70-84.

[11] Robert E. Lane, *The Market Experience*. Cambridge: Cambridge University Press (1991), 108.

[12] Howard, *op. cit.*, 3.

Howard's second basic principle (of three) is that BDIs earn superior returns. There is, however, a certain emotional cost. He writes:

> It would seem easy to build superior performing portfolios, but doing so would mean taking positions that are opposite the crowd. The powerful need for social validation acts as a strong deterrent for many investors, discouraging them from pursuing such an approach. It is tough to leave the emotional crowd and become a BDI.[13]

Howard does not simply identify rational investing with contrarian investing ("taking positions that are opposite the crowd"); the BPM approach is considerably broader and more nuanced.[14] Nonetheless, in his framework, contrarians can qualify as rational investors. Let us consider how they might differ in thought, attitude, and behavior from the members of emotional crowds.

A superficial statement of the contrarian position would simply hold that the emotional crowd is foolish and will sooner or later be proven dead wrong. No doubt there are contrarians who earn superior long-term returns without much mental effort. Nonetheless, if the contrarian approach is rational, then its view on the pricing mechanism can be articulated and justified.

One important version of contrarian investment theory sees security prices as "noisy." In information theory, noise in a transmission channel distorts the information-bearing signal. (**Figure 1.**) Think of static interfering with a radio broadcast.

---

[13] *Ibid.*, 9.

[14] For example, Howard recommends that investors implementing BPM be aware of market sentiment; create buckets for short-term income and liquidity, long-term capital growth, and alternative investments; and select managers on the basis of their strategy, consistency, and willingness to take high-conviction positions. *Op. cit.*, 18-22, 25.

**Figure 1.** Schematic Diagram of a General Communication System

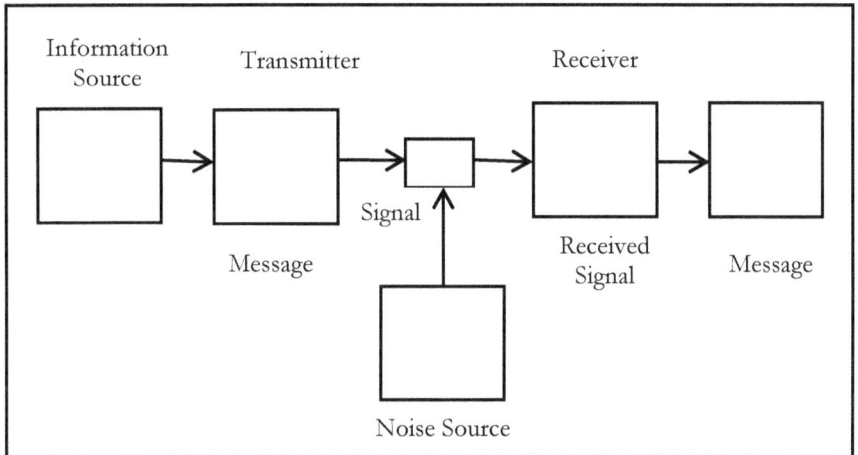

Source: Claude E. Shannon and Warren Weaver, *The Mathematical Theory of Communication*. Urbana and Chicago: University of Illinois Press (1963), 34.

By analogy, in modern portfolio theory, financial markets—the transmission channels—are at least fairly efficient (or clear), and security prices primarily reflect information (or news). In the contrarian view, however, markets are more than a little inefficient because many participants initiate transactions inspired by static. "Perhaps they think the noise they are trading on is information," wrote Fischer Black. "Or perhaps they just like to trade."[15]

In addition, the contrarian approach (unlike BPM)[16] recognizes that, although stocks exhibit short-term momentum, over the long run both the level of the equity market and the prices of individual securities are mean-reverting.[17] Empirical studies demonstrate that stocks whose prices

---

[15] Fischer Black, "Noise," *The Journal of Finance*, vol. 41, no. 3 (1986), 531.
[16] Howard asserts in passing that patterns of short-term momentum and mean reversion "tend to be transitory in nature." *Op. cit.,* 25.
[17] Ryan Larson and Vitali Kalesnik, respectively, provide clear and well-supported explanations of momentum and mean reversion. See Ryan Larson, "Hot Potato: Momentum As An Investment Strategy," Research Affiliates (August 2013), and Vitali Kalesnik, "Smart Beta and the Pendulum of Mispricing," Research Affiliates (3rd Quarter 2013).

have been trending have a pronounced tendency to turn around and head in the direction of their long term average prices. For example, Fama and French found "consistent evidence that stock returns are positively serially correlated over short horizons, and negatively autocorrelated over long horizons."[18] Mean reversion can continue for up to 10 years, but the strongest effect shows up over the period from two to five years after a reversal.[19]

Contrarian investors profit from long-term mean reversion in noisy security prices by contra-trading against prices when they rebalance their portfolios. In this context, rebalancing means selling winners (stocks which have appreciated) and buying losers (stocks which have lately declined in price). Winners are more likely to be overvalued; losers, undervalued. Contrarian investors are unaffected by subsequent mean reversion in the overvalued, high-price stocks they have divested, and they stand to gain if and when the undervalued, low-price stocks reverse direction and start to rise. Ironically, contrarian investing—taking positions opposite the emotional crowd—simply comes down to buying low and selling high. Contrarians are eminently rational.[20]

With this background, let's explore how contrarian investors might differ from the emotional crowd along the two key psychological dimensions Howard identified. Are contrarians also loss-averse? Do they stand equally in need of social validation?

---

[18] Eugene F. Fama and Kenneth R. French, "Dividend Yields and Expected Stock Returns," *Journal of Financial Economics*, vol. 22, no. 1 (1988), abstract and pages 3-4.

[19] See Kalesnik, "Smart Beta and the Pendulum of Mispricing, *op. cit.*

[20] They may also be smarter than the average bear. The fascinating study of IQ and trading behavior in Finland conducted by Grinblatt et al. did not specifically consider intelligence in relation to investment strategy. Nonetheless, the study found that high-IQ investors were more likely than low-IQ investors to hold (sell) stocks that hit a monthly low (high). "High IQ investors thus appear to be more contrarian than low-IQ investors with respect to these reference prices." This is especially true when extreme price movements occur. Nor is this pattern necessarily motivated by the disposition effect. Citing other studies, Grinblatt and his co-authors state, "by selling stocks at monthly highs and holding stocks at monthly lows, high-IQ investors are more likely to be following a rational liquidity provision strategy than a psychological bias that diminishes returns." See Mark Grinblatt, Matti Keloharju, and Juhanni T. Linnainmaa, "IQ, Trading Behavior, and Performance," *Journal of Financial Economics*, vol. 104, no. 2 (May 2012), 339-362.

People typically love to win and hate even more to lose. Winning is rewarding; it makes people feel good about themselves. Correlatively, losing is not only a disappointing outcome with a certain cost; it can be sharply experienced as a self-inflicted insult to the ego, particularly if the one who loses has narrowly framed the competition as a singularly important event. Kahneman said, "When you sell a loser, you don't just take a financial loss; you take a psychological loss from admitting you made a mistake. You are punishing yourself when you sell."[21]

Loss aversion refers to the experimentally established fact that decision makers have a natural tendency to weigh losses more heavily than gains. Richard Thaler states, "losses hurt roughly twice as much as gains feel good," and he observes that "even investors with long-term horizons appear to care about short-term gains and losses."[22]

Contrarian investors may sustain deep market value losses, but they are generally in position to sidestep the underlying psychological issue with which other investors have to contend: overcoming their reluctance to *realize* a loss. Rebalancing a contrarian portfolio entails selling the stocks which have appreciated and reinvesting the proceeds in low price stocks, including those whose market values have recently declined. Consequently, contrarian investors are more likely to realize gains than losses.

Nonetheless, contrarians do not avoid absolute market value losses in bear markets, and they may have to tolerate months or even years of relative underperformance when prices are trending upward. If they are somewhat less vulnerable to short-term loss aversion, it is probably because they have chosen a long-term investment strategy; and it is possible that this choice reflects a persistent attitude toward the future.

---

[21] Quoted in Jason Zweig, *Your Money and Your Brain: How the New Science of Neuroeconomics Can Help Make You Rich.* New York: Simon & Schuster (2007).
[22] Richard Thaler, "The End of Behavioral Finance," *Financial Analysts Journal,* vol. 55, no. 6 (November/December 1999), 15. Benartzi and Thaler made note of investors' propensity to check investment performance frequently and attributed the equity premium in part to what they called "myopic loss aversion." Shlomo Benartzi and Richard H. Thaler, "Myopic Loss Aversion and the Equity Premium Puzzle." *Quarterly Journal of Economics,* 110/1 (February 1995), 73-92. Kahneman wrote, "The combination of loss aversion and narrow framing is a costly curse. Individual investors can avoid that curse, achieving the emotional benefits of broad framing while also saving time and agony, by reducing the frequency with which they check how well their investments are doing." *Thinking, Fast and Slow, op. cit.,* 339.

Joseph Nuttin, a psychologist who studied personality and motivation, wrote, "Generally speaking, one could say that the future is the 'mental space' in which human needs are processed into long-term goals and behavioral projects."[23]

Although the future is a mental representation, it appears to have greater reality for achievement-oriented people. Indeed, there is a telling connection between individuals' outlook on the future and their self-understanding as active persons in a dynamic relationship with the world and other people. Psychological studies reveal that, while some subjects see the future as determined by chance, others regard it as largely dependent upon their own actions.[24] I would hazard that active long-term investors chiefly belong to the latter group.

In principle, surveys and experiments could establish whether contrarian investors have a greater-than-average future time orientation. However, the measurement issues are thorny, especially when future time orientation is considered as an abiding personality trait rather than a situation-specific or experimentally induced response.[25] Future time orientation may also be strongly influenced by cultural and historical factors; one would not expect similar averages from studies conducted in Belgium in the 1980s and the United States in the 2010s.

Investments are risky; that's in the nature of the game. But investment decision-making itself is fraught with uncertainty. Investors may doubt their assumptions ("Am I using the right discount rate?") or experience misgivings about their knowledge ("Why is the other side willing to enter this transaction?"). And, as Robert Cialdini explains, it is precisely in such conditions of uncertainty that people turn to the "principle of social proof," which holds that one of the ways we go about determining what is correct, or what to do, is to seek out what other people think is right. "In general," he wrote, "when we are unsure of ourselves, when the situation is unclear or ambiguous, when uncertainty reigns, we are most likely to look to and accept the actions of others as correct."[26]

---

[23] Joseph Nuttin, with the collaboration of Willy Lens, *Future Time Perspective and Motivation: Theory and Research Method*. Leuven, Belgium: Leuven University Press and Hillsdale, NJ: Lawrence Erlbaum Associates, Inc., Publishers (1985), 40.
[24] Nuttin, *op. cit.*, 29.
[25] Torgrim Gjesme explains the measurement issues in "On the Concept of Future Time Orientation: Considerations of Some Functions' and Measurements' Implications," *International Journal of Psychology*, 18 (1983), 443-461.

Adam Smith remarked that the more we mistrust our own feelings and opinions, the more weight we give others'. In his words:

> The agreement or disagreement both of the sentiments and judgments of other people with our own, is, in all cases, it must be observed, of more or less importance to us, exactly in proportion as we ourselves are more or less uncertain about the propriety of our own sentiments, about the accuracy of our own judgments.[27]

The question for a psychology of contrarian investing is whether contrarians are less influenced than average market participants by other investors' "sentiments and judgments." I have mentioned that active long-term investors, in general, seem likely to believe that their behavior in the present can affect the future. This perspective implies a proactive attitude and a certain self-reliance.[28] It seems reasonable to anticipate that contrarians will be predisposed to gather information, analyze it, and reach an independent conclusion. It also seems sensible not to expect the same of the emotional crowd, whose members may tend to see mental effort as an avoidable transaction cost. Recall that System 1 is their characteristic mode of thinking.

Within the financial services industry, all investment professionals are ethically obligated to use reasonable care and exercise independent judgment; and there is no *a priori* reason to suppose that contrarians are distinctively less (or, for that matter, more) reliant upon social validation than other practitioners.

Taking investment decisions seriously means not only acting competently but also understanding and accepting the affective consequences of making choices whose outcomes cannot be known in advance. This is tough on all investors, but arguably hardest on contrarians. Although they may expect to earn superior returns over full market cycles, they fall

---

[26] Robert B. Cialdini, *Influence: The Psychology of Persuasion*. Revised edition. New York: HarperCollins e-books, Chapter 4.

[27] Adam Smith, *The Theory of Moral Sentiments*. Edited by D.D. Raphael and A.L. Macfie. Indianapolis, IN: Liberty Fund (1982), III.2.16.

[28] Here, too, the social environment matters; even within a single culture and economy, prevalent attitudes change over time. Citing a major study, Lane reports that many more Americans saw the self as efficacious, and independence as a source of well-being, in 1976 than in 1957. *The Market Experience, op. cit.*, 173.

behind (and managers risk losing clients) when stocks are rising and everybody else is making money. Contrarian investors might sometimes feel isolated and embattled. It is natural to wonder whether they have characteristic personality traits and modes of thought that uniquely equip them to handle the stress of standing against the emotional crowd.

At least one way of articulating contrarian thought sees security prices as noisy and mean-reverting. Adopting this viewpoint may reflect the contrarian's personal preference, but it is not a purely arbitrary choice; noise-in-price models have proven theoretically sound and empirically sensible. The potential long-term outperformance of contrarian investing depends upon profiting from mean reversion at the level of the market and/or individual stocks. As Kalesnik points out, the emotional cost of the contrarian strategy may be reduced by investing in a transparent fundamentals-weighted index fund or ETF that rebalances through rules-based trading against price movements.[29]

Finally, I have suggested that contrarian investors may exhibit a number of normal traits to a higher-than-average degree. They include a proclivity for self-reliance and critical thinking, an active orientation toward the future, and a relatively low need for social validation. Hypothesis testing might determine whether contrarians actually have these characteristics.

*The author would like to acknowledge thoughtful comments and suggestions from Denis Chaves, Vitali Kalesnik, Engin Kose, Michele Mazzoleni, and Katy Sherrerd.*

---

[29] In "Smart Beta and the Pendulum of Mispricing," *op. cit.*, Kalesnik stated, "It is exceedingly difficult for investors and managers alike to hold fast when the market continues to move against them. One potential solution is to strip contrarian investing of its emotional component by committing long-term assets to a transparent algorithmic rebalancing strategy. Smart Beta strategies—a recent innovation in financial management—are transparent, non-price weighted solutions. Transparency and dispassionate rebalancing rules help significantly mitigate the agency problems facing regular managers."

## Searching for a New Investment Paradigm
May 2013

Investment management is supposed to be built on brilliant minds' novel insights and innovative approaches—or so our training and traditions have led us to believe. We celebrate our best investors, such as Warren Buffett, Peter Lynch, and Bill Gross, and our best financial theories, such as modern portfolio theory (MPT) and the efficient markets hypothesis (EMH). Yet it seems a long time since we have seen true genius or radically new ideas; and, even more unsettling, recent literature suggests that investors of the future may be deprived of the kind of revolutionary thinking that energized the investment profession in the last half-century.

Does the apparent dearth of financial genius mean the investment industry is in crisis? Will the lack of new investment theories lead to mediocre performance? We don't think so. In fact, we believe that the time is ripe for a new synthesis and that, in the interim, progressive investment management firms will continue to explore the possibilities and improve the investment process.

We are accustomed to think of scientific and technological advances as the work of individual creative geniuses. Albert Einstein's theories of relativity are, of course, classic cases in pure science, and examples in engineering also come readily to mind. Thomas Edison's perfection of the incandescent light bulb is taken for granted today, but, when Nikola Tesla's development of alternating current generators made long-distance power transmission practical, lighting changed the world by extending the natural day.[1] The cultural, economic, and personal effects of these inventions are immeasurable. In Robert J. Gordon's view, the electric light and the electric motor constitute the first of five clusters of great inventions in the late 19th and early 20th centuries that have shaped modern life.[2]

Likewise, the investment management industry has benefited tremendously from transformative ideas. Notably, MPT, EMH, and the

---

[1] Edison violently opposed the spread of Tesla's technology. It is not an edifying story.
[2] Robert J. Gordon, "Does the New Economy Measure Up to the Great Inventions of the Past?" *Journal of Economic Perspectives*, vol. 4, no. 14 (Fall 2000), 59.

capital asset pricing model (CAPM) were developed by financial geniuses—Markowitz, Sharpe, Miller, Fama, Treynor, and others— whose work in the 1960s and 1970s revolutionized investment theory. The conceptual framework they constructed and the equations they devised have equipped several generations of investment professionals to make sense of the markets, develop powerful analytical engines, estimate fair values under normal conditions, and vastly increase the range of available strategies and instruments for taking on and laying off risk.

But the role geniuses have played in the past is changing, according to Dean Keith Simonton, an expert in the psychology of scientific creativity. Simonton distinguishes between creative scientists, who come forward with original and useful ideas, and scientific geniuses, who propose ideas that are original, useful, and *surprising*. Historically, some geniuses have established new specialties, and others have revolutionized existing fields; but, in Simonton's opinion, it is no longer possible for individual scientists—however gifted, accomplished, unconventional, and industrious they may be—either to found or to transform a discipline. "Natural sciences," he wrote, "have become so big, and the knowledge base so complex and specialized, that much of the cutting-edge work these days tends to emerge from large, well-funded collaborative teams involving many contributors."[3]

In this environment, scientists are merely "tidying up loose ends" rather than blazing new paths.[4] Indeed, Simonton suggests that in the improbable event a solitary genius were to get scientists' attention, it is unlikely they would endorse a costly shift to a new paradigm. Such a conceptual revolution generally takes place in a state of crisis resulting from the incapacity of the received paradigm to account for phenomena it can only call "anomalies." According to Thomas S. Kuhn, "Failure of existing rules is the prelude to a search for new ones."[5]

---

[3] Dean Keith Simonton, "After Einstein: Scientific Genius is Extinct." *Nature*, vol. 493, no. 7434 (January 31, 2013).

[4] Simonton concedes, "A possible exception is theoretical physics, which is as yet unable to integrate gravity with the other three forces of nature." *Op. cit.*

[5] Thomas S. Kuhn, *The Structure of Scientific Revolutions*, 3rd ed. Chicago: University of Chicago Press (1996), 68. In Kuhn's influential theory, the natural sciences are subject to sudden, comprehensive "revolutions" or "paradigm shifts," particularly when scientists who are not irrevocably committed to the prevailing theory can no longer disregard contradictory findings.

In a 2013 cover story on the current pace of innovation,[6] *The Economist* concluded that pessimistic appraisals may be overblown, and suggested that economic growth in the emerging world might free millions of minds to "share the burden of knowledge." Tellingly, however, the article reports—and does not dispute—a conclusion reached by Pierre Azoulay and Benjamin Jones: "Though there are more people in research, they are doing less good." According to *The Economist*, Azoulay and Jones estimate that the average U.S. research and development (R&D) worker in 1950 added seven times more "total factor productivity" to economic growth than did an R&D worker in 2000. The article suggests that one element in this decline may be the vast amount of knowledge that individuals must acquire to reach the conceptual frontier of their discipline. I submit that Simonton's tidying up is another plausible factor.

Although the institutional setting is quite different, the investment industry is, in some ways, tracking the natural sciences. There are cracks in the paradigmatic theory of capital markets. Facts do not support it.

In its semi-strong form, EMH represents a textbook world of frictionless markets in which publicly available information zips to rational, tax-exempt mean-variance optimizers who promptly grasp its implications for asset values in the context of their total portfolios. Low latency trading, which reacts instantaneously to momentary variances in mean-reverting processes, approaches this ideal state, at least within the limits of each model's perceptual field. Nonetheless, there is incontrovertible evidence that financial markets are in varying degrees inefficient, and it is widely acknowledged that, individually and collectively, flesh-and-blood investors are at best imperfectly rational.

Exceptional minds have responded ingeniously to important aspects of this situation. For example, alternative approaches to index investment recognize that securities are commonly mispriced, and smart beta strategies exploit persistent market patterns such as the low-volatility anomaly. These new approaches stand to transform the way investment professionals allocate assets. In addition, some of the best minds in the field are investigating a range of macro- and microeconomic factors in pursuit of a more robust construct than standard discount models to explain the equity risk premium. Behavioral finance offers increasingly rich accounts of the biases to which investors are prone; a deeper

---

[6] *The Economist*. "Innovation Pessimism: Has the Ideas Machine Broken Down?" (January 12, 2013).

understanding of their cognitive styles and the stories they tell may lead theoreticians to rethink the industry's valuation models. It is also reasonable to anticipate significant contributions from emotional finance and neuroeconomics in the near future. In short, investment theory may not have entered a full-blown crisis, but fundamentally contrary ideas are in the air, and this is an exciting time for basic as well as applied research.

Will these alternative ideas be embraced? Or, as Simonton and Kuhn suggest, will they be resolutely ignored by established theorists and practitioners? Our experience tells us that many people are reluctant to explore, let alone endorse, new ideas. Some may feel they haven't enough time and energy to appraise the logic of and evidence for novel hypotheses. Others might thoroughly understand the rationale yet more or less consciously shrink from the career risk that accompanies nonconformist thinking. These are comprehensible concerns. Practitioners face relentless demands at work and, often, in their personal lives, and, when economic growth is slow and unemployment high, the loss of a job can be catastrophic.

Nonetheless, investment professionals are ethically obligated to put their clients' interests before their own. Careerism does not trump fiduciary responsibility. Moreover, once published, new ways of thinking are subjected to intense scrutiny—by academics and leading practitioners alike—at a phenomenal pace. We are optimistic that people will become more comfortable with alternative approaches to investing as the new ideas, in their turn, become conventional.

With these notions in mind, what can firms do to foster, or at least recognize, financial genius and healthy innovation in the investment management industry?

Fortunately, the options are within reach of most firms. Capital markets research requires neither funding on the scale of the CERN collider nor as many contributors as those who took part in the human genome project. Investment management firms organize relatively small workgroups or teams to conduct research in fairly well delineated topic areas such as asset classes. Large firms may additionally have more specialized research units exploring distinct geographical regions, economic sectors, or market segments. However they are organized, many firms' research efforts revolve around security analysis. Let us assume, however, that most investment organizations dedicate some resources and devote some time to thinking about theoretical issues such as identifying, investigating, and exploiting previously unrecognized or under-appreciated patterns of mispricing.

Academics and senior managers concerned with company culture, organizational design, and motivation have thought about the productivity of individuals and groups since the early days of the modern corporation more than a century ago. However, the challenges are all the greater in post-industrial, knowledge-based organizations, and they are especially acute when groups—even small groups—include the smartest and most independent people. Can investment research teams accommodate inventors and iconoclasts? Can truly original thinkers function as members of a team?

The familiar criticisms of assertedly nonjudgmental brainstorming call attention to the potential downside of group dynamics. No longer as fashionable as it once was, this technique for stimulating creativity in teams has not always proven effective because, despite the stated objective of generating new ideas in a safe haven, brainstorming naturally tends toward facile consensus-building. Some participants may fear they'll sound foolish, as original thinkers often do, and their suggestions will be quietly but nonetheless roundly dismissed. Others may keep their thoughts to themselves because they habitually defer to those who enjoy higher standing due to their hierarchical position, publishing record, or social status within the group. The exercise seems bound to end with fist-bumping after the team precipitously settles on the least disruptive rather than the most original idea.

Personalities differ, of course, but many creative people need encouragement, a quiet place, time alone, and, ironically, deadlines. And, far from being nonjudgmental, the workgroup should listen to their ideas critically—listen attentively, but find fault with their logic and evidence. Hugo Mercier and Dan Sperber do not see the confirmation bias[7] as a cognitive defect; they maintain instead that the human mind was made for arguing, and that reasoning itself is primarily a search for persuasive arguments in support of one's position.[8] That's why we're so bad at

---

[7] Daniel Kahneman concisely explains the confirmation bias: "Contrary to the rules of philosophers of science, who advise testing hypotheses by trying to refute them, people (and scientists, quite often) seek data that are likely to be compatible with the beliefs they currently hold." *Thinking, Fast and Slow*. New York: Farrar, Strauss and Giroux (2011), 81.

[8] Hugo Mercier and Dan Sperber, "Why Do Humans Reason? Arguments for an Argumentative Theory." *Behavioral and Brain Sciences*, vol. 34, no. 2 (March 2011),

criticizing our own ideas and so good at finding the weaknesses in others'. Argumentative theory compellingly suggests that the proper function of the team is to *evaluate* alternative hypotheses and solutions. At its best, small group research is an agonistic process, combative but never hostile.

The reticent and deferential individuals who hold back in brainstorming sessions will not be reassured when the firm encourages their teammates to criticize their ideas. However, there are steps senior managers, notably including research directors, can take to establish and maintain a collegial atmosphere. It is most important to ensure that team members have what Mercier and Sperber call "a shared interest in the truth." In other words, the participants should be concerned, not with winning a debate, but with finding the most promising answer, however outlandish it might sound at first. Moreover, a corporate culture and workgroup ethic that emphasizes interpersonal honesty, trust, and respect substantially improves the likelihood that all participants will openly share their opinions and offer constructive advice. Research directors and, in the best case, leadership coaches should freely guide participants who seek their advice, just as they should help chronic free riders and arrogant, sarcastic individuals understand that some other firm would probably prove more congenial.

In a recent talk at a Research Affiliates conference, Bradford Cornell proposed a series of simple economic principles modeled on fundamental physical laws such as the conservation of energy.[9] One of those principles is, "Growth in productivity over the long term is limited by the rate of technological innovation." Innovation that improves productivity is a necessary, and ultimately a limiting, condition for per capita GDP growth. But Cornell emphasized that it is not a sufficient condition; improvements in the standard of living further depend upon the social exploitation of new, more efficient technologies. Cornell was addressing a critical determinant of economic history with his customary rigor and attention to the data, but, simplified and expressed in more general terms, his insight also applies to investors and investment managers. We derive no advantage from better ways of doing things if we don't adopt them.

---

57–74. See also my essay below, "For the Sake of Argument."
[9] Bradford Cornell, "Six Easy Economic Pieces: A Lecture Honoring the Spirit of Richard P. Feynman." Delivered April 27th at the Research Affiliates 2013 Advisory Panel.

In our view, a new, principles-based investment theory, one that promises to work as well as CAPM did while accounting for recalcitrant facts about functioning capital markets, is in the offing. We don't know what form it will take—recall that genius is surprising—but we predict that it will emerge from the collective efforts of many gifted, accomplished, argumentative, sleep-deprived thinkers. In the interim, healthy small groups may succeed in discovering specific anomalies, hypothesizing about their causes, conditionally formulating restricted laws, vigorously criticizing them, and publishing their test results. This is not to suggest it's a good plan to leap a chasm in stages; it is merely to recognize the difference between tidying up and making real but admittedly incremental improvements in the professional practice of investment management. While the industry awaits a new synthesis, investors stand to profit from unexploited opportunities as well as the lower costs that may result from operational efficiencies. And they certainly benefit from transparency.

## The Valuation Puzzle
June 14, 2013

Let's take it for granted that the standard model of investment management—broadly including Graham-Dodd security analysis, Markowitz mean-variance portfolio optimization, the Capital Assets Pricing Model, the Efficient Markets Hypothesis (EMH), Arbitrage Pricing Theory, and Black-Scholes option pricing—cogently describes how exemplary investors would value securities under normal conditions in ideal markets. But let's also agree that it does not describe how markets function and investors arrive at decisions *in actuality*. In particular, it does not account for the extreme swings we've already seen in two equity market cycles this century. The stock market seems to go too far in both directions, up and down, and the amplitude of these movements cannot be satisfactorily explained within the cool analytical framework of the standard model. Some other forces or factors must be at work.

One hypothesis is that many market participants view mental effort as an avoidable transaction cost. Disinclined to gather and analyze solid information about the stocks that interest them, they are carried along by the crowd, trading on rumors and momentum. In Keynes's terms, they prefer speculation ("forecasting the psychology of the market") to enterprise ("forecasting the prospective yield of assets over their whole life"). Keynes wrote in the *General Theory*,

> Speculators may do no harm as bubbles on a steady stream of enterprise. But the position is serious when enterprise becomes the bubble on a whirlpool of speculation. When the capital development of a country becomes a by-product of the activities of a casino, the job is likely to be ill-done.[1]

Although there are many active portfolio management strategies and styles, at their transactional core they generally come down to Keynes's "enterprise": they are an attempt to discern what used to be called the inherent value of financial assets by estimating the present value of

---

[1] John Maynard Keynes, *The General Theory of Employment, Interest and Money*, Chapter 12, Section VI (Kissimee, FL: Signalman Publishing, 2009), Kindle edition.

future cash flows. Once they settle on inherent values—today we call them fair values—investors can observe that some assets are attractively priced while others fetch more than they are worth. Active portfolio management is a matter of buying the former and selling the latter while aligning market risk and expected return by maintaining an adequate level of diversification. And active managers are said to have added value when the portfolio return exceeds the return of a valid benchmark, usually an unmanaged, capitalization-weighted index that captures key features of the intended portfolio strategy.

Active management has never been a breeze; these days it's arguably harder than it ever was. Ironically, it isn't even clear whether conventional valuation techniques are reasonable in strongly trending markets. By any traditional measure, one of my portfolio holdings is overvalued. Should I sell it now? Or wait and see if its market price is higher this afternoon, or tomorrow? But I mustn't hold it too long because those on the other side of the trade might lower the bid, even, in the worst case, drop it below my historical cost. So: sell now, realize a gain, and possibly fall behind by forgoing a greater one? Or later, and possibly suffer an opportunity cost or realize a loss? When the stock market is a casino, and the penalties for underperformance are severe, active equity portfolio management all too easily becomes speculation— "the activity of forecasting the psychology of the market." Then it is an act of will to adhere to the agreed-upon strategy and the firm's established valuation process rather than trying to time the market or defaulting to a closet index. And more often than not even highly disciplined active management doesn't pay.[2]

How to value financial assets in momentum-driven markets is not the standard model's only conundrum.[3] Vernon L. Smith observes, "Along with the Valuation Puzzle, we also have the Trading Volume Puzzle that

---

[2] According to the SPIVA Scorecard compiled by S&P Dow Jones Indices, for periods ended December 31, 2012, 74.35% of actively managed U.S. equity funds underperformed benchmark indices for three years, 68.56% for five years, and 57.3% for ten years.

[3] The standard model is also confronted with the persistent low volatility anomaly—the well-established fact that, in violation of the fundamental financial principle that risk and return are positively correlated, low-volatility or low-beta stocks produce higher returns than high-volatility or high-beta stocks. (It is an anomaly, of course, only from the perspective of the standard model.) In the last few years, low-volatility index investing has emerged as a major smart beta strategy.

seems far beyond the grasp of traditional theory populated by agents using the same maximizing model and looking at pretty much the same data, yet they seem to be in constant disagreement!"[4] Richard H. Thaler explains the issue:

> Standard models of asset markets predict that participants will trade very little. The reason is that in a world where everyone knows that traders are rational (I know that you are rational, you know that I am rational, and I know that you know that I am rational), if I am offering to buy some shares of IBM Corporation and you are offering to sell them, I have to wonder what information you have that I do not.[5]

But in fact trade volumes are very high indeed. In the month of June 2013, the average *daily* volume traded on or through the New York Stock Exchange was approximately 1.6 billion shares of equity securities and exchange-traded funds (ETFs).[6] Let's assume algorithmic trading accounts for about half the trading volume.[7] That means every trading day some 800 million shares are changing hands as the result of conscious purchase and sale decisions on the NYSE alone.

Behavioral economists have described the biases that affect individuals' choices under uncertainty. In addition—although I believe the usefulness of fMRI research has been greatly overstated[8]—the field of neuroeconomics has also contributed to our understanding of the autonomous brain which leaps to conclusions while our minds are still deliberating. (Reasoning, it appears, is often rationalizing choices we may not know we've already made.) The insights into investor psychology

---

[4] E-mail dated June 14, 2013.
[5] Richart H. Thaler, "The End of Behavioral Finance," *Financial Analysts Journal*, vol. 55, no. 6 (November/December 1999), 13-14.
[6] NYSE Euronext Monthly Volume Summary, June 2013.
http://www.nyse.com/financials/1143717022567.html. Accessed July 13, 2013.
[7] Matthew Philips, "How the Robots Lost: High-Frequency Trading's Rise and Fall," Bloomberg Businessweek, June 6, 2013.
http://www.businessweek.com/articles/2013-06-06/how-the-robots-lost-high-frequency-tradings-rise-and-fall. Accessed July 13, 2013.
[8] Despite its provocative buy-the-book title, Sally Satel and Scott O. Lilienfeld's sustained critique, *Brainwashed: The Seductive Appeal of Mindless Neuroscience* (New York: Basic Books, 2013), offers a realistic appraisal of fMRI as an instrument for probing the workings of the brain.

and decision-making we've gained from these fields go a long way toward explaining noise in prices.[9]

Thus far, however, the new theories lack the quantitative apparatus that made the standard model so powerful for half a century. Andreas Steiner commented insightfully on an earlier version of this essay, "There were also no formulas in Adam Smith's *Wealth of Nations*; only several hundred years later did we have mathematical proof that a general market equilibrium is feasible (under specific assumptions). I think we will see a similar development with behavioural finance." As evidence that this effort is already well under way, he cited the mental accounting framework developed by Das, Markowitz, Scheid, and Statman. Their paper, which may prove to be a seminal contribution to the formalization of individual investment decision-making, integrates mean-variance theory and behavioral portfolio theory so as to accommodate return thresholds and attitudes toward risk that vary by sub-account.[10]

It is immensely worthwhile, of course, to understand how individuals, including ourselves, actually make investment decisions. Nonetheless, the new ideas will not—cannot—solve the valuation puzzle until they account for the price effects of interactions among countless market participants under the assumptions that the most knowledgeable have partial information and many, perhaps the majority, are noise traders. Until serious investors—optimally including boutique managers and retail investors—have an empirically sound basis for valuing securities in trending markets, the discoveries and intuitions of behavioral finance, neuroeconomics, experimental economics, and evolutionary psychology will remain, at best, philosophically interesting.

In the meantime, it's no longer clear to me that capitalization-weighted indices are appropriate benchmarks for appraising the results of active portfolio management. I realize this is heresy in the performance measurement community. But the stock market increasingly appears to be driven more by mass psychology than by sober professional judgment

---

[9] See especially Daniel Kahneman, *Thinking, Fast and Slow* (New York: Farrar, Strauss and Giroux, 2011); Arnold S. Wood, ed., *Behavioral Finance and Investment Management* (Charlottesville, VA: Research Foundation of CFA Institute, 2010); and Jason Zweig, *Your Money and Your Brain: How the New Science of Neuroeconomics Can Help Make You Rich* (New York: Simon & Schuster, 2007).

[10] Sanjiv Das, Harry Markowitz, Jonathan Scheid, and Meir Statman, "Portfolio Optimization with Mental Accounts," *Journal of Financial and Quantitative Analysis*, vol. 45, no. 2 (April 2010), 311-334.

based upon disciplined valuation techniques. Clients who seek superior risk-adjusted returns would more suitably evaluate managers against target Sharpe ratios, for all their limitations, than against cap-weighted indices. And those who have a specific hurdle rate really should consider satisficing.

## Back to the Basics: Value and Growth Investing
June 7, 2012

In a recent article entitled "Equity Investing: From Style Box to Global Unconstrained," PIMCO's Andrew Pyne wrote that the traditional equity style boxes have "constrained managers and limited their opportunity set."[1] The emphasis on cyclical, narrowly benchmarked capitalization and valuation styles has, he argued, encouraged clients to make disadvantageous short-term hiring and firing decisions and managers to become closet indexers. The "style box construct," he suggested, "has morphed into an expensive index strategy."

The prevalence of style classifications may very well have had unintended consequences in the competition to gather and retain assets. Moreover, I, too, have little patience for arbitrary constraints. In my experience, many investment policy statements are much too long and far too detailed. But the classic investment styles are neither conceptually misguided nor empirically unsupported; on the contrary, they capture well-established differences among stocks and essential dimensions of the investment decision process.[2] Using index data from Russell Investments, I will focus on value and growth investing in this piece.

Total return is one of the most rudimentary concepts of performance measurement, and its basic constituents are price changes and investment income. Relatedly, investors evaluate the relative attractiveness of stocks on the basis of potential price appreciation and prospective earnings. In this context, the price-earnings (P/E) ratio is a key measure. Christopherson, Cariño, and Ferson observe, "The 'growth' investor is concerned primarily with the earnings component of the ratio." If a stock's P/E is steady, the price is likely to rise with the growth of earnings. "The 'value' investor, on the other hand, is primarily concerned with the price component of the ratio and generally cares less about the future earnings growth of the company." If the P/E is too low, the

---

[1] Andrew Pyne, "Equity Investing: From Style Box to Global Unconstrained," AdvisorAnalyst.com, May 16, 2012. Accessed August 8, 2012. http://advisoranalyst.com/glablog/2012/05/16/equity-investing-from-style-box-to-global-unconstrained-pyne/

[2] Laurence B. Siegal explains the conceptual foundations and traces the evolution of style investing in his Research Foundation of CFA Institute monograph, *Benchmarks and Investment Management* (2003), 65-74. The PDF is available gratis from the publisher. Accessed August 8, 2012. http://www.cfapubs.org/toc/rf/2003/2003/1

stock's price is likely to rise to a level that properly reflects the company's earning power.[3]

Thus, growth and value investors place the emphasis on one aspect of valuation or the other: growth, earnings; value, price. Nothing could be more fundamental.

It is not surprising that growth and value portfolios and benchmarks have distinctive characteristics. **Table 1** shows that the Russell 3000® Growth Index[4] has a lower dividend yield than the corresponding value index, but higher price/book and P/E ratios as well as apparently accelerating earnings.

**Table 1.** Russell Style Index Characteristics as of April 30, 2012

|  | Russell 3000® Value Index | Russell 3000® Growth Index |
|---|---|---|
| Price/Book | 1.56 | 4.01 |
| Dividend Yield | 2.54 | 1.47 |
| Price/Earnings (ex-negative earnings) | 14.33 | 17.34 |
| IBES Long-Term Growth Forecast % | 9.19 | 13.66 |
| EPS 5-Year Growth | 1.06 | 15.3 |
| Source: Russell Investments |  |  |

**Table 2** provides additional statistical information; it is noteworthy that the value index has a higher Sharpe ratio and a lower beta than the

---

[3] Jon A. Christopherson, David R. Cariño, and Wayne E. Ferson, *Portfolio Performance Measurement and Benchmarking* (McGraw-Hill, 2009), 276-277. If I were teaching a college-level course on performance measurement, I would use this book.

[4] Russell's style index construction methodology uses three variables and a nonlinear probability algorithm to assign value and growth weights to individual stocks. The variables are the book-to-price ratio, the I/B/E/S forecast medium-term growth (2 year), and sales per share historical growth (5 year). Russell Investments, "Russell U.S. Equity Indexes Construction and Methodology," May 2012. Accessed August 8, 2012. http://www.russell.com/indexes/documents/Methodology.pdf. The design and construction of style indexes are beyond the scope of this article, but Siegal discusses the trade-offs in style index construction (*op. cit.*, 78-84), and Christopherson *et al.* explain the rationale for key features of the Russell style indexes (*op. cit.*, 320-323).

growth index. Also included in Table 2 are the two series' mean returns, monthly standard deviation of returns, kurtosis, and skewness.

**Table 2.** Statistical Measures

| Measure* | Russell 3000® Value Index | Russell 3000® Growth Index |
|---|---|---|
| Mean Monthly Return | 0.58 | 0.48 |
| Standard Deviation | 4.76 | 5.57 |
| Kurtosis | 1.43 | 0.62 |
| Skewness | –0.67 | –0.59 |
| Correlation | 0.79 | |
| Sharpe Ratio | 0.27 | 0.18 |
| Beta vs. Russell 3000® Index | 0.91 | 1.09 |
| *Based upon monthly total returns from June 1997 through May 2012 | | |

**Figure 1** presents side-by-side frequency distributions of monthly returns over the fifteen-year period from June 1997 through May 2012. The shaded columns represent the bins containing a return of zero. Historical information like this can help financial advisors guide clients toward the style that makes most sense in light of their investment objectives, time frame, and risk tolerance.

**Figure 1.** Monthly Total Returns

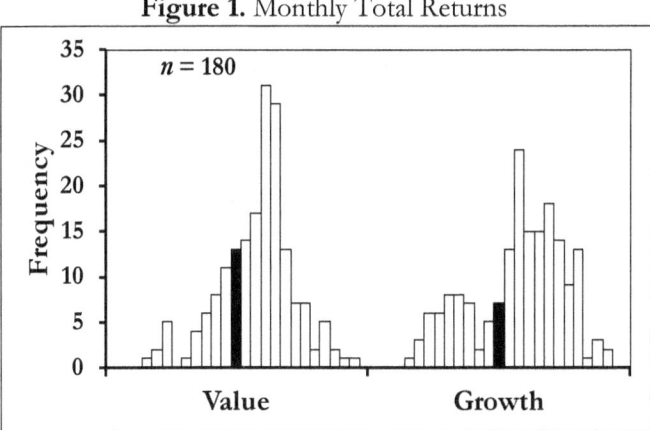

It is not unexpected that style portfolios and benchmarks exhibit cyclicality as they follow their disparate return paths.[5] In **Figure 2**, for

---

[5] Jason Hsu points out that the value premium is mean-reverting in his article,

example, growth outperformed value in the period October 1998–October 2000. However, the styles abruptly reversed their relative positions in November 2000, when the domestic equity market first started to decline after the dot-com boom of the 1990s (a decline that became a dead fall in February 2001). Value remained "in favor," that is, it continued to dominate growth, through March 2003. Interestingly, the opposite reversal occurred with the outbreak of the subprime crisis in September 2007.

**Figure 2**. Trailing 12-Month Total Returns
June 1997 through May 2012

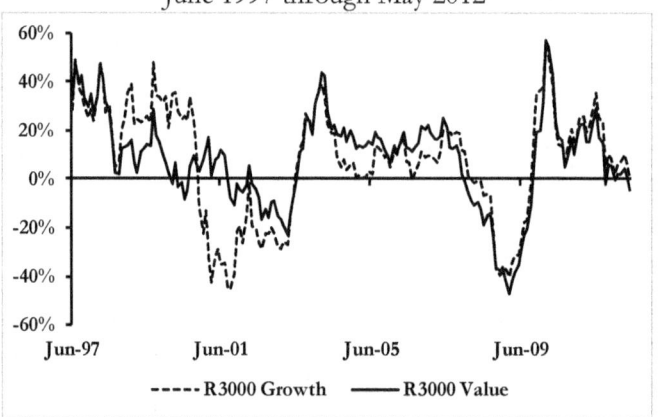

These conflicting outcomes suggest it might be exceedingly difficult to tease out signals that one style is about to dominate the other. Nonetheless, managers who believe they can anticipate or promptly identify such turning points might consider using futures contracts to adjust a core equity portfolio's exposure to growth and value stocks. (For example, futures on the Russell 1000® Growth and Value indexes trade on ICE.) Complementing the actively managed style portfolios, this openly index-based approach would presumably enable managers to advise and accommodate clients wishing to engage in tactical asset allocation.

The triangle chart in **Figure 3** offers a different view of the relationship between value and growth returns. It displays the spread or arithmetic difference in annualized returns for periods beginning in June and ending in May. For example, from June 2002 through May 2007, the Russell

3000® Value Index outperformed the Russell 3000 Growth Index by 4.88% per year, and from June 2006 through May 2010 the annualized total return of the growth index exceeded that of the value index by 3.38%.

**Figure 3.** Triangle Chart from June 2002 through May 2012

| From June... | Value Index Returns Minus Growth Index Returns (Annualized %) | | | | | | | | | |
|---|---|---|---|---|---|---|---|---|---|---|
| | Through May... | | | | | | | | | |
| | 2012 | 2011 | 2010 | 2009 | 2008 | 2007 | 2006 | 2005 | 2004 | 2003 |
| 2002 | −0.54 | 2.12 | 0.56 | 0.42 | 1.68 | 4.88 | 4.85 | 4.50 | 0.88 | 0.18 |
| 2003 | −0.63 | −0.71 | 0.62 | 0.47 | 2.03 | 6.32 | 6.73 | 7.15 | 1.78 | |
| 2004 | −0.89 | −0.29 | 0.46 | 0.25 | 2.09 | 7.76 | 9.00 | 12.04 | | |
| 2005 | −2.64 | −2.26 | −1.67 | −2.34 | −1.19 | 5.48 | 5.94 | | | |
| 2006 | −3.98 | −3.81 | −3.38 | −4.62 | −4.65 | 4.95 | | | | |
| 2007 | −5.41 | −5.57 | −5.42 | −7.59 | −11.88 | | | | | |
| 2008 | −3.66 | −3.27 | −2.28 | −4.33 | | | | | | |
| 2009 | −3.11 | −2.01 | 1.77 | | | | | | | |
| 2010 | −5.31 | −5.91 | | | | | | | | |
| 2011 | −4.78 | | | | | | | | | |

Note: Growth outperformed value in the shaded cells.

Over the 10-year period ended May 31, 2012, the annualized return of the Russell 3000 Growth Index was 4.81% and the corresponding return of the Russell 3000 Value Index was 4.27%.[6] This calendar year the growth style has been running substantially ahead of value. The growth index earned 6.88% year-to-date through May, appreciably better than the 3.51% return of the value index.[7]

Pyne's article raises interesting and important issues, including short-termism, due diligence in manager selection, and the uses of benchmarks in actively managed portfolios. I suspect we'd agree on the first two questions and not the third, but exploring these issues would take me far afield. My purposes here have simply been to recall the elementary thinking behind value and growth investing and to bring the evidentiary record up to date. In my view, there's a lot to be said for simple, straightforward, workmanlike equity investment management in accordance with well-tested strategies.

---

[6] For the full 15-year period ended May 31, 2012, the annualized return of the Russell 3000 Value Index was 5.76%, and the corresponding return of the Russell 3000 Growth Index was 3.94%. Thus, over the timeframe reflected in Table 2, Figure 1, and Figure 2 above, value outperformed growth by 182 basis points.

[7] Update: YTD through July 2012, the index returns are 11.2% (Growth) and 9.6% (Value), a difference of 160 basis points.

# Part Two: Leadership, Ethics, and Training

# Anatomy of a Calamity—Stage 2: "Calamity"

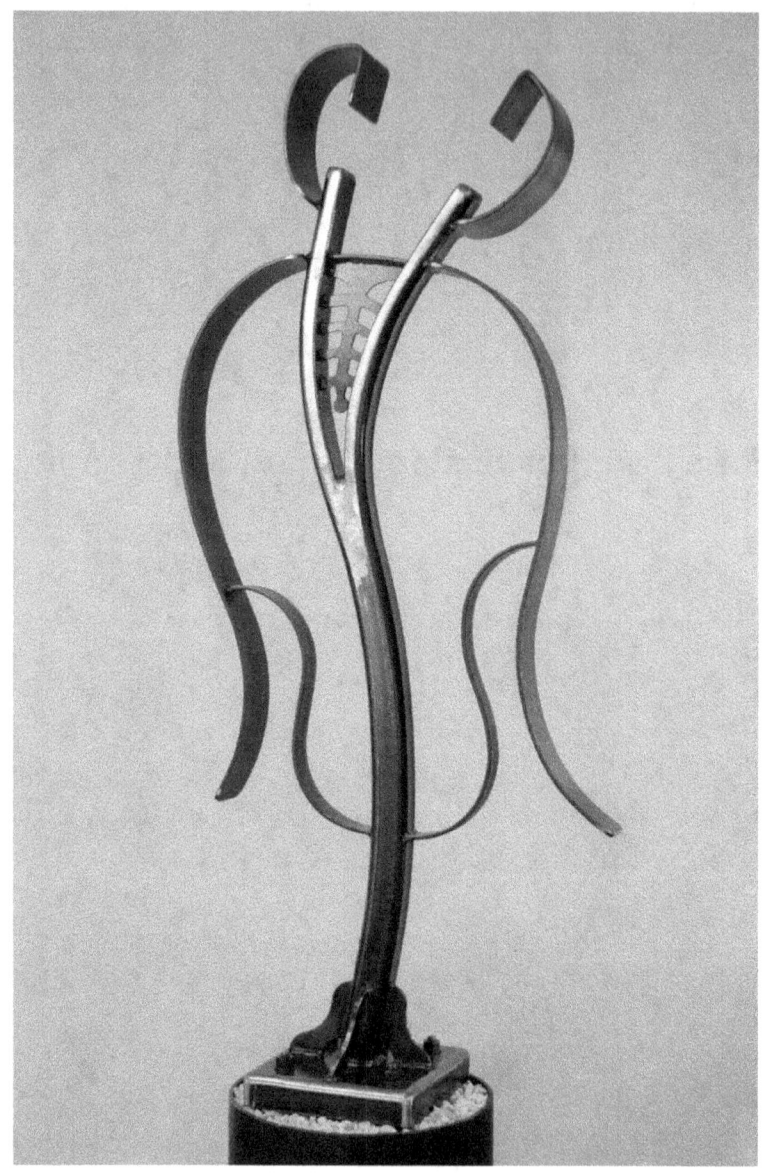

*Initially, when a traumatic event occurs, whether it is a severe illness, accident, assault, abuse or other trauma, it only affects the point of contact. Everything else disappears into the background.*

# The Motivation to Work
November 19, 2012

The Belgian psychologist Joseph Nuttin wrote, "it is a notorious fact that many people are not motivated to do the work they do; they work for *extrinsic* reasons: in order to do certain things alongside or after their work." Nonetheless, many others, he observed, "are deeply involved and find their pleasure in the work they accomplish."[1] What factors account for the difference?

Nuttin, who died in 1988, was an original thinker who brought creative insight as well as experimental ingenuity and analytical power to the study of general psychology. Unlike Freud, whose starting point and abiding interest was psychopathology, he primarily sought to understand well-adjusted, highly functioning people at all levels of their activity. Unlike Thorndike, Hull, and their respective epigones, he recognized and explained the rôles of cognition, intentionality, and self-concept in human behavior. Nuttin developed a dynamic, relational model of personality, one in which "it is suitable to say that personality is not simply *situated in* a world and *open to* this world, but that *this world enters as an integrating element into the personality itself.*"[2] And he expounded a theory of motivation that is, in my opinion, incomparable for its richness and subtlety.

There is no question of summarizing, let alone criticizing, Nuttin's theory of personality in this short piece. All I can do right now is to mention a theme that is germane to an understanding of the motivation to work. Nuttin objected to the thesis that people are driven primarily by physiological needs—sex, hunger, thirst, self-defense—and its corollary that higher-order needs are at best secondary or derivative. In his view, for example, the organism's fundamental need to maintain its existence against the external environment is equally present in the hunt for food and the endeavor to be someone in the social world. "We can easily recognize the psychic energy this 'drive' contains by imagining, just for an instant, all the effort and tedious work that the education and preliminary training for one *career* or another, precisely due to which a

---

[1] Joseph Nuttin, *Théorie de la motivation humaine: Du besoin au projet d'action*, 5e édition (Presses Universitaires de France, 2000), 195.
[2] *La Structure de la personnalité*, 6e édition (Presses Universitaires de France, 1985), 214.

young human being will become 'someone' among the others, requires of the one who submits to it."[3]

Nor, of course, can Nuttin's theory of motivation be adequately presented in this space. Given that he places personality, behavior, and motivation in a unified conceptual framework,[4] I can at most indicate some key elements. Building upon his insight that there is no personality without a world and no world without the personality that constructs it, Nuttin states that a person is "a being in situation doing something,"[5] and he defines behavior as "a meaningful response to a situation that also has a sense."[6] A situated subject acts on a perceived state of affairs in view of a conceived state—a goal—which is more or less 'realized' or achieved in the result of the action.[7] The fact that behavior has a *goal* is central to Nuttin's understanding of motivation.

With this sketchy introduction, let's turn to Nuttin's account of the motivation to work. One of the most striking aspects of human behavior, he observes, is that people can't leave things in the condition they find them. If they don't undertake to destroy what disturbs them, people are tempted "to intervene, to change, to restructure, to improve." Human beings also try to intervene in their own development, to become who they want to be, and this tendency is "personalized and made concrete—at least in our culture—in a vocational project." People generally seem to be motivated to achieve or create something which would not be accomplished or produced without *their* action. Often they identify with the things they succeed in making real; their opus is an extension of themselves.

In the ideal case, Nuttin says, individuals' intervention in producing things—their work—is incorporated in the project of their personal

---

[3] *Psychanalyse et conception spiritualiste de l'homme*, 3e édition (Publications Universitaires de Louvain, 1962), 261. Coming full circle, Nuttin wrote, "the different forms of needs pervade one another like the physiological and psycho-social activities themselves. Thus the need for nourishment is concretely manifested as a need to earn one's living and, even more concretely, as a need to maintain and develop one's social standing." *Tâche réussite et échec: Théorie de la conduite humaine* (Publications Universitaires de Louvain, 1953), 428. "Social standing" is in English in the original.

[4] *Théorie de la motivation, op. cit.*, 122.

[5] *Ibid.*, 104.

[6] *Ibid.*, 38.

[7] *Ibid.*, 78.

development and the realization of their self-concept. In most cases, however, one observes the contrary: "the work one must in fact execute consists in collaborating in the realization of *other persons' projects* without the least effort toward a certain integration of projects having been undertaken." Such extrinsically motivated work remains connected with the need for self-development in the sense that collaborating in an impersonal, collective project provides the feeling of being useful, a feeling which affects one's self-esteem, as the unemployed will attest. "Nonetheless," Nuttin writes, "intrinsically motivated work is accompanied by profound satisfaction, and the quality of the work supplied is generally superior."

Knowledge workers and those who are their own bosses seem to have less difficulty than others in finding tasks that really occupy them. Nuttin realistically acknowledges, however, that, independently of financial problems, few people appear capable of giving themselves work that "counts."[8] Moreover, an exaggerated fear of taking risks and an immoderate desire for security are factors that, in our society, impede the motivation for accomplishment and the tendency to pursue constructive personal projects. Insofar as there is a solution, the theoretically coherent remedy Nuttin suggests consists in "establishing lines of communication by which the person can find a certain personal development through and in his work." He cites measures to engage employees, such as involving them in enterprise planning and assigning them responsibility for the results obtained. "But," he writes, "psychology still seems a very feeble instrument in this struggle against differently powerful social and economic forces."[9]

---

[8] Nuttin found the widespread incapacity for constructive self-direction worrisome because, when he was writing, leisure time was expected to increase substantially. That prediction certainly hasn't come true. Many workers are compelled to sacrifice almost all their free time and hold more than one job just to make ends meet. [Added in 2018: Nonetheless, from personal observation, Nuttin's underlying concern is sensible, given that many people who can afford to retire seem to lead rather vacant lives after they stop working. In addition, the ongoing deployment of robots in manufacturing, mining, and medicine, and of artificial intelligence applications in service industries, now rather more credibly threatens to exclude vast numbers from the labor force (and, among them, knowledge workers such as accountants and financial advisors). People have fretted about automation and unemployment since the early 19th century, but this time might actually be different. Nor could providing universal basic income make up for the loss of meaningful work.]

[9] *Ibid.*, 194-199.

In my view, Nuttin's pessimism on this point may be unjustified. He might have underestimated how much a strong manager in a progressive corporate culture can do on behalf of employees who are open to the possibility of integrating work and personal growth. And creating the conditions for rewarding work that is, incidentally, of superior quality seems well worth the struggle.

# Smarts

January 27, 2013

One of the many things Howard Gardner has taught us is that displaying a talent for logico-mathematical thinking (or, in our line of work, quantitative modeling) is not the only way of being smart. His theory of multiple intelligences, first set out in *Frames of Mind* (Basic Books, 1983), holds that there are other, separate kinds of intellection, including for example linguistic, spatial, musical, and interpersonal competencies: other ways of learning and exhibiting intelligent behavior.

Gardner has profoundly enriched our understanding of intelligence. But his influential early work comes to mind now because *New Yorker* staff writer Adam Gopnik unexpectedly made an interesting observation about bright people and their cognitive styles in an article on the science of sound. Gopnik is a writer of exceptional range and subtlety. "Among highly intelligent people," he said, "there are two kinds of minds, the sharp and the soft. We expect smart people to have minds like swords, made to fight and slash and slay. Soft smart minds, though, are of another, rarer sort. They absorb great quantities of data and opinion, often silently, even sluggishly, and turn them around slowly until a solution appears."[1]

Traders, at least those who survive their first year or two, have sharp minds. They are paid well to see evanescent opportunities, exploit asymmetrical information, and execute advantageous decisions swiftly. They use their minds like sabers, and, eyes on the Bloomberg, they "fight and slash and slay" in an arena where relentless self-regard and aggressive behavior are not only acceptable but mandatory. On the trading floor there are the living—the "quick"—and the dead.

Is there any place in the investment industry for Gopnik's soft smart minds?

Contrasting "sharp" and "soft" is a curious move. The opposite of sharp is dull; of soft, hard. In ordinary language, to say that someone is "not the sharpest knife in the drawer" is no more a compliment than calling him "soft in the head." It's just common sense, it seems, that investment organizations competing in fast-moving, impersonal, zero-sum markets

---

[1] Adam Gopnik, "Music to Your Ears: The Quest for 3-D Recording and Other Mysteries of Sound," *The New Yorker*, January 28, 2013, p. 35.

need hardheaded men and women who will spot the opening and go for the kill. And it seems equally clear that soft minds—one is tempted to say flaccid minds—belong in philosophy departments, or rather in the caring professions. In my experience, academics, armed with pen-is-mightier vocabularies and finely honed instincts for one another's vulnerabilities, have shown themselves intensely competitive. Popper said Wittgenstein threatened him with a fireplace poker.[2]

Yet in Gopnik's usage soft smart minds are anything but weak. They merely have another, less familiar way of ingesting and processing complex and often contradictory information: they ruminate. This is a form of high intelligence that is difficult to describe favorably; Gopnik chose the unfortunate adverb "sluggishly," and I've inadvertently fallen into a bovine metaphor. Nonetheless, precisely because they don't reach conclusions precipitously, soft smart minds may be more likely to see remote connections, and less likely to overlook significant but unobvious trends.

Some investment management firms appear to value unhurried deliberation, not, of course, on the trading desk, but on the part of business and portfolio strategists. In my opinion, many more would do well to hire a few good, soft minds—in Gopnik's special sense—and supply them with economic and capital markets data. After a while they might come back with surprising insights.

---

[2] David Edmonds and John Eidinow, *Wittgenstein's Poker: The Story of a Ten-Minute Argument Between Two Great Philosophers* (Faber and Faber, 2001).

# Speed Bumps
September 23, 2012

There is a long block in a 25 miles-per-hour stretch of Robin Hood Road in Norfolk, Virginia, that has three speed bumps at intervals of about 150 feet. (They're called "speed humps" in these parts.) Although speeding is dangerous in any residential neighborhood, there is nothing distinctive about this one.

A friend told me the speed bumps in question were constructed in the early 1970s, when a developmentally impaired youngster lived on that block. The child has long since grown up and relocated; he may have children of his own in some other city. But the speed bumps remain and will probably slow traffic for decades or generations to come. "And when folks my age move away or die," said my friend, "nobody will have any idea why those blasted speed humps are there."

So think about your operations. Is your group mechanically doing something whose purpose is inapparent? Does anybody remember why? If not, it may be an unnecessary step, and the process can be simplified or streamlined by omitting it. But, to be sure, don't neglect to inform downstream operational teams before you change the routine. That's good corporate citizenship, and it may reduce the number of complaints you receive as the remote and unobvious consequences of your change come to light.

## The Sociology of Morality
March 6, 2013

Do you see yourself as a morally strong person? Are your actions consistent with your self-conception? How would you feel if you did something bad?

These simple questions are never asked in employment interviews; candidates' declarations of integrity would be inherently unreliable. Few recruiters and managers in the investment industry are trained in reading the facial micro-expressions that indicate whether someone is responding truthfully.[1] Moreover, nobody's actions are entirely predictable. Yet there is empirical evidence that individuals' internal moral standards are indirectly related to their conduct. It seems desirable for gatekeepers—indeed, for anyone who is concerned about an organization's culture, values, and reputation—to understand the factors that make some people more prone to misdeeds than others in like circumstances.

In a study published last year, two sociologists proposed and tested a theory of the self that explicitly links the cognitive, behavioral, and affective facets of moral choice. Jan E. Stets and Michael J. Carter wrote, "To understand the illicit behavior of some, we need to study the moral dimension of the self and what makes some individuals more dishonest than others within and across situations." They cited the "practices of stock brokers, investment advisors, and mortgage lenders whose behavior facilitated the recent economic recession" as an example.[2]

Among many other issues, philosophers have investigated the status of ethical codes, the nature of personhood, the meaning of virtue, and the relationships between thought, language, and action. Psychologists have examined motivation, the desire for external validation, and the affective consequences of inner conflict. Now Stets and Carter have enriched the study of moral choice by framing testable hypotheses on the basis of a

---

[1] Online training is available from Paul Ekman Group at www.paulekman.com. Accessed March 4, 2013.

[2] Jan E. Stets and Michael J. Carter, "A Theory of the Self for the Sociology of Morality." *American Sociological Review*, 2012, 135. http://asr.sagepub.com/content/77/1/120. Accessed March 2, 2013. DOI: 10.1177/0003122411433762. Many thanks to Sharon Gould for bringing this research to my attention.

sociological model of the internal operations of the self. They found that model in identity theory.

Identity theory sees people as actors, not merely reactors, and fully acknowledges the possibility of choice, but also recognizes that human action is constrained by social structure and social interaction. The theory crucially postulates that actions are shaped by the way individuals see themselves and the environment; and the meanings people attribute to themselves and to situations are developed through their interactions with others. In fact, people have as many identities as they have social roles—spouse, parent, child, sibling, manager, employee, colleague, and the like[3]—and those roles are structured in a "hierarchy of salience" defined by individuals' commitments to being a particular kind of person. (Salience, in this context, is the probability that a given role will be activated in a specific situation.) Sheldon Stryker, who largely developed identity theory, expresses its fundamental proposition in these terms: "Commitment impacts identity salience impacts role choice."[4]

In applying identity theory to the domain of moral choice, Stets and Carter emphasize the mechanism of "identity verification." They diagram the self in its environment and explain identity theory in the terminology of control systems, with inputs, outputs, and a feedback loop. The inputs are definitions of situations (interpretations that frame situations as calling for certain roles, behaviors, and feelings) and "reflected appraisals" (interpretations of others' reactions to one's behavior). These inputs are fed into a metaphorical "comparator" which relates them to stored identity standard meanings and produces error signals when it registers variances. If an actor thinks others perceive her as a just and caring person to the same extent that she so perceives herself—say a "moral identity score" of 7 on a scale of 1 to 10—then her identity is verified. However, if she thinks others see her as less, or more, moral than she considers herself, her identity is not verified.[5]

---

[3] [Added in 2018: Georg Simmel described the impact of functionally specialized roles on personal development in his classic work, *The Philosophy of Money* (1900). See Philip Lawton, *The King and the Poor Wretch: Simmel's Philosophy of the Actor*, Amazon/CreateSpace (2017), 9-13.]

[4] Sheldon Stryker, "Identity Theory," *Encyclopedia of Sociology* (Macmillan Reference USA, 2001), 1253-1258.

[5] Stets and Carter point out that non-verification of moral identity can result from surpassing as well as from falling short of one's identity standard. "Exceeding one's moral standard may generate the view that one is a moral fraud, while failing to meet a moral standard may result in feeling morally inadequate." *Op. cit.*, 135.

Similarly, there is a discrepancy if the meaning of a situation is unaligned with the person's salient identity. "For example," Stets and Carter said, "if meanings in a situation are about acquiring wealth rather than behaving morally, one will have difficulty verifying the moral identity."[6]

It is through the internal operation of identity verification that emotions come into play. Stets and Carter focus on two negative moral emotions that may follow from the experience of non-verification: guilt (an actor judges that he did something bad) and shame (an actor judges that he is a bad person). These emotions may trigger a variety of responses, including cognitive strategies such as rationalizing one's behavior, evading responsibility, minimizing one's participation, understating the consequences, and blaming the victim. Often, however, they result in behavioral changes intended to reduce the inconsistency. Stets and Carter stress the social significance of these emotions. "Ultimately," they wrote, "guilt and shame keep people integrated into society through internal monologues with the self and feedback from others."[7]

Stets and Carter formulated five hypotheses and designed an experiment to test them. For instance, one hypothesis was, "The higher a person's moral identity score, the more likely the person will behave morally." Another was, "The more a person defines a situation as containing moral meanings, the more likely the person will behave morally." The authors recruited 369 undergraduate sociology students and conducted the study in two parts. In the first phase, they administered a survey that measured the participants' moral identity, behavior, and emotions in scenarios that were relevant to the students' lives. In the second phase, conducted three months later, the same population—there was no attrition—responded to a survey that measured moral meanings and feeling rules (cultural expectations about the emotions that ought to be experienced in moral situations).

Stets and Carter's article in the *American Sociological Review* presents the design, results, and limitations of their study in considerable detail. In general, they state, their hypotheses were supported. For example, both the moral identity and situations with moral meanings are positively associated with moral behavior, and reports of moral emotions are positively associated with identity non-verification.

---

[6] *Ibid.*, 125.

[7] *Ibid.* The authors cite Jonathan H. Turner, "Natural Selection and the Evolution of Morality in Human Societies," in S. Hitlin and S. Vaisey, eds., *Handbook of the Sociology of Morality* (New York: Springer, 2010), 125–145.

This brief treatment does not remotely do justice to Stets and Carter's meticulous study. Well written and insightful, it repays careful reading. What are the implications of their research for investment professionals? To open the dialogue, here are two rather obvious suggestions.

First, senior management should set clear expectations for ethical conduct.

Because role choices guide behavior, the firm should commit itself to creating a culture that prizes integrity and to defining its employees' role in terms that prominently include ethical behavior. Staff should know, for instance, that they are expected without reservation to place clients' interests ahead of the firm's and their own interests. Moreover, because codes of conduct are all too often seen as meaningless totems, managers throughout the organization should consistently enforce internal controls, taking care to ensure there are no mixed messages that would interfere with moral identity verification. Establishing solid cultural and social expectations within the firm, and communicating them in practice every day, might encourage moral behavior—or at least discourage wrongdoing.

Second, training should importantly include practice in identifying and articulating the moral meanings of situations.

People can change, even radically. Examples of moral conversion come to mind readily: Constantine. Augustine. Closer to our own times, the late Charles Colson. But these men may be so easily recalled precisely because their stories are extraordinary. Change is hard, and radical change betokens a profound spiritual experience. Identity theory appears to consider the actor's internal standards inalterable; and, realistically, an adult's moral identity is fixed, at least in the short term. Investment management firms may, however, be able to influence the *other* input to the comparator, the moral meanings of situations that are likely to arise in the course of business. Helping staff perceive the ethical dimensions of their work might facilitate moral identity verification.

Understanding identity theory, and especially the mechanics of identity verification, is not particularly helpful in spotting likely miscreants, but it does suggest why they might make unfortunate choices. They may have relatively low internal standards; define their professional role in a way that minimizes or excludes ethical obligations; overlook moral meanings in situations; and/or fail to experience moral emotions, at least with the same intensity as others.  Because these are hidden characteristics, it remains possible that bad actors will occasionally slip through the hiring process—all the interviews, reference calls, and background checks—and disrupt the organization or put its reputation at risk.  Let them find themselves alone at investment management firms that take ethical conduct seriously.

# Managing the Firm
July 20, 2011

En route from Boston to Charlottesville, I went to a noontime meeting of the Institute of Management Accountants' Richmond chapter. My purpose was primarily to catch up with friends whom I haven't seen recently; I probably would not have gone out of my way to hear the guest speaker talk about managing costs at his company, a closely-held supplier of bricks to the residential construction industry. In fact, however, his presentation and the ensuing discussion were intriguing. The event took me back to the very basics of running a business.

Years ago, while still an MBA candidate, I worked in the finance department of a manufacturing company with international sales subsidiaries. I joined the company as a consolidations accountant and, under the tutelage of a capable controller, I learned the intricacies of transfer pricing. Later I became an analyst in the corporate financial planning group where, guided by another exceptional manager, I effectively had an apprenticeship in business economics. After completing my degree and earning the Certified Management Accountant (CMA) designation, I relocated to another city and, more or less by chance, entered the financial services industry.

The differences between manufacturing and distribution, on one hand, and financial services, on the other, are so great and so obvious that they scarcely bear mentioning. The former contribute to GDP; the economic value of a zero-sum game like financial services may not be so evident. In the financial services industry, research and development costs generally are not capitalized; there is no need to manage and track inventories of raw materials, work in progress, and finished goods; distribution expenses are unaffected by such factors as the price of diesel fuel. Manufacturing and distribution concerns are more likely to hedge against adverse changes in commodity prices than changes in corporate bond spreads.

Yet the similarities are remarkable. Just as in manufacturing and distribution, financial services organizations have workflows, hand-offs, bottlenecks, and errors, as well as compensation, infrastructure, and tax expenses. They have to meet clients' needs, control their operations, deal with counterparties, manage cash, and compete with domestic and foreign outfits. Oddly, they seem to do all this, for the most part, without taking advantage of managerial accounting disciplines that are well established in corporations whose products are tangible. I would hazard that few investment management organizations know the profitability of their individual products, because they do not know the underlying expenses, for example, the total cost of a trade—not merely the commission and the bid–ask spread, but additionally the cross-departmental costs of settlement and reconciliation.

In 1759 Adam Smith offered a word of advice that is all too often disregarded by bloggers like me. He wrote, "a certain reserve is necessary when we talk of our own friends, our own studies, our own professions. All these are objects which we cannot expect should interest our companions in the same degree in which they interest us."[1] Unquestionably, I could have made these points without hauling in my personal experience, but it was a long drive from Richmond to Charlottesville, and I had plenty of time to think about the topic. I cannot promise to be more reserved in the future.

---

[1] Adam Smith, *The Theory of Moral Sentiments*, ed. D.D. Raphael and A.L. Macfie (Oxford University Press, 1976), 33-34.

# The Compleat Securities Examiner
July 26, 2011

The Ponzi schemes that came to light in 2008–2009 were unspeakably damaging, not only to the investors who were defrauded, but also to the credibility and trustworthiness of the investment profession. They may, however, have had one socially positive outcome: they seem to have prompted regulatory agencies to reconsider the knowledge, skills, and abilities needed across their professional staff. In-depth knowledge of the regulations is necessary but not sufficient; securities and bank examiners should additionally understand the moving parts of the investment management and banking businesses.

The SEC website states that people with accounting or finance degrees are ideal candidates for entry-level positions as examiners. To its credit, the SEC has also made room for industry professionals with expertise in such areas as risk management, structured products, and valuations, and has created a market abuse unit charged with acquiring specialized knowledge for the investigation of large-scale, hard-to-detect frauds. The FDIC employs financial analysts and offers its bank examiners training, not only in compliance, but also in information technology and risk management.

So what, beyond the regulations, must seasoned securities examiners know? In my opinion, they should grasp the firm's investment strategies; have sufficient quantitative skills to validate portfolio rates of return; and understand investment operations. Many investment professionals might disagree, but I think the third desideratum, the expectation that examiners know the ropes, is the most important.

Once, years ago—yes, indeed, here comes another anecdote—I led a team conducting a company-wide cash management study at a large multiline insurer. In one department after another, we asked how long it took to get premium checks to the bank, and we were invariably told, "Our standard is 24 hours." More often than not, however, the team would find live checks growing old in filing cabinets and desk drawers.

Similarly, when evaluating controls, securities examiners ought not merely rely upon the firm's representations. They should look *with understanding* at what actually happens—for example, in addition to reviewing system diagrams and workflows, they should track trades through their entire life cycle—in order to identify weaknesses that employees might exploit, whether for nefarious purposes or simply to keep up with the pace of work.

The securities regulators are to be applauded for their efforts to extend examiners' skill sets and support their ongoing professional development. Investors will be well served if they succeed. Investment management firms also stand to benefit: the prospect of being examined by more knowledgeable regulators might motivate senior management to pay greater attention to operational controls. Excelsior!

# Employee Loyalty
August 31, 2011

My father only worked for two companies over some thirty-odd years, and both were in the insurance industry. When I joined the treasurer's department at Aetna Life & Casualty in the early 1980s, he told me that, as long as I showed up on time and did an honest day's work, I'd never have to look for another position.

He was speaking from his own postwar experience, but by then the employment relationship had permanently changed. These days new hires are emphatically advised that their employment is "at-will." Job offers and employee handbooks explain the legal concept in plain language: "This means that either you or the company may terminate your employment at any time, for any reason, with or without cause."

Please sign here.

Ironically, even as the social ties have weakened, employee commitment seems to have grown stronger. After putting in long days at the office, many professionals *normally* work nights and weekends at home. Yet it isn't always easy to sort out the motivations for working so hard. In some cases, at least, it may be more a personal choice (or a psychological compulsion) than a requirement of the job. The philosopher Brian Schrag remarks, "there cannot be a duty to act above and beyond the call of duty."[1]

What does the duty of loyalty to the employer require?

A widely accepted, ethically minimalist view holds that employees must not act against the company's interests. For example, the CFA Institute *Standards of Professional Conduct* states, "In matters related to their employment, Members and Candidates must act for the benefit of their employer and not deprive their employer of the advantage of their skills and abilities, divulge confidential information, or otherwise cause harm to their employer."[2]

---

[1] Brian Schrag, "The Moral Significance of Employee Loyalty," *Business Ethics Quarterly*, vol. 11 no. 1 (2001), 47.

[2] CFA Institute, *Code of Ethics and Standards of Professional Conduct* (2010). Accessed August 1, 2012. http://www.cfapubs.org/doi/pdf/10.2469/ccb.v2010.n14.

But going public with allegations of internal wrongdoing is indisputably damaging to the company. Does it follow that whistleblowers are disloyal?

Suppose William J. Harrington had come forward in 2005, when he was a Moody's analyst, and described the firm's credit rating process as he did in his comments to the SEC last week. Managers allegedly intimidated analysts and manipulated credit committees to keep "the CDO plant" humming. "The goal of [Moody's] management," Harrington claimed, "is to mold analysts into pliable corporate citizens who cast their committee votes in line with the unchanging corporate credo of maximizing earnings of the largely captive franchise."[3]

Would Harrington have been disloyal to Moody's if he had contacted the SEC while he still worked there?

I have argued elsewhere that whistleblowers ought not be accused of disloyalty. On the contrary, they may be committed to the identity, culture, and values of a firm whose reputation for excellence is in jeopardy.[4] Harrington's statement seems to support this reasoning. "In the author's experience," he said, "analysts once came to Moody's solely to do work of which they would be proud, not to kowtow to their superiors and certainly not to prostrate themselves in front of whichever external entity happened to be footing the bill on a given day."[5]

In any specific case, an employee's decision to blow the whistle on her employer may be over-determined, driven by a mix of emotions (for example, healthy self-respect and petty resentment) and serving several purposes (such as stopping an injustice and, say, getting even). In other words, an informant's decision may not always be wholly disinterested, especially now that there are financial incentives. But whistleblowing is not *inherently* disloyal.

---

[3] William J. Harrington, "Comment on SEC Proposed Rules for Nationally Recognized Statistical Rating Organizations, August 8, 2011, 8. Accessed August 1, 2012. http://www.sec.gov/comments/s7-18-11/s71811-33.pdf

[4] Philip Lawton, "Ethics in Practice" (CFA Institute, 2005), 3. Accessed August 1, 2012. http://www.cfainstitute.org/learning/products/publications/readings/Documents/ser_lev3_reading3.pdf

[5] Harrington, *op. cit.*, 21.

Finally, questioning the character and motives of whistleblowers who provide verifiable, actionable information is unhelpful. It takes courage for employees to pursue remedies they find unavailable within the company; and quality tips serve the public interest in trustworthy advisors, reliable services, and efficient markets. That's all we need to know.

## Series 99
September 21, 2011

The new Series 99 exam is vitally important for operational personnel at U.S. broker-dealers. As of this writing, there is no comparable credential for operations professionals at investment management organizations. However, if you have supervisory responsibilities at a buy-side firm, then along with everything else you are probably expected to train new hires. Without minimizing the differences between investment managers and broker-dealers, you may find this necessarily concise overview of the Series 99 exam instructive.

For background, effective October 2011, most back-office managers and staff at U.S. broker-dealers will be required to register as Operations Professionals with the Financial Industry Regulatory Authority (FINRA). Rule 1230(b)(6) describes who must register and lists sixteen functions for which they might be responsible.[1] The covered functions range from on-boarding clients to approving pricing models used for valuations.

With some exceptions, individuals are additionally required to pass a qualifications exam within 120 days of registering as Operations Professionals. (The exceptions are people who have been registered in specified categories within the last two years. FINRA may also recognize alternate qualifications.) The three-hour exam will contain 110 multiple-choice questions. Of these, 100 will be scored; the other ten are unidentified pre-test questions scattered through the exam.

FINRA provides a content outline[2] with three sections: basic knowledge associated with the securities industry (32 of 100 questions on the exam); basic knowledge associated with broker-dealer operations (48 questions); and professional conduct and ethical considerations (20 questions). The content outline goes into considerably more detail than I'll attempt to survey here.

---

[1] Rule 1230(b)(6), *FINRA Manual.* Accessed August 2, 2011.
http://finra.complinet.com/en/display/display.html?rbid=2403&record_id=13962&element_id=10203&highlight=1230#r13962
[2] FINRA, Operations Professional Qualification Examination (Test Series 99), Content Outline. Accessed August 2, 2012.
http://www.finra.org/web/groups/industry/@ip/@comp/@regis/documents/industry/p124124.pdf

- The section on the securities industry addresses the purpose of the marketplace; characteristics of securities and products; and characteristics of broker-dealers, including regulatory requirements.

- The centrally important section on broker-dealer operations includes account opening and maintenance; cashiering and account transfers; custody and control of securities; trade reporting and corrections; corporate actions; margin and securities lending; settlement; account statements and confirmations; and books and records.

- The section on professional conduct and ethical considerations covers employee conduct; relationships and dealings with customers, vendors, and associated persons of the firm; customer privacy; the importance of escalating complaints and/or potential red flags; and broker-dealer supervision and control.

At present, FINRA does not offer readings or courses to help Operations Professionals prepare for the exam. Given their experience with e-learning, however, it is to be hoped that they will make such materials available in the future. (It is also reasonable to anticipate that commercial test prep course providers will bring Series 99 products to market fairly quickly.) For now, the content outline brochure has an appendix with a list of rules and regulations that is intended to serve as a reference guide for exam preparation. The brochure also includes some sample questions.

I know a little about developing a professional credentialing program, and, while the lack of educational resources is regrettable, the Series 99 exam certainly appears to have been properly constructed. The questions were written and validated by practitioners under the guidance of FINRA staff, and each one is directly related to an element of the content outline. The passing score is based upon standard-setting, reflecting best practice in the testing field. FINRA staff will use statistical techniques to monitor the performance of exam questions, and the content will be modified over time to keep pace with regulatory developments and industry practice. These are all signs of a valid qualifications exam.

I'll come back in the next week or two with suggestions for effective internal training programs, including on-the-job training, in risk management, performance measurement, and investment operations.

# Effective Internal Training
September 28, 2011

Two managerial challenges that heads of risk management and performance measurement departments contend with are staff training and turnover. They are not necessarily related problems. However, in addition to boosting productivity, effective internal training programs may incidentally improve the quality of work-life and reinforce employees' commitment to the organization. The time you spend thinking about your staff's educational needs and planning to meet them may have a greater payoff than you expect.

Unlike investment operations, the fields of risk management and performance measurement have credentialing programs with established bodies of knowledge that provide a framework for conceptual advances and technical refinements: the Financial Risk Manager (FRM®), Professional Risk Manager (PRM™), and Certificate in Performance Measurement (CIPM®) programs. In addition, the membership associations behind these credentials—GARP, PRMIA, and CFA Institute—constantly refresh their continuing professional education products, including publications and webinars. These offerings can easily be incorporated into internal training programs.

On-boarding new staff should involve more than showing them where to find the coffee station, copying machines, and restrooms. Even if new employees have already been given an overview of the company as a whole, the department head has to explain how their assignment fits into the business. Work is generally more meaningful when seen in its organizational context.

In the case of performance measurement, this explanation might well start with the firm's investment mandates and decision-making processes. It is also important for staff to understand how the performance measurement department interfaces with other groups, including portfolio management, compliance, accounting, marketing, and client relations. Similarly, new members of the risk management team should be told about the organization's investment strategies and products, including the types of instruments held; the regulatory regimes under which the company operates; and the firm's approaches to budgeting, measuring, analyzing, and controlling risks. Up-to-date system diagrams and workflows are inexpressibly useful for giving new staff a clear view of operations.

Employees who understand how their activities contribute to the firm's success in gaining and keeping clients may view their work more positively than those who think of themselves as machine tenders. Staff who grasp the downstream consequences of failures may become more proactive in avoiding and correcting mistakes than those who just want to keep their heads down and meet minimum quality standards.

Inexperienced, uncredentialed risk and performance analysts will benefit from an introductory course in their field. If your budget permits, consider bringing consultants on site to conduct customized courses. Be sure to select someone who not only practices in these domains but also excels as an educator; it is surprisingly difficult to teach the fundamentals effectively.

It is most desirable to conduct a class or a workshop on ethical issues that risk and performance analysts may face at some point in their careers. The professional associations' codes of ethics and standards of conduct can help frame issues for discussion. The goal is not to answer all the questions but to raise awareness and give staff some practice in ethical reasoning. In my experience, holding these sessions off-site seems to encourage participation.

New hires also have to become proficient users of particular systems. Specific skills such as defining a query and generating a report are usually conveyed through on-the-job training (OJT), a phrase that all too often masks dereliction. As the manager, you should at least list the functions you expect capable analysts to perform, pair the novices with more accomplished staff, and monitor their progress. It can also be advantageous to have power users conduct short classes on selected topics. I'll have more to say about OJT in a future article.

It is much easier, and no less important, to meet the needs of senior risk and performance analysts. You might call upon a consultant to conduct a master class for your staff. In addition, employees with specific expertise in advanced analytical techniques can present their work internally, and everyone benefits—not least the employee, who gains valuable speaking experience in a supportive environment. Cross-unit presentations are useful not only for sharing information but also for breaking down organizational silos.

Finally, by all means keep an eye on your professional association's educational offerings. Gathering a group together for a webinar on a topic of interest or concern can be highly productive, especially if the group stays after the broadcast to discuss how the webinar concepts might be applied in your organization.

## Or Should Have Known
September 30, 2011

Today's *Wall Street Journal* reports that the Securities and Exchange Commission may file more civil cases in which individuals are accused only of negligence in activities that assertedly contributed to the financial crisis.[1] The reporter, Jean Eaglesham, characterizes this trend as "a major shift from the agency's traditional enforcement strategy." In the past, charges of negligence have typically accompanied other, more serious allegations, or they have figured in plea-bargaining to settle cases before going to court.

I am not qualified to opine on the legal and regulatory grounds for bringing a charge of negligence against an investment adviser. From an ethical point of view, however, negligence—not knowing or doing what one should have known or done—clearly violates a duty of loyalty to the client. Investment professionals who are subject to the CFA Institute *Code of Ethics and Standards of Professional Conduct*[2] must put their clients' interests ahead of their own, use reasonable care, and exercise prudent judgment. In addition, negligence violates an ethical obligation to exercise "diligence, independence, and thoroughness in analyzing investments, making investment recommendations, and taking investment actions." Negligence may also violate provisions of the Code and Standards related to client communications.

Eaglesham cites a case filed in June 2011—SEC v. Edward F. Steffelin[3]—as the biggest example of the change in enforcement tactics. The formal charge against Steffelin is fraud in violation of Sections 17(a)(2) and (3) of the Securities Act of 1933 and Section 206(2) of the Investment Advisers Act of 1940. Gibson Dunn explains, "What is significant is that the SEC charged the case under statutory provisions for which negligence alone (rather than intentional or even reckless conduct) could constitute a violation. The SEC's pursuit of an individual under a

---

[1] Jean Eaglesham, "At SEC, Strategy Changes Course," *The Wall Street Journal*, September 30, 2011, pp. C1-2.
[2] CFA Institute, Code of Ethics and Standards of Professional Conduct (2010). Accessed August 1, 2012.
http://www.cfapubs.org/doi/pdf/10.2469/ccb.v2010.n14.1
[3] SEC v. Steffelin, No. CV11-04204 (S.D.N.Y. June 21, 2011). Accessed August 1, 2012. http://www.sec.gov/litigation/complaints/2011/comp-pr2011-131-steffelin.pdf

negligence theory indicates the lengths to which the SEC is going to respond to calls to hold individuals accountable in the wake of the financial crisis."[4]

It is an instructive case. Steffelin, a dealmaker at GSC Capital who managed the structuring and marketing of a synthetic CDO called Squared, allegedly misrepresented the asset selection process and inadequately disclosed material facts in the pitch book, term sheet, and offering circular. According to the SEC complaint, a hedge fund, Magnetar, was involved behind the scenes in selecting assets for Squared; Magnetar took substantial short positions in the same assets; and, while portfolio selection was under way, Sheffelin was seeking employment at Magnetar. The law can bring these facts to light, but only a psychologist or a novelist could help us understand why they seemed acceptable. As the SEC observes in its complaint, "Synthetic CDOs like Squared contributed to the recent financial crisis by magnifying losses associated with the downturn in the housing market."

---

[4] Gibson Dunn, "2011 Mid-Year Securities Enforcement Update," July 18, 2011. Accessed August 2, 2012.
http://gibsondunn.com/publications/pages/2011Mid-YearSecuritiesEnforcementUpdate.aspx. I am grateful to Jean Eaglesham for correcting an earlier version of this paragraph and providing this reference.

## Silociology: The Study of Silos
October 26, 2011

Virtually unknown outside a small circle of initiates, silociology [sī-lō-sē-ŏl'-ə-jē] is an entirely spurious branch of political science which studies the characteristic isolation of functional units within dysfunctional organizations. Such isolated departments or workgroups are commonly known as "silos." In addition to categorizing organizational silos, the discipline seeks to explain the causes and consequences of their insularity.

An activist offshoot led by the controversial Charlottesville school contends that silociology should curtail or abandon its research program in favor of reintegration planning and consultative services. *The Silobusters' Manifesto* states, "The point is not to understand the organization but to remediate it." (Section 3.5.) Most silociologists—the reputable ones—distance themselves from the militant faction in order to maintain a posture of scientific detachment and academic futility.

The two major types of organizational silo are *missile* and *grain*. Although they differ in many important ways, both are explosive.

Almost any department can voluntarily become a missile silo; in the financial services industry, for example, portfolio management units with complex investment strategies sometimes opt for this stance. The fundamentally elective nature of this state may become unapparent with the passage of time, but missile silo managers value autonomy (which they see as strength) over collaboration (weakness). Their normal strategy is stonewalling. However, they tend to react aggressively when their territory is threatened and may take offensive action to prevent another department from engaging in any activity they see as rightly theirs. One way to identify missile silos is to mention the department in question to an internal auditor or compliance officer and watch for sighing or eye-rolling.

In contrast, grain silos—repositories of expertise and processed data, typically operating in a support capacity—are involuntarily isolated. Performance measurement departments occasionally find themselves in this situation. In some cases, grain silos are sidelined because a missile silo prefers to handle the pertinent function internally. In others, they are unintentionally isolated because they are seen as a cost of doing business rather than a potential contributor to organizational effectiveness.

Beyond calculating rates of return, for example, performance measurement groups might add value by identifying the sources of portfolio returns. Attribution analysis can offer senior management independent, objective feedback on the firm's decision-making process and help relationship managers explain investment results to clients and clients' consultants. The Charlottesville school advises grain silo managers to take the initiative by preparing illustrative value-added analyses and showing key people how their unit's skill set and access to information can make a difference.

The consequences of silos include duplication of effort and missed opportunities. In some large organizations, for instance, performance measurement may be unknowingly conducted by multiple groups using diverse systems and methodologies. Analytical talent, system licenses, and IT support are expensive, and the collective output from numerous organizational units is unlikely to give senior management a consistent and reliable view of firm-wide results. Missile silos' dogged resistance will impede re-engineering; a possible tactical response is to establish another unit with a transitional mandate to consolidate information gathered from existing groups. Change management is a political art.

For completeness, *feed silos* such as reference data management teams are a third type. Indeed, the word "silage" refers to feedstuff in the process of fermentation (*e.g.*, stale prices). Although typically self-contained, feed silos are mentioned infrequently in the literature because they usually are not completely isolated. Many industry observers expect to see continuing pressure for faster delivery of more data as well as rising demand for integration and aggregation solutions. Incessant incoming messages from the business lines may make ballistic missiles seem attractive to feed silo managers.

The nascent field of silociology has no endowed chair, no professional association, no journal, and—full disclosure—only one proponent. The career opportunities are nil. In fact, résumés containing gibberish like "silociology" stand to be balled up and tossed into the wastebasket. However, grain silo managers who succeed in overcoming obstacles and visibly supporting the organization's objectives truly deserve to be celebrated.

## On-the-Job Training
December 9, 2011

Let's say you have hired a new performance or risk analyst, a recent graduate, who demonstrated theoretical knowledge and intellectual curiosity in the course of several interviews. You have introduced her to the company; its investment strategies, products, and decision-making process; and the role of the performance measurement or risk management group in relation to other organizational units. Now it's time for on-the-job training. What will you do?

In general, there are two managerial approaches. One is to present the new analyst to her colleagues and ask them to show her the ropes. The other is more effortful, but most of the time it leads to substantially more satisfactory results. Here are some suggestions for planning an on-the-job training (OJT) sequence that will help new employees become competent practitioners.

The first step is to translate the responsibilities of the position into a task list from which you can derive the new person's training needs. If you have a comprehensive, up-to-date position description, that's a good resource (and, if you don't, surprise HR by writing one). The employment ad for the new analyst's job may be an alternative; you undoubtedly put some thought into it. The resulting task list may include such items as, "Produce and validate monthly performance reports for assigned portfolios," or "Update input data and produce assigned VaR analyses for the month-end Board package." Then ask yourself what the analyst needs to *know* and *do* to accomplish each task.

The second step is to gather and review the available documentation. Training new staff is one of the ways useful, up-to-date documentation of policies and procedures contributes to effective management.[1] The firm's GIPS® policies are required reading for new performance analysts at firms that claim compliance with the Global Investment Performance Standards. System vendors' user manuals are also essential. Make sure your copy corresponds with the software release your firm is currently using.

---

[1] See "Playbooks: Workflow Documentation" in Holly H. Miller and Philip Lawton, *The Top Ten Operational Risks: A Survival Guide for Investment Management Firms and Hedge Funds* (Stone House Consulting, 2010). Accessed August 2, 2012. http://www.stonehouseconsulting.com/OpRisk/BookDesc.html

System vendors generally offer instructor-led user training as part of the initial implementation. It is most unfortunate that they don't routinely develop e-learning modules that all their clients could incorporate into internal training programs. In actuality, the best way to get a new employee started with an unfamiliar system is to pair her with an experienced user—but this, too, requires thoughtful planning, not only in selecting and motivating the trainer but also in establishing clear expectations of both participants.

- The most accomplished users may not be the most effective trainers. For example, a staff member who exhibits methodical thought processes will prove to be a better teacher than one who thinks holistically and proceeds by intuitive leaps. Similarly, a patient, team-oriented person will get better results than one who has acquired dazzling keyboard skills in the single-minded pursuit of individual productivity. It is not enough for trainers to know what they are doing; they also have to be able to explain and demonstrate discrete operations as well as to encourage and correct learners.

- Staff who are given training responsibilities in addition to their regular, deadline-driven work may not consistently make choices in the best interest of their new colleague. If at all feasible, try to lighten their workload during the training period. If the group had excess capacity and a complete skill set, however, you probably would not have needed to hire another analyst. In any case, it is vitally important that trainers be confident their added effort will be recognized and rewarded.

- Tell the trainer and trainee they are *jointly* responsible for the trainee's progress towards self-sufficiency. Review the list of training requirements with them so they clearly understand what is expected. Meet with them together—brief conversations will generally suffice—to ensure the training is on track and proceeding smoothly. If they've encountered a problem, help them figure out how to resolve it.

On-boarding new employees is costly. Good managers will help them succeed.

# The Volunteer's Dilemma
February 20, 2012

Outside academia, game theory is best known for its contributions to political and military thinking during the duck-and-cover years of the Cold War.[1] These days the dilemmas of game theory seem as outmoded as the quandaries of existentialism. They certainly don't come up very often in discussions of risk management. It is all the more intriguing, then, to read in the Bank of England's *Financial Stability Paper No. 11*, "Liquidity provision in a payment system has much in common with the Volunteer's Dilemma."[2] Let's explore this notion.

The volunteer's dilemma is a game for many players in which each repeatedly chooses between sharing the production cost of a collective good (cooperating) and taking a free ride (defecting). Douglas Hofstadter's account of defection is convoluted enough to cause injuries among turnstile-hoppers, but it expresses a central idea: "A defection is an action such that, if everyone did it, things would clearly be worse (for everyone) than if everyone refrained from doing it, and yet which tempts everyone, since if only one individual (or a sufficiently small number) did it while others refrained, life would be sweeter for that individual (or select group)."[3]

A true dilemma, this one has no rational solution. All utility-seeking people—all players—will see that defecting is the logical strategy, unless, of course, many or all choose to defect.

It might be helpful at this point to present a few working definitions. First, a strategy is said to be dominant if it earns a player the highest possible payout *regardless* of other players' choices. Second, a game is in

---

[1] Two-person games of strategy found ready application in analyses of the nuclear arms race between the United States and the former Soviet Union during the 1950s. William Poundstone offers a fascinating, non-mathematical history of game theory in *Prisoner's Dilemma* (Doubleday, 1992).

[2] Allan Ball, Edward Denbee, Mark Manning, and Anne Wetherilt, *Financial Stability Paper No. 11*, "Intraday liquidity: risk and regulation" (Bank of England, June 2011), 5. Accessed August 2, 2012.
http://www.bankofengland.co.uk/publications/Documents/fsr/fs_paper11.pdf

[3] Douglas Hofstadter, *Metamagical Themas: Questing for the Essence of Mind and Pattern*, Chapter 31, "Irrationality is the Square Root of All Evil" (Basic Books, 1985), Kindle edition.

equilibrium when each player's strategy is optimal *given* the strategies of all other players. Third, maximin is a strategy whose objective is to maximize the minimum payoff.

With these concepts in hand, **Figure 1** describes the volunteer's dilemma under the simplifying assumption that the collective good is unavailable only if *nobody* cooperates. Andreas Diekmann, who formalized the volunteer's dilemma, points out that defection is not a dominant strategy and maximin is not an equilibrium strategy. "But if one expects the other players to apply maximin, a better choice might be D [defection]."[4]

The volunteer's dilemma applies to any situation in which the availability of a public good—clean air, for example, or potable water, or peace and quiet—depends upon the cooperation of many or all. But defection is always an option. In a payment system, banks can delay their own outflows and use the liquidity furnished by other banks' payments as a funding source that has no monetary cost. Ball *et al.* write, "In this type of game the strategic solution can result in the underprovision of liquidity."[5]

**Figure 1.** $N$-Person Game ($N \geq 0$)

| | Number of Choices | | | | |
|---|---|---|---|---|---|
| | 0 | 1 | 2 | ... | $N$–1 |
| Cooperate | 0 | $U$–$K$ | $U$–$K$ | ... | $U$–$K$ |
| Defect | 0 | $U$ | $U$ | ... | $U$ |

$K$ = Production costs
$U$ = Utility of the collective good
$U$–$K > 0$

Based upon Andreas Diekmann, "Volunteer's Dilemma," *Journal of Conflict Resolution*, Vol. 29 No. 4 (December 1985), 606-607.

If all the players, whether individuals or organizations, are inclined to do what is best for themselves, then a volunteer's dilemma gives rise to a practical problem. Derek Parfit writes, "Unless something changes, the actual outcome will be worse for everyone. This problem is one of the chief reasons why we need more than laissez-faire economics—why we need both politics and morality."[6]

---

[4] Andreas Diekmann, "Volunteer's Dilemma," *Journal of Conflict Resolution*, Vol. 29 No. 4 (December 1985), 606-607.

[5] *Financial Stability Paper No. 11*, loc. cit.

[6] Derek Parfit, *Reasons and Persons* (Oxford University Press, 1984), Section 24. See also *On What Matters*, Vol. One (Oxford University Press, 2011), 301-307. Parfit uses the terms "contributor's dilemmas" and "each-we dilemmas."

Political action can resolve volunteers' dilemmas by changing the conditions. Taxes, if unavoidable, make "cooperation" involuntary, and fines, if equally certain, modify the payoffs. In the context of liquidity risk management, regulation by the payment system or a governmental agency might be more effective if defection inevitably triggered swift, substantial monetary penalties.

Morality can resolve the dilemma by changing the players' dispositions. One formulation of Kant's categorical imperative states, more or less, that we should always act the way we could logically want everyone to act.[7] Hofstadter calls people who adopt this rule "*superrational,* or for short, *sane.*"[8] Diekmann acknowledges, "Payoffs are higher if players are superrational in Hofstadter's sense (1983). This is to say that all participants in the game maximize their expected utility under the restriction of Kant's categorical imperative."[9]

Ball *et al.* rightly note that repeated games tend to foster cooperation, and, indeed, in normal times the volunteer's dilemma does not lead to liquidity shortages. However, Hofstadter tells about an airline flight on which he was to be seated in a low-numbered row. He waited with others similarly situated while the flight was boarded back-to-front by passengers in higher-numbered rows. But then a few impatient travelers broke ranks, and soon there was a stampede. "At that point, some sort of phase transition, or collective shift, took place, and the stable state of patient cooperation collapsed into a chaotic scrambling for places."[10] Given the velocity of information and the interconnectedness of financial institutions, it is not hard to imagine a few players' actions triggering a wave of defections that create a liquidity crisis. Our understanding the volunteer's dilemma may not help the central banks restore order, but at least we'll know what's happening.

---

[7] "Act only in accordance with that maxim through which you can, at the same time, will that it should become a universal [*algemeines*] law." Immanuel Kant, *Grundlegung zur Metaphysik der Sitten*, 2er Abschnitt (Felix Meiner Verlag, 1965), 42.

[8] "Such individuals—individuals who will cooperate with one another despite all temptations toward crude egoism—are more than just *rational*; they are *superrational,* or for short, *sane.*" Douglas Hofstadter, op. cit., Introduction to Section VII, "Sanity and Survival."

[9] Diekmann, *op. cit.,* 608.

[10] Hofstadter, *op. cit.,* "Post-Scriptum" to Chapter 29, "The Prisoner's Dilemma Computer Tournaments and the Evolution of Cooperation".

# Adding Value
February 29, 2012

It appears that buy-side organizations are committing significant resources to the middle office. In good part, larger technology investments and higher compensation expenses are driven by the need to meet new regulatory requirements. But the value of middle office operations (in particular, that of the risk management and performance measurement functions) is not limited to regulatory compliance. The middle office additionally satisfies clients' demands and potentially enhances the investment decision-making process. Let's take a look at these further benefits.

As a rule, institutional investors will not engage external managers who cannot demonstrate a sound program of risk management or do not claim to comply with the Global Investment Performance Standards (GIPS®). In fact, the gatekeepers, the consultants who conduct manager searches, simply don't present firms whose policies and practices fall short of industry standards or their own and their clients' expectations. Accordingly, investment management firms competing for institutional business know that the marketplace requires them to develop, staff, and support robust risk management and performance measurement systems and processes. Credibility in these areas is a necessary condition for gathering and retaining institutional assets.

It is also widely recognized, in principle if not in fact, that performance measurement can contribute to effective firm management by providing useful analyses of investment results. **Figure 1**, a classic representation of a top-down investment process, shows performance measurement in this internal role. By estimating the return impact of portfolio decisions, performance attribution can help firms re-examine their portfolio policies, investment strategies, and capital market expectations while evaluating the investment process itself. Given sufficiently granular holdings and benchmark data, over time the firm can determine what it consistently does well (for example, identifying undervalued bank stocks, or adjusting market weights in the energy sector, or using derivatives to modify foreign currency exposures, or anticipating changes in the shape of the yield curve), and what not so well, or so reliably. Departmental managers may succeed in communicating the value of performance analysis by offering insights like these.

Originally published almost 30 years ago, Figure 1 assumes that risk management is inherent in the investment process. For instance, portfolio policies include constraints, and capital market expectations are expressible in terms of returns, volatilities, and correlations. Charles D. Ellis wrote at the time, "the basic responsibility of portfolio managers— since the invention of insurance and pooled risk accounts in merchant shipping on sailing vessels hundreds of years ago—is to control risk."[1] Ellis's statement is still true, but in the interim risk management has emerged as a specialized, credentialed discipline in its own right.

**Figure 2** is an attempt to position risk management as a distinctive competence that is nonetheless fully integrated into the investment decision-making process. This exhibit differs from the traditional representation by the addition of (1) "risk management policies and strategies" in the planning phase, (2) "risk analytics" in the feedback phase, and (3) an arrow from the feedback to the portfolio revision box, indicating that performance and risk analysis can directly provide corrective information. It is in the planning stage of the investment

**Figure 1.** Portfolio Construction, Monitoring, and Revision Process

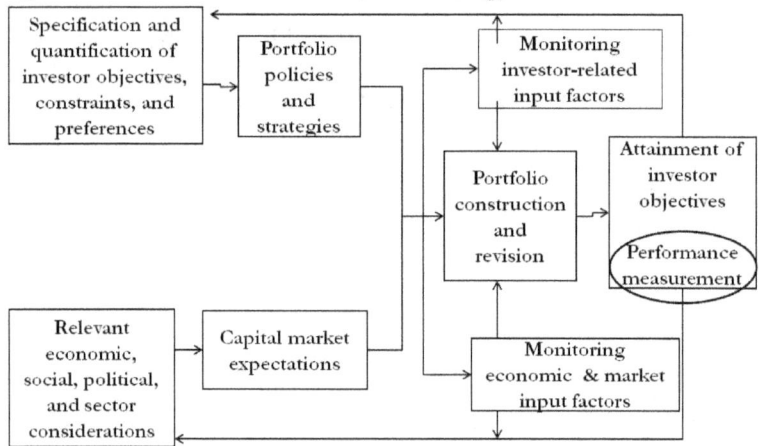

Source: *Managing Investment Portfolios: A Dynamic Process*, 3rd ed., edited by John L. Maginn, Donald L. Tuttle, Jerald E. Pinto, and Dennis W. McLeavey (Wiley, 2007), Exhibit 1-1, 6.

---

[1] Charles D. Ellis, "Conceptualizing Portfolio Management," Chapter 2 in John L. Maginn and Donald L. Tuttle, eds., *Managing Investment Portfolios: A Dynamic Process*, Student Edition (Warren, Gorham & Lamont, 1983), p. 11.

process that risk professionals stand to make the more significant contributions. Investment decisions belong to the portfolio manager but, much like economists' views on industries, risk managers' independent input on markets may sharpen the thinking behind those decisions.

**Figure 2.** Adding Value in the Investment Process

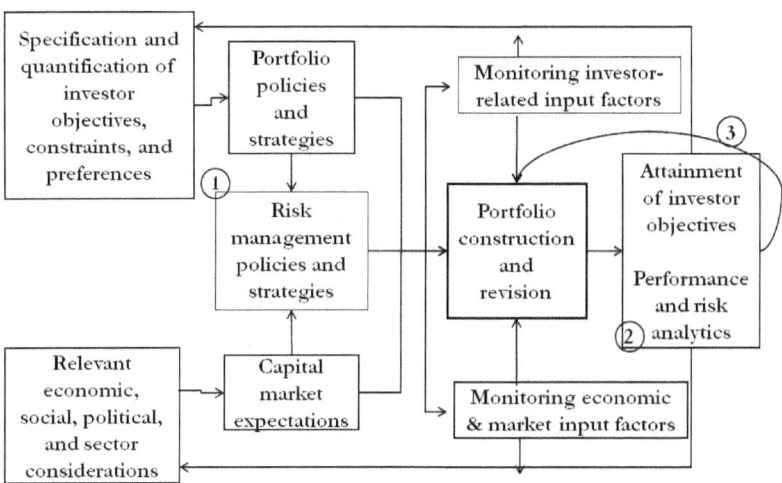

Based upon *Managing Investment Portfolios: A Dynamic Process*, 3rd ed., edited by John L. Maginn *et al.* (Wiley, 2007), Exhibit 1-1, 6.

Admittedly, all of this presupposes a corporate environment where trust is possible and a culture that prizes both collegiality and critical thinking. It is more difficult to add value in firms with silos. This takes us into issues of leadership, governance, and organizational design that we'll save for another day.

## Best Practice
March 12, 2012

The phrase "best practice" is so widely used in professional circles that its ambiguity may pass unnoticed. Because the expression seems conventional and authoritative, we assume we know what it means and rarely ask for clarification. In fact, the term straddles theory and practice (or, in postmodern parlance, argument and narrative), and that very straddling is the source of its ambiguity. It may be worthwhile, just once, to unpack the normative and descriptive senses of the phrase.

In my observation, when consultants and vendors speak of "best practice," they generally have in mind a policy or methodology utilized by industry-leading firms. However, this descriptive usage often isn't clearly defined. The industry leaders may not be named and the selection criteria, if any, may not be stated. In this case, "best practice" may prove to be nothing more than an unfounded way of tendentiously referring to a particular solution. It is, let's say, a manner of speaking.

Nor are explicit selection criteria unproblematic. For example, it seems sensible to identify the most profitable firms as industry leaders. Survey results might then show some level of correlation between the use of a given process and firm profitability as measured by return on sales or equity. These ratios, however, are affected by extraneous factors. Return on sales typically varies with scale, and return on equity is heavily influenced by capital structure. In addition, one profitable firm may have chosen a specific approach because it is the most practical, in view of the company's current capabilities and technology priorities, while another might have determined that, assuming a certain utility function or discount rate, the same solution meets core business requirements at an acceptable cost. Whether a methodology is theoretically optimal may not be a decisive factor.

In my interpretation, standard-setters who use the term "best practice" mainly intend it to stand for an objective norm or ideal. "Best practice" refers to the way something should be done. But this *should* invites the charge that a given standard merely represents a disputable opinion. If the standard-setting board or committee is unanimous, then the supposed "best practice" is a product of groupthink. If the so-called "best practice" reflects the thinking of a majority of committee members, then it is, in the pejorative sense, a product of politics. In this characterization, norms represent nothing more than the standard-setters' subjective values, and any particular "best practice" is simply the preference of people in positions of influence.

"Best practice" might rather be defined as "the way something is done when it is done properly." And, as a rule, standard-setting organizations take measures to ensure that industry norms are established as objectively as possible. I consider the International Organization for Standardization (ISO) a model in this regard. Consensus-building is one of the ISO's fundamental principles; there are cogent criteria for selecting people to lead the technical work; and stakeholder feedback occurs at several points in the six stages of the standard-development process.[1] The ISO Code of Conduct for the Technical Work[2] emphasizes impartiality and specifically excludes collusive and anticompetitive behavior.

Nonetheless, standard-setters don't necessarily take implementation costs into account. When they do recognize that norms require project planning and presuppose an infrastructure, they may provide extended lead times. For example, the GIPS Executive Committee stated at least five years in advance of the effective date that valuing portfolios upon the occurrence of large external cash flows was expected to become a requirement.[3] This gave existing investment managers more than ample opportunity to enter contracts for intraperiod valuations and to modify their systems accordingly. I do not question this requirement. Now that it is in effect, however, it may constitute an impediment for small or newly organized firms that might otherwise have chosen to claim compliance with the Standards.

Perhaps, when talking about voluntary standards, we should use the term "ideal practice," or get in the habit of saying, "ideally, the best practice

---

[1] ISO, "Stages of the Development of International Standards." Accessed August 2, 2012.
http://www.iso.org/iso/home/standards_development/resources-for-technical-work/stages_of_the_development_of_international_standards_.htm
[2] "ISO Code of Conduct for the Technical Work." Accessed August 2, 2012.
http://www.iso.org/iso/codes_of_conduct.pdf
[3] The 2003 *Guidance Statement on Calculation Methodologies* stated, "the GIPS standards will *require* time-weighted rates of return that adjust for *daily-weighted* cash flows by 1 January 2005 and will likely *require* time-weighted rates of return with valuations at the time of external cash flows by 1 January 2010." Accessed August 2, 2012.
http://www.gipsstandards.org/standards/guidance/develop/pdf/calcmethod.pdf

is…." The latter phrasing would make it clear that we are using "best practice" in the normative sense. It would also acknowledge, implicitly, that firms have different resources and capabilities. In some cases the best solution within reach—the best *practical* approach—is theoretically suboptimal.

# Book Review: *The Wrong Answer Faster*
April 8, 2012

Michael Goodkin's delightfully unpretentious memoir, *The Wrong Answer Faster: The Inside Story of Making the Machine that Trades Trillions* (John Wiley & Sons, 2012), is at once an autobiographical narrative, a business history, and a case study in the commercial application of academic ideas in the second half of the 20th century.[1] Two case studies, in fact, because Goodkin tells about founding Arbitrage Management Company, Inc. with economists John Shelton, Harry Markowitz, Paul Samuelson, and Robert Merton in 1968 as well as Numerix LLC with physicists Mitchell Feigenbaum, Alexander Sokol, and Nigel Goldenfeld in 1996. (Arbitrage Management Company thrived, was sold, and is now defunct; Numerix is today a dominant factor in cross-asset deal structuring, valuation, and risk analysis.) In addition, *The Wrong Answer Faster* spans the industrial revolution of the investment management business—the arrival of desktop computers, the ascendancy of quantitative methods, and the engineering of new, complex, and transformative financial instruments. Goodkin tells his own story in a book that reads like a long, companionable chat, but the changes he helped bring about contributed to revamping the financial services industry and, arguably, reshaping the global economy.

Regrettably, the book would have benefited from another round of copy-editing and proofreading. The author's occasional repetitiousness is natural and excusable; this is, after all, a work of memory. There are, however, far too many sentences that are poorly constructed if not grammatically incorrect. Indeed, one has the impression the published work is simply an unedited transcript in the manner of an oral history. For example, Goodkin says, "Unlike with the bookmaker, who if I lost I was losing his money and that would be the end of it, the financier required…."[2] There are also errors of the sort an automated spell-checker won't catch, such as "orders being executed with lightening speed," two instances of "waived" where "waved" was meant, and misspelt names ("Carl Ichan" and, twice, "Solomon Brothers;" the latter

---

[1] The title expresses Goodkin's discovery that traders did not want more precise valuations as much as they wanted conventional results sooner than other traders could calculate them.

[2] Michael Goodkin, Prologue, *The Wrong Answer Faster: The Inside Story of Making the Machine that Trades Trillions* (John Wiley & Sons, 2012), Kindle edition.

misnomer is slavishly reproduced in the index). It is disappointing to see a distinguished publishing house overlook flaws like these.

Goodkin's account opens with his formative high-school experiences as a card shark and shoe salesman, and carries through his undergraduate career at the University of Illinois and his successful graduate studies in law at Northwestern and business at Columbia. Despite his academic credentials, he was not a scholar, and, coming late to the study of mathematics, not a quant, either. While at Northwestern he started a company that employed his fellow students as contract research staff for small law firms, and of his first meeting with Markowitz in 1968 he writes, "It soon became obvious we were very different sorts of people. I was a pragmatist, only concerned with whether things worked. He, despite his commercial success, was an intellectual. He wanted to know why things worked. As much as he was soft-spoken, gentle, and calm, I was blunt and intense."[3] Goodkin taught himself backgammon in order to socialize with prospective investors, and, after selling Arbitrage Management Company, he moved to London, played competitive backgammon, and idled with the beautiful people. In 1986, he recalls, he stumbled across a book entitled *Chaos;* "not seeing too many mathematical formulae or complex graphs," he says, "I bought it."[4] Goodkin's notion that there might be a connection between chaos theory and derivatives pricing led, eventually, to the formation of Numerix.

Goodkin's role, then, was entirely entrepreneurial. It would be a mistake, however, to think that he merely retailed other people's original work. He himself had extraordinary ideas: he saw how concepts and techniques developed in one domain might solve problems in another. This betokens a distinctively creative mental process. Arthur Koestler wrote, "The creative act does not create something out of nothing, like the God of the Old Testament; it combines, reshuffles and relates already existing but hitherto separate ideas, facts, frames of perception, associative contexts. This act of cross-fertilization—or self-fertilization within the same brain—seems to be the essence of creativity, and to justify the term 'bisociation.'"[5] Goodkin's intuitions seem to have been bisociative in Koestler's sense.

---

[3] *Ibid.*, "Recruiting the Brain Trust," in Chapter 7, "Stepping Out in the World."
[4] *Ibid.*, Chapter 12, "Does God Play with Loaded Dice?" Goodkin allows that "some events appear out of precise chronology." (Acknowledgments.) I suspect the book he perused was James Gleick's bestseller, *Chaos: Making a New Science,* published by Viking Penguin in 1987.

Moreover, as an entrepreneur, Goodkin recruited theoreticians before the universities took a serious proprietary interest in the inventions of their faculty members, and he turned to private investors for financing before the venture capital industry was fully organized. The most interesting, and often amusing, parts of Goodkin's memoir are those in which he tells about pitching his ideas to bemused professors and skeptical financiers. For instance, he describes a meeting with Sir Sigmund Warburg in 1970: "'A computer,' he said once more. 'Fancy that.' And then his eyes lost their twinkle. 'Preposterous! Utterly preposterous!'"[6] The meeting ended on that note.

All autobiographies, of course, are suspect. "It is impossible," Goodkin avows, "to be objective when writing a memoir."[7] Other people might remember or interpret the same events differently and recall ambiguous or unflattering incidents that are not mentioned in this book. Nonetheless, we are most fortunate to have Goodkin's first-person account of a career that contributed so much to crystallizing contemporary modes of thought and practice in the investment profession.

---

[5] Arthur Koestler, *The Ghost in the Machine* (Viking Penguin, 1967), p. 184. See also Koestler's earlier book, *The Act of Creation* (Viking Penguin, 1964), p. 35 seq., and my article on creativity and the unconscious: Philip Lawton, "Art, Science, and the Clear Blue Sky," *International Studies in the Philosophy of Science*, vol. 7, no. 2 (1993), p. 111.

[6] Goodkin, *op. cit.*, "An American Capitalist in Sir Sigmund's Court," in Chapter 10, "Too Good to Be True."

[7] *Ibid.*, Acknowledgments.

## Leadership in Complex Organizations
June 18, 2012

"[Banks] of the size and complexity of J.P. Morgan Chase (JPM), Citi (C), and Bank of America (BAC) are just too difficult to manage, even for talented managers like [Jamie] Dimon," says Sheila Bair. "Whatever economies the megabanks achieve from their size are more than offset by the challenges in managing trillion-dollar institutions that are into trading, market making, investment banking, derivatives, and insurance, in addition to the core business of taking deposits and making loans." In her opinion, the banks' leadership should take the initiative to downsize. "The best way for Dimon to provide a better return to his investors is to recognize that his bank is worth more in smaller, easier-to-manage pieces."[1]

For the record, as of the close of the first quarter, JPMorgan Chase & Co. had total assets of $2.3 trillion and a headcount of 261,453 employees across seven business lines: Investment Bank, Retail Financial Services, Card Services & Auto, Commercial Banking, Treasury & Securities Services, Asset Management, and Corporate/Private Equity.[2] It is the biggest U.S. bank by assets but not by the number of employees: Citi had assets of $1.9 trillion and approximately 266,000 employees across four to eight business groups,[3] depending upon how you count them, and Bank of America, with assets of $2.2 trillion, had 278,688 employees in five business segments.[4]

---

[1] Sheila Bair, "Breaking Up Chase: Good for Shareholders and Taxpayers," Fortune, May 25, 2012. Accessed August 2, 2012.
http://finance.fortune.cnn.com/2012/05/25/jp-morgan-chase-breakup/
[2] JPMorgan Chase & Co., First Quarter 2012 Earnings Release Financial Supplement (Revised as of May 10, 2012). Accessed August 2, 2012.
http://files.shareholder.com/downloads/ONE/1926972419x0x568607/530d9a03-89dd-4123-b57e-094e47a4f842/1Q12_ERF_Supplement_FINAL_5.10.12.pdf
[3] Assets and business groups: Citigroup, Quarterly Financial Data Supplement, 1Q12. Accessed August 2, 2012.
http://www.citigroup.com/citi/investor/data/qer112s.pdf?ieNocache=0 Direct staff: Citigroup Financial Snapshot, 2011. Accessed August 2, 2011.
http://www.citigroup.com/citi/investor/snapshot.htm
[4] Bank of America, First-Quarter 2012 Financial Results. Accessed August 2, 2012. http://investor.bankofamerica.com/phoenix.zhtml?c=71595&p=irol-newsArticle&ID=1684843&highlight=#fbid=scCziZ1--F5.

I am strongly inclined to agree with Bair: outsize banks should be dismembered in the interest of mitigating systemic risk and maximizing shareholder value. But other financial services concerns, including some which aren't large enough to qualify as systemically important, may also be too unwieldy to control and too inflexible to respond creatively to changing conditions.

Calling themselves complexity leadership theorists, some thinkers in the field of organizational behavior suggest that the limitations of management arise not from the scope and scale of operations but, rather, from the application of an outmoded command-and-control theory of leadership that is unsuitable for complex, post-industrial, knowledge-based companies. In this view, the traditional ideal of heroic leadership impedes the exploration of possible responses to new environmental pressures. Mary Uhl-Bien, Russ Marion, and Bill McKelvey state, "This new perspective is grounded in a core proposition: *Much of leadership thinking has failed to recognize that leadership is not merely the influential act of an individual or individuals but rather is embedded in a complex interplay of numerous interacting forces.*"[5]

Complexity theory—"the study of the dynamic behaviors of complexly interacting, interdependent, and adaptive agents under conditions of internal and external pressure"[6]—traces its lineage to theoretical biology, chaos theory, and complex adaptive systems (CAS) theory, among other sources.[7] Complexity leadership theory focuses on strategies and behaviors that promote creativity, learning, and adaptability by engaging CAS dynamics within hierarchical or bureaucratic organizations. It recognizes three kinds of leadership: administrative, enabling, and adaptive.

Conducted by individuals in formal managerial roles, administrative leadership builds the strategic vision, engages in planning, allocates

---

[5] Marion Uhl-Bien, Russ Marion, and Bill McKelvey, "Complexity Leadership Theory: Shifting Leadership From the Industrial Age to the Knowledge Era," Chapter Eight in *Complexity Leadership, Part I: Conceptual Foundations*, edited by Mary Uhl-Bien and Russ Marion (Charlotte, NC: Information Age Publishing, 2008), Kindle edition. Authors' emphasis. Reprinted by permission of Elsevier, this chapter was originally published in Vol. 18, No. 4, of *The Leadership Quarterly*.
[6] Russ Marion, "Complexity Theory for Organizations and Organizational Leadership," Chapter 1 in *Complexity Leadership, Part I, op. cit.*
[7] Jeffrey Goldstein, "Conceptual Foundations of Complexity Science: Development and Main Constructs," Chapter 2 in *Complexity Leadership, Part I, op. cit.*

resources, coordinates tasks, and manages crises. Occurring at all levels of the organization, enabling leadership fosters the conditions in which creativity, learning, and adaptability can thrive, and facilitates the flow of knowledge from adaptive to administrative structures. Middle managers are well positioned to engage in enabling behaviors. And adaptive leadership is, in the words of Uhl-Bien, Marion, and McKelvey,

> an emergent, interactive dynamic that produces adaptive outcomes in a social system. It is a collaborative change movement that emerges nonlinearly from interactive exchanges, or, more specifically, from the "spaces between" agents…. That is, it originates in struggles among agents and groups over conflicting needs, ideas, or preferences; it results in movements, alliances of people, ideas, or technologies, and cooperative efforts. Adaptive leadership is a complex dynamic rather than a person (although people are, importantly, involved); we label it leadership because it is *a*, and, arguably, *the*, proximal source of change in an organization.[8]

In cognitive science, consciousness emerges from neural activity in the brain; similarly, in complexity leadership theory, adaptive leadership arises from the interaction of parties engaged in problem-solving at all levels of an enabled organization. It is a by-product of stakeholder involvement.[9] Far from the heroic model, adaptive leadership is anonymous, organic, epiphenomenal: leadership without a leader. Organizations in which adaptive leadership flourishes may be well equipped to survive under pressure, find creative solutions to new trials, and prosper in the face of adversity.

---

[8] Uhl-Bien, Marion, and McKelvey, "Complexity Leadership Theory: Shifting Leadership From the Industrial Age to the Knowledge Era," *op. cit.* The authors formally define adaptive leadership as "emergent change behaviors under conditions of interaction, interdependence, asymmetrical information, complex network dynamics, and tension."

[9] In my understanding, the participants' interdependence in complexity leadership theory is compatible—or at least not incompatible—with the independent thinking that James Surowiecki identified as a necessary condition for crowds to be wise. See *The Wisdom of Crowds: Why the Many are Smarter than the Few and How Collective Wisdom Shapes Business, Economies, Societies, and Nations* (New York: Random House, 2004).

# For the Sake of Argument
June 30, 2012

If it is valid, a new theory of reasoning has important ramifications for leadership and decision making. In the classic view, reasoning acts to increase knowledge and improve decisions. It is widely recognized, however, that people often reason poorly, leaning too heavily on evidence that supports their position and discounting or disregarding evidence to the contrary. Hugo Mercier and Dan Sperber adopt another perspective: reasoning emerged in the evolutionary context of human communication; it is primarily social; and its main function is argumentative. "Reasoning enables people to exchange arguments that, on the whole, make communication more reliable and hence more advantageous."[1] In argumentative theory, what behavioral economists call the confirmation bias is a feature rather than a flaw of reasoning; it "clearly serves the goal of convincing others."[2] Let's consider these ideas.

Mercier and Sperber's hypothesis is consistent with one aspect of critical thinking as it is generally understood. The ability to evaluate the soundness of an argument—that is to say, to appraise the truth of its premises and the logical strength of the inferential link between those premises and the conclusion—helps one avoid being misinformed or duped. Because there are no indubitable markers of honesty, people have to "exercise epistemic vigilance," questioning both the veracity of the speaker and the validity of the argument. "The task of epistemic vigilance," Mercier and Sperber state, "is to evaluate communicator[s] and the content of their messages in order to filter communicated information."[3] They also report that people are generally competent in evaluating others' arguments, and they attribute poor performance in standard reasoning tests to the lack of an argumentative context.[4]

---

[1] Hugo Mercier and Dan Sperber, "Why Do Humans Reason? Arguments for an Argumentative Theory," *Behavioral and Brain Sciences*, vol. 34 (2011), 60.

[2] *Ibid.*, 63.

[3] *Ibid.*, 60.

[4] *Ibid.*, 61-62. Independently, the results of an fMRI study assertedly indicate that "motivated reasoning is *qualitatively distinct* from reasoning when people do not have a strong emotional stake in the conclusions reached." (Emphasis added.) Drew Westen, Pavel S. Blagov, Keith Harenski, Clint Kilts, and Stephan Hamann, "Neural Bases of Motivated Reasoning: An fMRI Study of Emotional Constraints on Partisan Political Judgment in the 2004 U.S. Presidential Election," *Journal of Cognitive Neuroscience*, November 2006, Vol. 18, No. 11, 1947-1958.

It is in describing the production, not the evaluation, of arguments that Mercier and Sperber's work departs most meaningfully from traditional accounts. In their view, reasoning is not a process in which independent thinkers dispassionately formulate and weigh alternative solutions in order to find the truth or make the best, or fairest, decision. Instead, it is a search only for supporting arguments that will justify their preferred answer and persuade others to endorse it. Accordingly, most people do not demonstrate skill in criticizing their own arguments. Distancing themselves from their opinions and considering alternatives "involves exercising some imperfect control over a natural disposition that spontaneously pulls in a different direction."[5]

To my mind, the argumentative theory of reasoning is persuasive and, if not literally true, then at least verisimilar. In addition, it appears to be supported by the results of numerous psychological experiments that the authors cite and, when appropriate, plausibly reinterpret. Argumentative theory cautions us how taxing epistemic vigilance can be, especially when directed towards our own arguments, but it does not require us to abandon the ideal of critical thinking or forswear the tools of logical analysis; on the contrary, it underscores the importance of healthy skepticism and hardheaded deliberation. Argumentative theory also rehabilitates the once-familiar idea that reasoning takes place in the social world. Sixty years ago the French phenomenologist Maurice Merleau-Ponty said, "our rapport with the true passes by others. Either we go to the true with them, or it is not to the true that we are going."[6]

As a practical matter, argumentative theory suggests that alternative solutions to issues should be evaluated by groups rather than solitary individuals. Leaders should ensure that a minimal but necessary condition is satisfied: the participants must have what Mercier and Sperber call "a shared interest in the truth." In other words, they must be concerned to find the best answer, not win a debate. I would add that shaping an organizational culture which values honesty without sacrificing trust may improve the odds of success.

The authors acknowledge that the soundness of participants' opening arguments is not necessarily improved in a group setting. However, they write, "When different answers are initially proposed and all of them are

---

[5] Mercier and Sperber, *op. cit.*, 72.
[6] Maurice Merleau-Ponty, "Eloge de la philosophie," in *Eloge de la philosophie et autres essais*, Gallimard, 1953, p. 39.

incorrect, then all of them are likely to be rejected, and wholly or partly new hypotheses are likely to be proposed and filtered in turn, thus explaining how groups may do better than any of their individual members."[7] For financial institutions, in my view, this approach to decision making would be especially beneficial in the areas of strategic planning and scenario forecasting.

---

[7] Mercier and Sperber, *op. cit.*, 72.

## Truth in Managerial Costing
July 20, 2012

The IMA's draft *Conceptual Framework for Managerial Costing*[1] is a surpassing achievement. If the IMA task force chaired by Larry R. White had merely filled a gap in the management accounting literature by developing a theoretical basis for managerial costing, its members would deserve a prominent place in the intellectual history of the discipline. In fact, however, they have done much more. In my opinion, the IMA framework of principles, concepts, and constraints stands to reinvigorate the profession of management accounting and guide the core practice of managerial costing for at least the next generation.

Managerial costing, properly understood, supports the achievement of strategic objectives by informing the operational decision-making that creates sustainable economic value. The objective of managerial costing is to determine the monetary value of resource utilization on the basis of cause-and-effect relationships among quantifiable factors. In an investment organization, for example, managerial costing would answer questions such as these:

- Are operational costs primarily driven by the amount of assets under management, the number of client accounts, the volume of transactions, or something else?
- Across the sales, compliance, and accounting functions, what does it cost to onboard a new client?
- What is the all-in cost of a trade, including order entry, commission and spread, confirmation, settlement, and reconciliation? What is the cost of a failed trade?
- How would raising or lowering the minimum account size affect costs?
- What does it cost the firm to accommodate a hedge fund client's request for a separate account?

Managerial costing is not to be confused with cost accounting. The latter applies financial reporting conventions to inventory valuation, transfer

---

[1] IMA, Conceptual Framework for Managerial Costing: Draft Report of the IMA Managerial Costing Conceptual Framework Task Force. Accessed August 2, 2012.
http://www.imanet.org/PDFs/Public/Research/CFMC%20Draft%20for%20R eview.pdf

pricing, and the cost of goods and services sold, and it serves the informational requirements of external parties, including investors, creditors, regulators, and tax authorities. Managerial costing is intended for internal use; it supports the decisions that managers make to optimize operations. The authors observe, "The stock market clearly does not value a company for excellently prepared financial statements if operational excellence is lacking." Moreover, in order to capture outputs and their required inputs, well-executed managerial costing uses data drawn from operational and logistical systems rather than general ledger accounts. In this way, operational quantities and costs are tied to the organization's internal value chain.

The IMA framework additionally recognizes that money is "the meta-language of economic activity and not the activity itself;" accordingly, it analytically separates the quantitative but non-monetary representation of cause-and-effect relationships from their monetary valuation. This conceptual approach equips management accountants to base their analyses of current and prospective operational costs upon empirically grounded insights into the underlying workings or operational dynamics of the firm.

The framework is not a methodology. Rather, it sets out the fundamental principles of causality and analogy,[2] which might be construed as rules of deductive and inferential thinking pertinent to managerial costing; defines modeling and information concepts such as responsiveness, traceability, and interdependence; and, similarly, formulates modeling and information constraints, including among others measurability, materiality, and impartiality. The concepts and constraints effectively constitute standards that any valid method should meet.

A short article cannot adequately cover the scope, much less convey the subtlety, of the IMA managerial costing framework, but a few words about the modeling concept of responsiveness might at least be indicative. Responsiveness, defined as "the correlation between a particular managerial objective's output quantity and the input quantities required to produce that output," replaces the conventional idea that total cost varies monotonically with total volume. A more robust concept, responsiveness captures indirect and shared costs, reflects fixed

---

[2] Adapting a definition proposed by the late Gordon Shillinglaw, the task force presents causality as "the relation between a managerial objective's quantitative output and the input quantities consumed if the output is to be achieved." Analogy is "the use of causal insights to infer past or future causes or effects."

and proportional causal relationships, and represents the consumption and cost relationships of resources that interact within a process, that is, below the aggregate level. It focuses on the point where managers make operational decisions. The draft document states, "Responsiveness is the cornerstone of the marginal/incremental information that the managerial costing model will provide."

Finally, in an extraordinary move—one rarely sees philosophical ideas, let alone epistemological positions, explicitly articulated in business or technical writing—the task force identifies truth as the bedrock of managerial costing. In the traditional correspondence theory of truth, a statement is true if it faithfully represents a state of affairs in the world, or, more or less equivalently, a statement is true if what it corresponds to is a fact. "Truth in cost modeling means reflecting the reality of the operations being modeled."

In a seven-page appendix, the authors distinguish between truth and precision, introduce the logical laws of rational inference and non-contradiction, explain the sense in which truth is pertinent, endorse the correspondence theory, and preemptively reply to a series of common objections. I won't quibble with the philosophical argument they advance because, however simplistic their notion of truth, the task force brings such a fund of good sense to this discussion. "We can all spot a wayward allocation from a mile away," they write, "in fact every manager can, particularly when it looms large on a cost report with no clear causal relationship to the outputs. The statement that the managerial costing framework is based on a foundation of truth captures this reality."

At this writing, the exposure draft of the conceptual framework is open for comment. I anticipate that, once finalized, the framework will become the context in which research is conducted. It will also be presented at industry conferences, incorporated into the management accounting curriculum, and, most importantly, put to good use in all sorts of enterprises. The IMA's publication of the *Conceptual Framework for Managerial Costing* is a signal event for the management accounting profession.

# Part Three: Regulatory Compliance

# Anatomy of a Calamity, Stage 3: "Reaction"

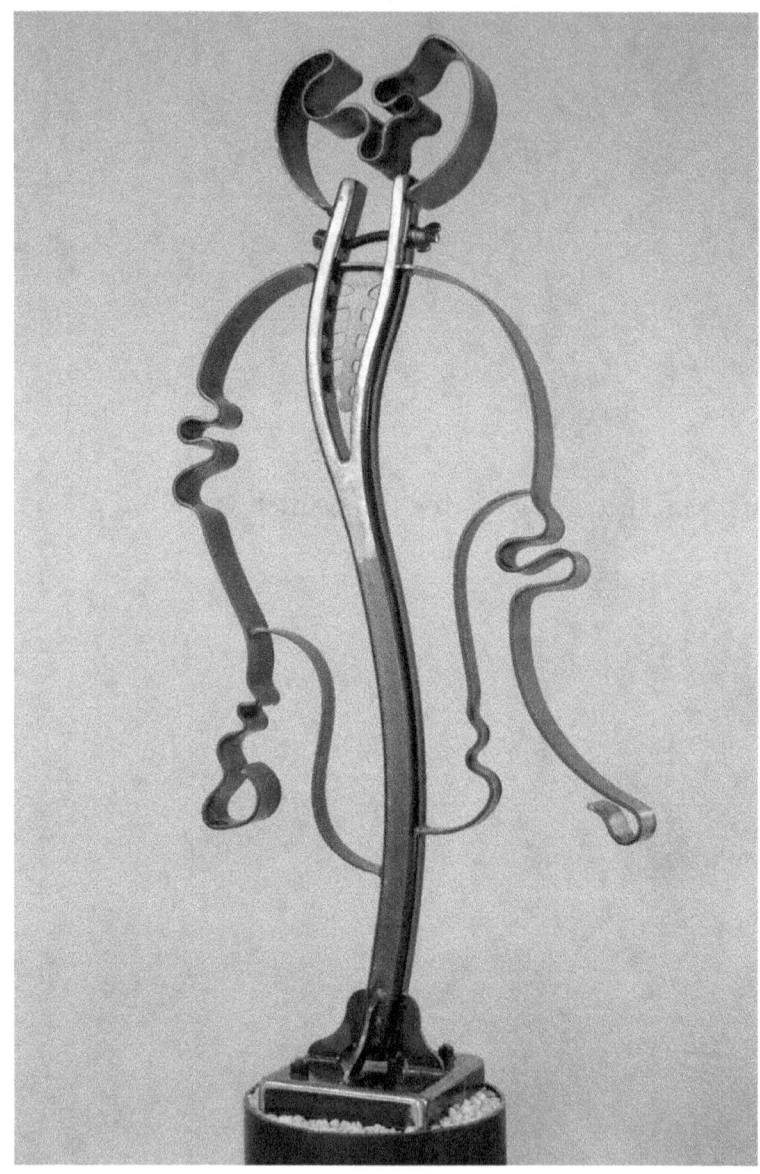

*Shortly after the incident the person reacts without any control. The trauma affects every portion of their being. Every bit of their physical, mental, social and spiritual self becomes part of the reaction.*

## Assessing the Cost of Basel III
October 5, 2012

The International Monetary Fund (IMF) recently released a working paper on the prospective credit impact of key Basel III regulations.[1] The authors, Douglas Elliott, Suzanne Salloy, and André Oliveira Santos, reckoned that, after a transitional period, the ongoing cost of bank lending would rise by 13 basis points in Europe, 10 basis points in Japan, and 20 basis points in the U.S. Unsurprisingly, the authors concluded their findings "strongly suggest" that the presumptive benefits "would indeed outweigh the costs of regulatory reforms in the long run."[2] Because the economic value of financial regulation is contested, and the results of cost-benefit analyses are highly sensitive to the initial assumptions, the IMF-sponsored study merits careful reading.

The scope of the study under consideration is at once broad and limited. It considers the cost of Basel III requirements related to capital and liquidity, derivatives, and taxes and fees, in three distinct markets, but it focuses principally on bank loans, to the relative neglect of other affected segments. It uses a simple formula that reflects the conventional accounting-based approach and reasonably assumes the interest rate on a loan has to cover the cost of funding, expected credit losses, and administrative expenses.

The authors made some crucial and instructive choices in framing their research. For the record, I generally agree with their assumptions. *Parti pris*. It must nonetheless be observed that their decisions predominately tend to attenuate the economic effects of regulatory reform. Moreover, the resulting reduction in the estimated credit impact of Basel III requirements is substantial. For comparison, in a less forgiving study released a year ago, the Institute of International Finance estimated markedly higher increases in the post-transition costs of lending: 3.28% in Europe, 1.81% in Japan, and 2.43% in the United States.[3] (See **Table 1**.) Let's consider salient positions adopted in the IMF working paper.

---

[1] Douglas Elliott, Suzanne Salloy, and André Oliveira Santos, "Assessing the Cost of Financial Regulation," IMF Working Paper WP/12/233 (International Monetary Fund, September 2012). Accessed October 5, 2012. http://www.imf.org/external/pubs/ft/wp/2012/wp12233.pdf.
[2] *Ibid.*, 6, 68.
[3] Institute of International Finance, *The Cumulative Impact on the Global Economy of Changes in the Financial Regulatory Framework* (September 2011). Accessed October 5, 2012. http://www.iif.com/emr/resources+1359.php

**Table 1**. Basel III Impact on Credit Spreads (bps)

|  | Europe | Japan | United States |
|---|---|---|---|
| IMF | 18 | 8 | 28 |
| IIF 2012-2019 | 328 | 181 | 243 |
| IIF 2011-2015 | 291 | 202 | 468 |

Based upon IMF Working Paper WP/12/233, Table 1

First, unlike the IIF report, the IMF-sponsored study heroically leaps the chasm of transitional costs. The authors don't deny that achieving compliance with Basel III entails costly adjustments. Nor are they cavalier about excluding those costs from the scope of their research. Indeed, they acknowledge, "Good policymaking requires true cost-benefit analyses and it would certainly be a mistake to ignore transitional costs. However, resource constraints required a narrower focus on the central question of the long-term effects on credit."[4]

This is a regrettable limitation. Merely to keep the doors open, banks—many of which are exceedingly complex organizations—are compelled not only to upgrade and integrate their governance, risk management, and compliance (GRC) systems but also to divert business and technological talent from other projects which might improve customer service or operational efficiency. Although ancillary benefits may surface over the long term,[5] implementing system and process changes to cope with regulatory reform on the scale of Basel III is not a trivial undertaking.

Second, the authors select year-end 2010 as the baseline in order to exclude the effects of the higher safety margins attributable to market forces after the subprime crisis. This decision is sound. Choosing a pre-crisis point in time for the baseline, as the IIF researchers appear to have done, arguably overstates the impact of new regulations. It is unfortunate the IMF-sponsored study could not similarly extract the credit impact of the Eurozone crisis.

---

[4] *Op. cit.*, 8. The authors avow, "It would be worthwhile to extend the quantitative analysis from this paper to take into account transitional as well as long-term effects." 67.

[5] For example, automated data collection to monitor liquidity indicators might help the treasury department centrally manage intraday positions. See "Basel's Proposal for Monitoring Intraday Liquidity," below.

Third, the authors assume that banks will respond to the new regulations by taking cost-cutting and other measures,[6] and they estimate the resulting economies will offset the unfavorable credit impact of Basel III by 13 basis points in Europe, 10 basis points in Japan, and 20 basis points in the United States. (These estimated offsets are included in the figures cited above.) In particular, the authors observe, "A substantial portion of the cost of credit provision comes from administrative and marketing expenses, where there is considerable room to cut expenses if necessary."[7] As a practical matter, then, reducing costs generally means lowering compensation and staffing levels. The authors do not address broader social and economic effects,[8] but it is apparent that a goodly portion of the cost of regulatory reform is borne by financial services employees and their families.[9] And those who don't lose their jobs must work all the harder.

Fourth, the authors assume that investors will lower their required rate of return (ROE) on bank equity due to the greater safety presumably resulting from regulatory reform. In applying the credit pricing formula mentioned above, they use required ROEs of 12% in Europe and the United States and 7% in Japan. As a reality check, **Table 2** displays ballpark estimates of actual and required ROEs for five U.S. banks that have been designated systemically important as of this writing: Bank of America (ticker symbol BAC), BNY Mellon (BK), Citi (C), JPMorgan Chase (JPM), and Wells Fargo (WFC). In this small sample, the rough-and-ready approximations of required ROE range from 10% to 13%, a fairly tight grouping, and the arithmetic mean is 11.5%. (These values will, of course, change as the banks announce third quarter earnings in the next few weeks.) Without leaning too heavily on the data in this

---

[6] In addition to cost-cutting, the mitigants available to management include, among others, improving internal risk models, changing the risk-weighted asset mix, restructuring the portfolio of businesses, lowering expected credit losses by strengthening covenants and rationing credit, and reducing the asset/liability mismatch by shortening assets and lengthening liabilities. Obviously, some of these actions affect banks' ability to serve the vital economic rôle of transforming maturities and providing liquidity.

[7] *Op. cit.*, 59.

[8] The IIF study extends the analysis to the estimated impact of regulatory reform on real GDP growth and end-point employment levels. The findings are summarized in Table I.1: IIF Cumulative Impact Results – Comparison of Scenarios, IIF, *op. cit.*, 10.

[9] See "The Employment Impact of Securities Regulation," below.

exhibit, as of this writing the paper's estimate of 12% seems reasonable for at least a handful of U.S.-headquartered banks.

**Table 2.** Estimated Rates of Return on Equity

| Bank | Trailing EPS (EPS$_T$) | 30 June 2012 Book Value (BV) | Expected EPS (EPS$_E$) | Price (P) | Estimated ROE | |
|---|---|---|---|---|---|---|
| | | | | | Actual (EPS$_T$/BV) | Required (EPS$_E$/P) |
| BAC | 0.93 | 20.16 | 0.93 | 9.32 | 4.61% | 9.98% |
| BK | 2.11 | 29.25 | 2.38 | 23.42 | 7.21% | 10.16% |
| C | 3.67 | 63.27 | 4.54 | 34.77 | 5.80% | 13.06% |
| JPM | 4.32 | 48.28 | 5.19 | 41.71 | 8.95% | 12.44% |
| WFC | 3.02 | 25.92 | 3.64 | 35.84 | 11.65% | 10.16% |
| Average | | | | | 7.52% | 11.50% |

Data Source: Zack's Investment Research (6 Oct 2012)

These notes do not remotely convey the value and interest of the IMF work paper. It is worthwhile to remark, however, that the sharp differences between the IIF and IMF-sponsored studies resurrect long-standing theoretical disagreements about the credibility of empirical research in economics and the other social sciences.[10] In view of the strongly partisan disagreement over the proper extent of regulation that is currently playing out in the United States, the philosophical questions of scientific independence and objectivity have real-world consequences. We are all stakeholders. As participants in the capital markets, the most we can reasonably expect of economists is a forthright statement of their assumptions, and of ourselves, critical thinking with openness to the possibility we are mistaken. Regulators charged with presenting cost-benefit analyses to legislative bodies have the far more difficult task of persuading the opposition to accept their conclusions.

---

[10] Gunnar Myrdal's classic study, *Objectivity in Social Research* (Pantheon, 1969), is indispensable. A recent publication is José Castor Caldas and Vitor Neves, eds., *Facts, Values and Objectivity in Economics* (Routledge, 2012).

# Principles-Based Regulation
November 22, 2011

The public comment period for the Securities and Exchange Commission's concept release on investment companies' use of derivatives[1] ended this month. The SEC received about 50 comments[2] from mutual fund providers, interest groups, securities lawyers, and private investors, including a few crackpots. Numerous respectable commentators suggested approaches to "segregating" or earmarking assets to cover mutual funds' senior debt, which, in the SEC's view, includes financial liabilities related to derivatives positions. Because segregated assets are unavailable for sale or disposition, they purportedly protect investors against adverse outcomes due to leverage.

In the past, the SEC has defined asset segregation requirements for senior debt on an instrument-by-instrument basis. For example, Release 10666,[3] a key document in mutual fund regulatory history, specifically has to do with reverse repo and deferred commitment agreements such as TBAs. Some commentators consider the customary method ill-suited to derivatives, which "come in too many varieties with too many different types of risk to be shoehorned effectively into a model based on Depression-era investment concepts." (Oppenheimer Funds.)[4] They call, instead, for principles-based regulation.

The letter addressed to the SEC by the Investment Company Institute[5] exemplifies the principles-based perspective. Funds would be required to

---

[1] Securities and Exchange Commission, "Use of Derivatives by Investment Companies under the Investment Company Act of 1940." Release No. IC-29776; File No. S7-33-11. Accessed August 2, 2012. http://www.sec.gov/rules/concept/2011/ic-29776.pdf
[2] Securities and Exchange Commission, "Comments on Concept Release: Use of Derivatives by Investment Companies under the Investment Company Act of 1940." Accessed August 2, 2012. http://www.sec.gov/comments/s7-33-11/s73311.shtml
[3] 44 FR 25188. Accessed August 2, 2012. http://www.sec.gov/divisions/investment/imseniorsecurities/ic-10666.pdf
[4] Oppenheimer Funds, letter to Elizabeth Murphy, Secretary, U.S. Securities and Exchange Commission (November 7, 2011). Accessed August 2, 2012. http://www.sec.gov/comments/s7-33-11/s73311-44.pdf
[5] Investment Company Institute, letter to Elizabeth Murphy, Secretary, U.S. Securities and Exchange Commission (November 7, 2011). Accessed August 3, 2012. http://www.sec.gov/comments/s7-33-11/s73311-46.pdf

adopt Rule 38a-1 compliance policies and procedures[6] to establish asset segregation standards in keeping with the way investment, risk, and compliance professionals manage portfolio exposures. The ICI proposal calls upon the SEC to provide guidance in the form of "guardrails" recommending, for instance, that advisers take measures to validate the models and assumptions used in determining the amount of assets to be segregated under extreme but plausible market conditions. Other commentators refer not to "extreme but plausible" scenarios but to "realistic, reasonable and current expectations of the potential for loss to the fund." (Loomis, Sayles.)[7]

In a principles-based regulatory environment, the directors and the Chief Compliance Officer (CCO) would be responsible for the reasonability of the fund's asset segregation policies. In practice, as an *Ignites* article[8] points out, the CCO would be on the line. The Independent Directors Council[9] remarks, "Fund boards rely on the fund CCO to test the effectiveness of and compliance with the policies and procedures and to report any concerns to the board."

Let's think about this.

The deficiencies of the established method must certainly be acknowledged. Rules-based regulation fosters a legalistic mentality, rewards evasive tactics, places regulators in a chronically reactionary position, and contributes to regulatory uncertainty as firms attempt to reason from existing rules to novel situations.

However, under a principles-based approach, it is realistic to expect utility-maximizing organizations to look for a competitive advantage by means of a liberal inflection tending to understate the amount of assets

---

[6] 68 FR 74714. Accessed August 3, 2012. http://www.gpo.gov/fdsys/pkg/FR-2003-12-24/pdf/03-31544.pdf. The same rule under the Investment Advisers Act of 1940 is 206(4)-7.

[7] Loomis Sayles, letter to Elizabeth Murphy, Secretary, U.S. Securities and Exchange Commission (November 7, 2011). Accessed August 3, 2012. http://www.sec.gov/comments/s7-33-11/s73311-25.pdf

[8] Peter Ortiz, "ICI's Ideas for Derivatives Reform Serve Up CCO Curveball," Ignites, November 18, 2011. Accessed August 3, 2011. http://www.ignites.com/c/276751/32861/ideas_derivatives_reform_serve_cur veball?referrer_module=issueHeadline&module_order=3

[9] Independent Directors Council, letter to Elizabeth Murphy, Secretary, U.S. Securities and Exchange Commission (November 7, 2011). Accessed August 3, 2012. http://www.sec.gov/comments/s7-33-11/s73311-24.pdf

to be segregated. "On its face," writes AQR Capital Management,[10] "it is logical that the place where oversight of derivative usage occurs primarily be the place where the trades occur. But we remain concerned that different funds could reach different determinations, perhaps some taking more aggressive positions to allow for greater use of derivatives to drive performance." This is a realistic concern. Recall that the widespread use of derivatives in the 1990s and 2000s was impelled not only by risk management objectives but also by competition in the structured investments marketplace and, in good part, by regulatory capital arbitrage.[11]

Moreover, not all CCOs may have the technical skill, let alone the moral authority, to evaluate internal asset segregation policies and ensure the adequacy of set-asides. Under Rule 38a-1, it is a violation to "coerce, manipulate, mislead or fraudulently influence the fund's chief compliance officer in the performance of her responsibilities." But everyone wants to be accepted. And employment ads for compliance officers are far more likely to require "strong interpersonal and communication skills" than "a solid grasp of derivatives and VaR."

AQR and others call for clear SEC guidance on internal asset segregation policies. If principles-based regulation is not to be an abdication, the regulators' firm expectations would indeed have to be plainly articulated and, as some commentators suggest, accompanied by examples. Equally important: frequent, vigorous examinations and credible enforcement.

Principles-based regulation may very well be preferable to the traditional approach, but let us be mindful of recent history and proceed advisedly. SEC staff might wish to have a private conversation with European supervisors about their experience with Basel II's Advanced measurement Approach (AMA)[12] for the calculation of operational risk capital charges. I can recommend a quiet little estaminet in Brabant.

---

[10] AQR Capital Management, letter to Elizabeth Murphy, Secretary, U.S. Securities and Exchange Commission (November 7, 2011). Accessed August 3, 2012. http://www.sec.gov/comments/s7-33-11/s73311-26.pdf
[11] Simon Johnson and James Kwak, *13 Bankers: The Wall Street Takeover and the Next Financial Meltdown* (Vintage Books, 2011 edition), pp. 138–139.
[12] Basel Committee on Banking Supervision, *Operational Risk—Supervisory Guidelines for the Advanced Measurement Approaches*, June 2011. Accessed August 3, 2012. http://www.bis.org/publ/bcbs196.pdf

## Passing Papers
December 6, 2011

Yesterday, two months after we started the ordeal, my wife and I closed on a new mortgage. The transaction was a simple rate-and-term refinancing on an owner-occupied house with a 35 percent loan-to-value (LTV) ratio, but the documentation was exhaustive to the point of obsessiveness. Nor were records pursued merely to pack a file or complete a checklist; the mortgage lender's underwriting department called us repeatedly to clarify facts about our household economy. We were asked, for instance, to account for several non-payroll bank deposits above a low threshold, and to back up our explanations with evidence. ("Please fax those items to us today.") Because the originating lender may not retain the mortgage, we additionally signed releases authorizing a purchaser to confirm pertinent financial information independently. This is the residential mortgage loan business in an age of reform.

Section 941 of the Dodd-Frank Act (DFA) inserted a new section, 15G, into the Securities Exchange Act of 1934. Section 15G requires securitizers to retain not less than five percent of the credit risk for assets transferred through the issuance of asset-backed securities, including collateralized mortgage obligations. There are, however, some exceptions, including an exemption for asset-backed securities that are collateralized exclusively by "qualified residential mortgages" (QRMs). DFA directed the Office of the Comptroller of the Currency, the Board of Governors of the Federal Reserve System, the Federal Deposit Insurance Corporation, the U.S. Securities and Exchange Commission, the Federal Housing Finance Agency, and the Department of Housing and Urban Development to collaborate in prescribing underwriting standards for QRMs. Accordingly, on March 31, 2011, those agencies proposed a Credit Risk Retention[1] rule which, with an extension, remained open for public comment through August 1st.

---

[1] Department of the Treasury, Federal Reserve System, Federal Deposit Insurance Corporation, U.S. Securities and Exchange Commission, Federal Housing Finance Agency, and Department of Housing and Urban Development, Proposed Rule, "Credit Risk Retention," March 31, 2011. Accessed August 4, 2012. http://www.sec.gov/rules/proposed/2011/34-64148.pdf

Under the proposed rule, only a closed-end first-lien mortgage to purchase or refinance a one-to-four family property, at least one unit of which is the principal dwelling of a borrower, is eligible for QRM status. The term to maturity mustn't exceed 30 years, points and fees are capped at three percent of the total loan value, and there are significant restrictions on payment terms and rate increases. For example, interest-only payments are prohibited, and regularly scheduled principal and interest payments may not result in an increase of the unpaid principal balance; balloon payments of size are prohibited; and interest rate increases on variable-rate mortgages cannot exceed two percent in any 12-month period or six percent over the life of the loan. The proposed QRM underwriting standards also include, among others, those paraphrased here:

- The borrower cannot currently be 30 or more days past due on any debt obligation, nor have been 60 or more days past due within the last 24 months.

- Minimum LTV ratios are 80 percent for a purchase mortgage, 75 percent for a rate and term refinancing, and 70 percent for a cash-out refinancing.

- If purchasing a house, the borrower must make a minimum cash down payment of 20 percent; an Appendix to the rule sets forth additional requirements pertaining to acceptable sources of the down payment.

- The rule proposes a front-end debt-to-income ratio limit of 28 percent and a back-end ratio limit of 36 percent. (The back-end ratio includes the pro forma effect of the mortgage loan under consideration.)

Given that Title XIV of DFA also addresses mortgage standards, we can hazard a few predictions about housing finance and living arrangements for the next generation.

First, the cost of originating and servicing all mortgages will rise, and the increase will be passed along to borrowers in the form of higher interest rates. (This effect may not become apparent until interest rates rise and banks pick up the pace of mortgage lending.)

Second, because QRMs will effectively have a lower cost of capital than other mortgage loans, two-tier pricing will emerge.

Third, occupancy of existing single-family residences will become denser as more adult children with limited financial resources make the difficult decision to raise their own families in their aging parents' homes.

Fourth, lifelong renting will become as commonplace in the U.S. as it is in other countries, and rental income will become a significant factor in residential appraisals.

There's a lot to think about, but this entry is quite long enough already. Let me conclude with gratuitous trivia. We call our house Shodwell in view of my wife's closetful of footwear and in wistful homage to Thomas Jefferson's birthplace, Shadwell, which stood nearby. This house, a rather modest dwelling by local standards, is our only residence, but sometimes I travel on business. My wife's FICO scores are higher than mine, and, upon reflection, I'm okay with that.

# Gearing Down: The Basel III Leverage Ratio
December 13, 2011

Appearing before a U.S. Senate subcommittee on 7 December, Sheila Bair testified, "In the near term…regulators' primary focus should be on constraining absolute leverage through an international leverage ratio that is significantly higher than the Basel Committee's proposed 3% standard."[1]

Is that so?

Leverage in the banking system was, indubitably, a significant contributor to the subprime crisis, and deleveraging intensified the ensuing credit crunch. The Basel Committee on Banking Supervision observed upon releasing Basel III, "In many cases, banks built up excessive leverage while still showing strong risk based capital ratios. During the most severe part of the crisis, the banking sector was forced by the market to reduce its leverage in a manner that amplified downward pressure on asset prices, further exacerbating the positive feedback loop between losses, declines in bank capital, and contraction in credit availability." In order to attenuate such cycles in the future, Basel III includes "a simple, transparent, non-risk based leverage ratio that is calibrated to act as a credible supplementary measure to the risk based capital requirements."

The present commentary considers the leverage ratio in isolation. A more complete treatment would assess it in the context of all the other capital-related provisions; there may be complex interactions and unintended consequences. Nonetheless, attending to the leverage ratio in its own right is not entirely inappropriate. One would do the same with any other backstop measure.

Presented in Section V of Basel III, the leverage ratio is the average monthly ratio of a "capital measure" to an "exposure measure." The capital measure is Tier 1 capital.[2] The exposure measure includes balance

---

[1] Sheila Bair, "A New Regime for Regulating Large, Complex Financial Institutions." Testimony of Sheila C. Bair before the Financial Institutions and Consumer Protection Subcommittee of the Senate Committee on Banking, Housing and Urban Affairs, December 7, 2011. Accessed August 3, 2012. http://banking.senate.gov/public/index.cfm?FuseAction=Files.View&FileStore _id=29da74f2-85f9-479e-8c23-836a718fd1e9Financial Institutions and Consumer Protection Subcommittee

[2] Tier 1 capital is defined in Basel III paragraphs 52–57.

sheet items; securities financing transactions (SFT) such as repurchase agreements, security lending, and margin lending; derivatives; and off-balance sheet items (OBS) including commitments, direct credit substitutes, acceptances, letters of credit, failed transactions and unsettled securities.[3] The inclusion of OBS and SFT items is, in my opinion, a significant advance.

The Committee stated that it will "test" a minimum Tier 1 leverage ratio of 3% over the four-year period beginning 1 January 2013. Expressed as a multiple rather than a percentage, the maximum on- and off-balance sheet exposure is 33 times Tier 1 capital. Two examples might make this measure more meaningful.

- As of September 30, 2011, Citigroup's Tier 1 capital was US$122.3 billion.[4] With a maximum leverage ratio of 33, Citigroup could support exposure up to some US$4.1 trillion or approximately 27% of U.S gross domestic product (GDP).[5]

- As of 30 September, Bank of America's Tier 1 capital was US$120.4 billion.[6] Bank of America's maximum exposure would be approximately US$4.0 trillion or about 26% of GDP.

I think regulators' primary concern should be reducing systemic risk, but limiting leverage in the banking system is an important element of any plan to prevent a cascade of failures. I fully agree with the second part of

[3] This summary does not reflect technical details of the leverage ratio calculation. The capital measure is set forth in Basel III paragraphs 154–156, and the exposure measure is explained in paragraphs 157–164.
[4] Citigroup, Report at the Close of Business September 30, 2011, Consolidated Reports of Condition and Income for a Bank with Domestic and Foreign Offices Only—FFIEC 031. Accessed August 3, 2012. http://www.citigroup.com/citi/fin/data/call110930cb.pdf?ieNocache=449
[5] Released on 22 November 2011, the Bureau of Economic Analysis's second revised estimate of seasonally adjusted annual GDP for the third quarter was US$15,180.9 billion. Bureau of Economic Analysis, U.S. Department of Commerce, National Income and Product Accounts: Gross Domestic Product, 3rd quarter 2011 (second estimate); Corporate Profits, 3rd quarter 2011 (preliminary estimate), November 22, 2011. Accessed August 3, 2012. http://www.bea.gov/newsreleases/national/gdp/2011/gdp3q11_2nd.htm
[6] Bank of America, Report at the Close of Business September 30, 2011, Consolidated Reports of Condition and Income for a Bank with Domestic and Foreign Offices Only—FFIEC 031. Accessed August 3, 2012. https://cdr.ffiec.gov/Public/ViewPDFFacsimile.aspx

Bair's argument. Basel III's proposed leverage ratio is well defined but the 3% minimum is indeed too liberal. A tighter international restriction on bank leverage would afford the global economy more protection.

## Home for the Holidays
December 22, 2011

Christmas 2011. Three years after the subprime crisis, the Bureau of Labor Statistics reports that 13.3 million U.S. workers are unemployed, 8.5 million are involuntarily working part-time, and 1.1 million have given up looking for jobs.[1] Uncounted are those with the relatively good fortune to have full-time work at substantially lower pay than they previously earned. In a related domain, the Office of the Comptroller of the Currency reports that 1.5 million home retention actions—loan modifications, trial period plans, and payment plans—were initiated in the first nine months of this year; nonetheless, more than half a million homes were forfeited in that period, and as of September 30, 2011, 1.3 million foreclosures were in process.[2] It is a hard time for many American families.

Last week the Securities and Exchange Commission charged six former executives of government-sponsored entities (GSEs) with securities fraud.[3] For the record, a complaint against past Fannie Mae officers names Daniel H. Mudd, Enrico Dallavecchia, and Thomas A. Lund. A similar complaint against former Freddie Mac officers names Richard L. Syron, Patricia L. Cook, and Donald J. Bisenius. According to the SEC documents, the defendants misled investors by materially understating the agencies' exposures to subprime and low-documentation mortgage loans.

The SEC managed a potential conflict of interest by entering non-prosecution agreements in which the GSEs consented to accept responsibility and not to call into question a damning statement of facts. In its complaints against the executives, the SEC catalogues many

---

[1] Bureau of Labor Statistics, U.S. Department of Labor, "The Employment Situation—November 2011." Accessed August 3, 2012. http://www.bls.gov/news.release/archives/empsit_12022011.pdf
[2] Office of the Comptroller of the Currency, U.S. Department of theTreasury, "OCC Mortgage Metrics Report, Third Quarter 2011." Accessed August 3, 2012. http://www.occ.treas.gov/publications/publications-by-type/other-publications-reports/mortgage-metrics-2011/mortgage-metrics-q3-2011.pdf
[3] Securities and Exchange Commission, "SEC Charges Former Fannie Mae and Freddie Mac Executives with Securities Fraud," December 16, 2011. Accessed August 3, 2012. http://www.sec.gov/news/press/2011/2011-267.htm

misrepresentations in regulatory filings, speeches, and calls with investors and analysts. Here are two examples.

- Fannie Mae: "At the time of this [2006 Form 10-K] disclosure [16 Aug 2007], Fannie Mae's total exposure to loans with 'lower or alternative documentation' (Alt-A) was actually 22% of its total Single Family mortgage credit book of business, not 12% as disclosed. Fannie Mae's reporting of its Alt-A [holdings] omitted approximately $238 billion worth of Fannie Mae's Single Family mortgage credit book of business, which consisted of reduced document loans as of June 30, 2007—almost equal to the $296 billion that was disclosed as Alt-A."[4]

- Freddie Mac: In May 2007, Syron stated at a UBS conference that "Freddie had basically no subprime exposure in our guarantee business" at the end of 2006. Cook made the same statement at a Lehman conference. However, according to the SEC, Freddie Mac's single family guarantee portfolio contained approximately $141 billion dollars of loans that the business internally characterized as "subprime," "otherwise subprime," or "subprime-like." This amount represented about 10% of the single family guarantee portfolio.[5]

The housing bubble was not the fault of Fannie Mae and Freddie Mac alone, but they had a hand in it. While their public mission is to support home ownership, they arguably facilitated questionable mortgage lending—in cases of fraud, they were the fence—and they are said to have denied investors a sound basis for evaluating credit risk. Assertedly, then, socially and economically harmful decisions were made and executed, not only by the organizations as legal persons, but by real people, individual men and women, allegedly including those charged in the SEC complaints. Suing them does not assist the unemployed or the uprooted in any practical, material way, but it might help put this sorry history to rest. And may this Christmas not be a time of anger, disappointment, or despair, but a season of love and hope.

---

[4] SEC v. Mudd, Dallavecchia, and Lund, No. CV 11-9202 (S.D.N.Y, December 16, 2011), para 181. Accessed August 3, 2012.
http://www.sec.gov/litigation/complaints/2011/comp-pr2011-267-fanniemae.pdf
[5] SEC v. Syron, Cook, and Bisenius, No. CV 11-9201 (S.D.N.Y., December 14, 2011), para. 86, 92, and 93. Accessed August 3, 2012.
http://www.sec.gov/litigation/complaints/2011/comp-pr2011-267-freddiemac.pdf

## FATCA: We Are Not Impressed
January 4, 2012

The Foreign Account Tax Compliance Act (FATCA), which entered U.S. law in 2010 as Title V of the Hiring Incentives to Restore Employment (HIRE) Act, originated with a legitimate concern to bolster U.S. tax receipts by reducing the incidence of tax evasion. Unfortunately, even a cursory perusal of its key provisions[1] reveals little else to praise in this legislation.

First, in a departure from civilized norms, FATCA apparently rests upon a presumption of guilt. Unless they file IRS Form 8938 with their annual income tax return,[2] American expatriates holding more than US$50,000 in foreign assets will be subject to a penalty of US$10,000. In addition, if they actually *are* tax evaders, they will be assessed 40 percent of the understated tax liability attributable to foreign assets.

Second, and much more pertinently for many *Middle Office* readers, FATCA imposes significant due diligence, reporting, and withholding requirements on non-U.S. financial institutions, including banks and asset managers. In brief, the law requires "foreign financial institutions" (FFIs) to search for U.S. accounts, compile and disclose information about them, and withhold 30 percent of certain transfers to non-participating institutions as well as certain payments to corporate or individual account holders who haven't provided enough information to determine whether they are U.S. persons.

Thus, in an overreach arguably unexampled since the British admiralty put a stop to impressment, FATCA effectively forces international banks and asset managers on board as agents of the U.S. Treasury. In economic terms, it's a prime example of a negative externality: The U.S. government will have the benefit of higher tax receipts, while the transaction costs will be largely, and involuntarily, borne by international banks and asset managers.

From the perspective of a non-U.S. financial institution, FATCA necessitates a stupefyingly unproductive use of corporate resources at a

[1] IRS, "Summary of Key FATCA Provisions." Accessed August 3, 2012. http://www.irs.gov/businesses/corporations/article/0,,id=236664,00.html
[2] IRS, Form 8938, Statement of Specified Foreign Financial Assets. Accessed August 3, 2012. http://www.irs.gov/pub/irs-pdf/f8938.pdf

time when other regulatory changes are already placing heavy demands on scarce technological and operational capabilities. From a wider viewpoint, FATCA represents a new and disadvantageous cost of business for non-U.S. banks and asset managers in a highly competitive global industry. Let us hope it does not impair international cooperation in vitally important areas of common interest such as, say, reducing systemic risk.

## Suitability
January 9, 2012

Whether brokers, dealers, and investment advisors should be held to a uniform standard of care when providing personalized investment advice remains an open issue.[1] As a practical matter, however, FINRA[2] has narrowed the regulatory gap between broker-dealers and investment advisors with two new rules scheduled to take effect July 9, 2012.

- Rule 2090, Know Your Customer,[3] requires FINRA members to "use reasonable diligence" to know and retain "the essential facts" about each customer and the authority of persons acting on the customer's behalf.

- Rule 2111, Suitability,[4] requires members and associated persons to have "a reasonable basis to believe" that an investment recommendation is "suitable for the customer." Compliance entails "reasonable diligence...to ascertain the customer's investment profile," including, among other things, "the customer's age, other investments, financial situation and needs,

---

[1] Under the uniform fiduciary standard recommended by the SEC, "the standard of conduct for all brokers, dealers, and investment advisers, when providing personalized investment advice about securities to retail customers...shall be to act in the best interest of the customer without regard to the financial or other interest of the broker, dealer, or investment adviser providing the advice." SEC, *Study on Investment Advisers and Broker-Dealers*, January 2012, 109-110. Accessed August 3, 2012. http://www.sec.gov/news/studies/2011/913studyfinal.pdf

[2] For the information of international readers: FINRA, the Financial Industry Regulatory Authority, , is the largest independent regulator of U.S. securities firms doing business with the public. It was formed by the merger, in 2007, of the National Association of Securities Dealers (NASD) and the member regulation, enforcement, and arbitration functions of the New York Stock Exchange. As a national securities association registered with the SEC, FINRA is obligated to comply with the Securities Exchange Act of 1934 and to enforce compliance by its members with the Exchange Act and its own rules. Obtaining SEC approval is key step in FINRA's rulemaking process.

[3] Rule 2090, FINRA Manual. Accessed August 3, 2012. http://finra.complinet.com/en/display/display.html?rbid=2403&record_id=13389&element_id=9858&highlight=2090#r13389

[4] Rule 2111, FINRA Manual. Accessed August 3, 2012. http://finra.complinet.com/en/display/display_main.html?rbid=2403&element_id=9859

tax status, investment objectives, investment experience, investment time horizon, liquidity needs, [and] risk tolerance."

The suitability rule, in particular, generally aligns brokers' and dealers' obligations with accepted practice in the advisory domain. The SEC set forth its expectations of investment advisors in Investment Act Release No. 1406,[5] effectively[6] requiring advisors "to make only suitable recommendations to a client, after a reasonable inquiry into the client's financial situation, investment experience, and investment objectives." Similarly, under the CFA Institute *Standards of Professional Conduct*,[7] members and candidates must make "a reasonable inquiry into a client's or prospective client's investment experience, risk and return objectives, and financial constraints prior to making any investment recommendation…and must reassess and update this information regularly." (III.C.1.a.) In addition, they must "have a reasonable and adequate basis, supported by appropriate research and investigation," for any recommendation. (V.A.2.)

The implementation guidance FINRA has offered to date is sparse and vague. For instance, Regulatory Notice 11-25 states that the suitability rule allows firms to adopt a risk-based approach to documenting suitability determinations, taking into account the complexity and/or risks of the recommended security or strategy. "However," we are advised, "firms should understand that, to the degree that the basis for suitability is not evident from the recommendation itself, FINRA examination and enforcement concerns will rise with the lack of documentary evidence for the recommendation."[8] Evidently, whether a broker has adequately memorialized the product- and customer-specific grounds on which she deemed an investment recommendation suitable

---

[5] 59 FR 6658. Accessed August 3, 2012. http://www.gpo.gov/fdsys/pkg/FR-1994-03-22/html/94-6658.htm

[6] Robert E. Plaze explains, "In Release No. 1406, the SEC proposed a rule under the Act's anti-fraud provisions requiring advisers give clients only suitable advice. Although the rule was never adopted, the SEC staff takes the position that the rule would have codified existing suitability obligations of advisers and, as a result, the proposed rule reflects the current obligation of advisers under the Act." *The Regulation of Investment Advisers by the Securities and Exchange Commission*, updated to November 22, 2006, 38 fn. 82. Accessed August 3, 2012. http://www.sec.gov/about/offices/oia/oia_investman/rplaze-042006.pdf

[7] CFA Institute, *Code of Ethics and Standards of Professional Conduct*, 2010. Accessed August 3, 2012. http://www.cfapubs.org/doi/pdf/10.2469/ccb.v2010.n14.1

[8] FINRA, Regulatory Notice 11-25, "Know Your Customer and Suitability," May 2011. Accessed August 3, 2012.

depends, in part, upon the examiner's perspicacity. Even seasoned, battle-hardened CCOs may find this intelligence unnerving.

Clearly, many broker-dealers are facing a monumental task, even in the ideal situation where their existing documentation is comprehensive, current, and electronically accessible. Within six months, they will minimally have had to formulate internal policies, ensure the account opening process is thorough, educate unenthusiastic brokers in unaccustomed responsibilities—they'd rather be producing!—and monitor their compliance, not merely with the firm's documentation guidelines, but also with the underlying suitability requirement. (FINRA cautions, "documentation by itself does not cure an otherwise unsuitable recommendation.") Buy-side operational consultants may be able to help; they know how investment managers with discretionary accounts handle suitability issues. But there's no getting away from the effort and expense of coming into compliance.

Are Rules 2090 and 211 worth the costs to the broker-dealer industry, the firms, branches, and brokers, and the retail investors whose fees may rise? Philosophically, yes. FINRA's action promotes greater professionalism among brokers while advancing its mission to "protect America's investors by making sure the securities industry operates fairly and honestly." In the short run, however, what a bear.

## The Employment Impact of Securities Regulations
January 16, 2012

It was reported last week that the SEC plans to request more data, including public comments, and conduct a cost-benefit analysis before finalizing its proposal for a uniform fiduciary standard.[1] This is no surprise; I wrote elsewhere about the politics of economic analysis following a Capital Markets Subcommittee hearing that addressed the contemplated fiduciary rule in September 2011. But it brings to mind once again the complex issues surrounding the social and economic value of new financial regulations.

For context, let's recall that the Great Recession of 2007–2009 was the deepest contraction since the Bureau of Economic Advisors (BEA) started releasing quarterly real GDP estimates in 1947. Moreover, the recovery has been sluggish; BEA most recently estimated that real GDP rose at an annual rate of 2.0% in the third quarter of 2011, while real disposable personal income *fell* 1.9%.[2] The Bureau of Labor Statistics said this month that nonfarm payroll employment rose by 1.6 million in 2011.[3] At this pace, it will take years to replace the nine million jobs lost during the recession while accommodating net new entrants to the workforce.

The financial services industry was by no means the hardest hit. Far from it. Nonetheless, BLS statistics show that in December 2011 the U.S. securities, commodity contracts, and investments industry[4] employed approximately 52,000 (6.1%) fewer than it had four years earlier.[5]

---

[1] Suzanne Barlyn, "New SEC Request May Stall Process 6 More Months," *Reuters*, January 13, 2012. Accessed August 3, 2012.
http://www.reuters.com/article/2012/01/13/us-sec-fiduciary-idUSTRE80C1YX20120113

[2] Bureau of Economic Analysis, U.S. Department of Commerce, "Gross Domestic Product: Third Quarter 2011 (Third Estimate); Corporate Profits: Third Quarter 2011 (Revised Estimate), December 22, 2011. Accessed August 3, 2012.
http://www.bea.gov/newsreleases/national/gdp/2011/pdf/gdp3q11_3rd.pdf

[3] Bureau of Labor Statistics, U.S. Department of Labor, "Employment Situation—December 2011." Accessed August 3, 2012.
http://www.bls.gov/news.release/archives/empsit_01062012.pdf

[4] North American Industry Classification System (NAICS) 523.

[5] Bureau of Labor Statistics, U.S. Department of Labor. Accessed August 3, 2012. http://data.bls.gov/timeseries/CES5552300001?data_tool=XGtable

Moreover, this point-to-point change undoubtedly masks the financial impact of protracted unemployment on individuals and their families. Some of those who were displaced in big-bank layoffs, for instance, may not find work in this field again.

In 1993 President Clinton opened Executive Order 12866, "Regulatory Planning and Review,"[6] with the words, "The American people deserve a regulatory system that works for them, not against them." EO 12866 requires regulators to "propose or adopt a regulation only upon a reasoned determination that the benefits of the intended regulation justify its costs." Specifically, EO 12866 requires regulatory agencies to submit cost-benefit analyses of "significant regulatory actions" to the Office of Information and Regulatory Affairs in the Office of Management and Budget. The order explicitly states, in pertinent part, that cost assessments must take into account "any adverse effects on the efficient functioning of the economy [and on] private markets (including productivity, employment, and competitiveness)."

The uniform fiduciary rule will most likely prove to be a significant regulatory action as E0 12866 defines the term.[7] With regard to one of the criteria, for example, it is easy to imagine that broker-dealers will, in aggregate, spend more than $100 million on training employees and monitoring their client communications.

Paul Noe contends that regulators routinely disregard the employment impact of proposed rules and cogently argues that, as a matter of transparency, analysts should consider the costs of job destruction, including the destruction of human capital when workers' skills become obsolete; wages lost during a period of unemployment; reduced earning potential; relocation expenses; and the cost of new job training. In addition, Noe holds, analysts should consider the "distributional impacts—equity or fairness concerns" of regulatory actions on particularly vulnerable subpopulations. The latter fall "outside the traditional cost-benefit framework but within the current regulatory impact analysis paradigm."[8] These are sound recommendations, and

---

[6] Executive Orders, Federal Register Vol. 58, No. 190. Accessed August 3, 2012. http://www.archives.gov/federal-register/executive-orders/pdf/12866.pdf
[7] EO 12866 defines "significant regulatory action" as one that is likely to result in a rule that may, among other criteria, "have an annual effect on the economy of $100 million or more or adversely affect in a material way the economy, a sector of the economy, productivity, competition, jobs, the environment, public health or safety, or State, local, or tribal governments or communities."

Noe's introduction of distributional impacts may advance the state of the art.

It is no criticism of Noe, however, to point out that, with its isolation and demarcation of significant regulatory actions, EO 12866 disregards the classic sorites problem. If I remove grains, one by one, from a heap of sand, at what point is it no longer a heap? Financial services organizations are facing a heap of regulations. The uniform fiduciary standard, on its own, may not cause a firm to put its employees on the street, but the cumulative effect of regulations introduced under the Dodd-Frank Act may very well make it uneconomical for investment organizations, especially smaller firms, to stay open.

Announcing its 2012 closing, Pacific West Financial Group stated, "In recent years, we have been faced with a steady increase in costs to operate a high quality broker-dealer, including the increased cost of regulation and supervision, as well as the need for investment in technology and platforms." (Pacific West has entered a recruitment agreement with Multi-Financial Securities Corp., a subsidiary of Cetera Financial Group, attenuating the impact on jobs.) It is reasonable to expect a spate of firm closings and business combinations this year.

Regulatory burdens are not the only decision factor; as Noe writes, "Forces such as international competition, changes in technology and preferences, product substitution, balance of trade, and the general state of the economy can have larger effects on employment than regulation." In addition, the current series of regulations is indubitably creating jobs in financial services, not only for regulators, compliance officers, securities lawyers, lobbyists, and consultants, but also for risk managers and technology professionals.

Unpacking multiple causes and effects will call for creative leadership and first-rate econometric talent. No matter how challenging and politically fraught it may be, we ought to understand the overall employment impact of new regulations, preferably before they become effective. The SEC has a terrific opportunity, in its study of the uniform fiduciary rule, to set a new standard for economic analysis in the regulatory domain.

---

[8] Paul Noe, "Analyzing the Destruction of Human Capital by Regulations," *Administrative Law Review*, vol. 63, special edition (2011), pp. 203-211. I am grateful to Joe Bartels for sending me this paper.

## Canada's New Credit Rating Regime
January 30, 2012

Last week the Canadian Securities Administrators (CSA) announced a new regulatory regime[1] for credit rating organizations. By adopting National Instrument 25-101, *Designated Rating Organizations*,[2] provincial securities commissions will impose requirements on credit rating organizations wishing to qualify their credit ratings for use in securities legislation.

We've learned a great deal in recent years about the regulatory and ethical issues surrounding credit rating organizations. Let's take a look at the Canadian approach.

At first glance it appears that Canada and the U.S. are moving in opposite directions. In accordance with a Section 939A of the Dodd-Frank Act, the SEC in July 2011 adopted amendments to disclosure rules and registration forms[3] promulgated under the Securities Act of 1933 and the Securities Exchange Act of 1934. The amendments, which are now in effect, *eliminate* long-standing references to credit ratings. Given Canada's disjointed regulatory structure, it may be the case that enabling firms to become designated rating organizations (DROs) facilitates bringing them under the purview of provincial securities commissions. In any event, the new Canadian national instrument addresses other important concerns, including the credit rating organizations' governance and internal controls, for which SEC rulemaking is, at this writing, still in progress.[4]

---

[1] Canadian Securities Administrators, "Canadian Securities Regulators Adopt Regulatory Regime for Credit Rating Organizations," January 27, 2012. Accessed August 3, 2012. http://www.securities-administrators.ca/aboutcsa.aspx?id=1016

[2] British Columbia Securities Commission, National Instrument 25-101, *Designated Rating Organizations*. Accessed August 3, 2012. http://www.bcsc.bc.ca/uploadedFiles/securitieslaw/policy2/25-101%20%5BNI%20Advance%20Notice%5D.pdf

[3] Securities and Exchange Commission, Final Rule, "Security Ratings." Accessed August 3, 2012. http://www.sec.gov/rules/final/2011/33-9245.pdf

[4] The SEC's "Proposed Rules for Nationally Recognized Statistical Rating Organizations" are set out in a 517-page document that was released for public comment in May 2011 (now closed). Accessed August 3, 2012. http://www.sec.gov/rules/proposed/2011/34-64514.pdf

Essential provisions of NI 25-101 may be paraphrased as follows:

- Credit rating organizations that apply to be DROs must complete and file a specified registration form.[5]

- A DRO must have a board with at least three directors, and at least half the board members, but not fewer than two, must be independent.[6]

- A DRO must establish, maintain, and comply with a code of conduct, incorporating specified provisions, which must be posted prominently on the DRO's website and filed with the regulatory authority.

- A DRO must not issue credit ratings unless it has a compliance officer who has direct access to the board of directors; who does not participate in the development of credit ratings, methodologies, or models, or in decisions affecting the compensation of employees other than his or her own direct reports; and whose compensation is not linked to the financial performance of the DRO.

- A DRO must keep such books, records, and documents as are necessary to account for its credit rating activities and the conduct of its business.

- Each DRO must meet certain ongoing filing requirements.

The most interesting, and substantive, part of the new regime is the code of conduct. Its required provisions are described under three major headings: Quality and Integrity of the Rating Process; Independence and Conflicts of Interest; and Responsibilities to the Investing Public and to Issuers.

---

[5] In brief, credit rating organizations which have offices in Canada must file Form 25-101F1; those which are incorporated in foreign jurisdictions and do not have a Canadian office must file Form 25-101F2, as must DRO affiliates. ("Affiliate" is a defined term.)

[6] The rule spells out conditions under which a member of the board of directors is *not* considered independent. Among other stipulations, a person who has served on the board of directors for more than five years in total is not independent for the purpose of NI 25-101. Note that under this instrument a DRO's code of conduct must contain additional provisions related to governance.

A few sample provisions may convey a sense of the whole. NI 25-101 does not regulate the content of a credit rating or the methodologies employed by a credit rating organization, but it requires a DRO to "include a provision in its code of conduct that it will use only rating methodologies that are rigorous, systematic, continuous and subject to validation based on experience, including back-testing." One of many provisions having to do with conflicts of interest states that credit ratings issued by a DRO will not be affected by existing or potential business relationships with any other person or company, "including, for greater certainty, the rated entity, its affiliates or related entities." When issuing or revising a rating, the DRO will provide an explanation of the key elements underlying the rating opinion.

The code of conduct is comprehensive, merits careful study, and cannot be adequately summarized here. On a first reading, however, in prescribing the elements of an acceptable code of conduct, the CSA brought to bear its customary thoroughness and good sense. Moreover, the new regime generally seems well conceived.

Nonetheless, NI 25-101 will serve its purpose only if it is stringently enforced. Some credit rating organizations have proven untrustworthy, and, given the business model, none can be relied upon to police itself. In order to ascertain whether DROs are consistently adhering to rigorous methodologies, Canada will have to call upon examiners who have subject matter expertise as well as critical thinking skills. I would contend, for instance, that chartered accountants—whom we know to be clear thinkers—are not fully qualified for the assignment unless they are also CFA charterholders with pertinent experience in fixed-income investing and credit analysis. And, should an examination uncover evidence that a DRO has not adhered to its code of conduct, then enforcement action must inexorably follow to set things right.

## The SEC's Measured Pace Toward Global Accounting Standards
March 29, 2012

In prepared testimony before the House Financial Services Committee this week,[1] chief accountant James L. Kroeker used stock language to explain the SEC's "conceptual support" for global accounting standards. "This position," he said, "advances the dual goals of improving financial reporting within the United States and reducing country-by-country disparity in financial reporting, which in turn facilitates cross-border capital formation and helps provide investors with the comparable and material information they need to make informed decisions about investment opportunities."

The same statement appeared verbatim in a work plan the SEC announced two years ago.[2] Nonetheless, there are clear signs of progress. In 2011 the Commission released a possible method of incorporating International Financial Reporting Standards (IFRS) into U.S. GAAP;[3] an extremely useful comparison of U.S. GAAP and IFRS;[4] and a review of accounting practices in a cross-industry sample of companies using IFRS.[5]

---

[1] James L. Kroeker, "Testimony Concerning Accounting and Auditing Oversight: Pending Proposals and Emerging Issues Confronting Regulators, Standard Setters, and the Economy," Subcommittee on Capital Markets and Government Sponsored Enterprises of the House Committee on Financial Services, March 28, 2012. Accessed August 3, 2012. http://financialservices.house.gov/UploadedFiles/HHRG-112-BA-WState-JKroeker-20120328.pdf

[2] Securities and Exchange Commission, "Commission Statement in Support of Convergence and Global Accounting Standards," 75 FR 9494, March 2, 2010. Accessed August 3, 2012. http://www.sec.gov/rules/other/2010/33-9109fr.pdf

[3] Securities and Exchange Commission Staff Paper, "Work Plan for the Consideration of Incorporating International Financial Reporting Standards into the Financial Reporting System for U.S. Issuers: Exploring a Possible Method of Incorporation," May 26, 2011. Accessed August 3, 2012. http://www.sec.gov/spotlight/globalaccountingstandards/ifrs-work-plan-paper-052611.pdf

[4] Securities and Exchange Commission Staff Paper, "Work Plan for the Consideration of Incorporating International Financial Reporting Standards into the Financial Reporting System for U.S. Issuers: A Comparison of U.S. GAAP and IFRS," November 16, 2011. Accessed August 3, 2012. http://www.sec.gov/spotlight/globalaccountingstandards/ifrs-work-plan-paper-111611-gaap.pdf

[5] Securities and Exchange Commission Staff Paper, "Work Plan for the

A final staff report to the Commission is expected within the next few months.[6]

The Financial Accounting Standards Board (FASB), which operates under the supervision of the Financial Accounting Foundation (FAF), and the International Accounting Standards Board (IASB) have also moved ahead in their continuing effort to reduce the differences between U.S. GAAP and IFRS. In 2011, among other accomplishments, the FASB and the IASB harmonized the accounting treatment for fair value measurement and comprehensive income, and they issued exposure drafts on revenue recognition. The Boards' ongoing work in two areas—financial instruments and leases—will have a tremendous impact on issuers and the financial services industry.

For Canadians, who converted to IFRS for reporting periods beginning 1 January 2011, the U.S. approach may seem ponderous to the point of torpor. Whether to align with international accounting standards is a fairly easy question (and the answer is pretty much a foregone conclusion); when and, above all, how to come into alignment are the tough ones. Under the proposed approach, the SEC will retain sovereign authority over U.S. financial reporting requirements; the FASB will remain the national standard-setter;[7] and, to avoid disturbing countless legal agreements, "U.S. GAAP" will stay in place as the statutory basis for U.S. issuers' financial reporting. The FASB will incorporate IFRS into U.S. GAAP over an extended transition period (five to seven years).

In its thoughtful comments on the SEC's possible method of incorporation,[8] the FAF articulated potential evaluation criteria for the

---

Consideration of Incorporating International Financial Reporting Standards into the Financial Reporting System for U.S. Issuers: An Analysis of IFRS in Practice," November 16, 2011. Accessed August 3, 2012.
http://www.sec.gov/spotlight/globalaccountingstandards/ifrs-work-plan-paper-111611-practice.pdf
[6] Speaking in London, the SEC's Meredith Cross clarified that a few months means "more than a couple and less than many." "Keynote Address at PLI - Eleventh Annual Institute on Securities Regulation in Europe," March 8, 2012. Accessed August 3, 2012.
http://www.sec.gov/news/speech/2012/spch030812mc.htm
[7] The SEC officially recognizes FASB standards as authoritative.
[8] Financial Accounting Foundation, Letter to Elizabeth M. Murphy, November 15, 2011. Accessed August 3, 2012.
http://www.accountingfoundation.org/cs/BlobServer?blobcol=urldata&blobtable=MungoBlobs&blobkey=id&blobwhere=1175823317850&blobheader=appli

FASB's decisions to incorporate specific international standards into U.S. GAAP. In paraphrase, the FAF holds that standards must:

- improve or, at minimum, maintain the quality of financial reporting;
- support the primary purpose of providing decision-useful information to investors;
- reflect independence and objectivity in standard-setting;
- result from robust, thorough, transparent, and participatory due diligence;
- offer benefits greater than costs; and
- provide sufficient clarity and adequate guidance to be consistently and uniformly applied.

Provided the SEC reduces uncertainty by committing to a final plan in the upcoming months, it makes sense to afford registrants and market participants a long transition period. Financial services organizations, in particular, are contending with historic regulatory change across jurisdictions, business lines, products, and instruments. There is no compelling reason to compound the demands on people, processes, and systems by hustling companies into a new accounting framework. Five to seven years seems about right.[9]

---

cation%2Fpdf

[9] [Added in 2018: IFRS 9, *Financial Instruments,* is now in effect for annual periods beginning on or after January 1, 2018. See Philip Lawton and Jonathan Leonardelli's articles on the Financial Risk Group blog at https://www.frgrisk.com/blog/.]

## Leveraged Lending
April 3, 2012

The Federal Reserve, the Office of the Comptroller of the Currency (OCC), and the Federal Deposit Insurance Corporation (FDIC) have jointly released proposed guidance on leveraged lending.[1] (In one definition, "leveraged lending" is the banking industry's infelicitous term for lending to borrowers who have, or will have, debt ratios that exceed the norm in their industry. In other words, the prospective obligor, not the lending, is leveraged.) The proposed guidance is intended to replace interagency guidance issued in 2001.[2]

The regulatory agencies warn that the "lack of robust risk management processes and controls in institutions with significant leveraged finance activities could contribute to a finding that the institution is engaged in an unsafe and unsound banking practice." In view of the subprime crisis, they also observe that poorly underwritten transactions can contribute to systemic risk, and they state that the proposed guidance on leveraged lending builds upon the proposed guidance on stress testing that was released for public comment in January.[3] In addition, the agencies remark, "An institution's apparent failure to meet its legal or fiduciary responsibilities in underwriting and distributing transactions can damage its reputation and impair its ability to compete."

The regulators call upon banks to shape leveraged financing transactions so as to reflect a sound business premise, an appropriate capital structure, and reasonable cash flow and balance sheet leverage. They further enjoin banks to spell out their definition of leveraged finance;

[1] Department of the Treasury, Federal Reserve, and Federal Deposit Insurance Corporation, "Proposed Guidance on Leveraged Lending," March 26, 2012. Accessed August 3, 2012.
http://www.federalreserve.gov/boarddocs/press/foiadocs/2012/20120423/foia20120423.pdf
[2] *Leveraged Financing: Sound Risk Management Practices* was issued by the Office of the Comptroller of the Currency (OCC), the Board of Governors of the Federal Reserve System, the Federal Deposit Insurance Corporation (FDIC), and the Office of Thrift Supervision on April 9, 2001. The OCC published it as Bulletin 2001-18. Accessed August 3, 2012. http://www.occ.gov/news-issuances/bulletins/2001/bulletin-2001-18a.pdf
[3] U.S. Department of the Treasury, Notice of Proposed Rulemaking, "Annual Stress Test," 77 FR 3408, January 24, 2012. Accessed August 3, 2012. http://www.gpo.gov/fdsys/pkg/FR-2012-01-24/pdf/2012-1274.pdf

erect a credit limit and concentration framework that is consistent with their risk appetite; define clear underwriting standards setting out acceptable levels of leverage and stating management's amortization expectations; develop systems to identify, aggregate, and monitor exposures; and establish strong pipeline policies and procedures.

The proposed guidance explicitly covers a long list of topics. Rather than attempting to summarize the entire document within the confines of this medium, I will focus on an area that strikes me as especially interesting and important (qualities I tend to conflate). Specifically, I will describe and comment on the agencies' minimum regulatory expectations related to internal reporting and analytics.

The regulators state that comprehensive reports and summaries should be provided to management and the board of directors, respectively, at least every quarter. The reports will present characteristics of and trends in the institution's exposures to higher-risk credits, including leveraged loans. Policies should specify the data to be captured for accurate and timely reporting. ("Timely" means, one supposes, not too long after quarter-end.) The reporting "may include" elements described, or at any rate listed, in 15 bullet points. Among the more challenging ones are these:

- Risk rating distribution and migration analysis. The regulators refer to previously issued guidance on internal credit rating systems and processes,[4] limiting themselves here to a few remarks on using realistic repayment assumptions and considering enterprise value as a secondary or contingent source of repayment only if that value is well supported. Clearly, the distribution of credit exposures across rating categories gives

---

[4] See the Federal Reserve's FRB SR 98-25, "Sound Credit Risk Management and the Use of Internal Credit Risk Ratings at Large Banking Organizations" (September 1998) at http://www.federalreserve.gov/boarddocs/SRLETTERS/1998/sr9825.htm; OCC Handbooks "Rating Credit Risk" (April 2001) at http://www.occ.gov/publications/publications-by-type/comptrollers-handbook/rcr.pdf and "Leveraged Lending" (February 2008) at http://www.occ.gov/publications/publications-by-type/comptrollers-handbook/_pdf/leveragedlending.pdf; and "Loan Appraisal and Classification" in the FDIC Risk Management Manual of Examination Policies, Section 3.2, Loans (last updated in April 2005), at http://www.fdic.gov/regulations/safety/manual/section3-2.html#loanAppraisal. Sites accessed August 3, 2012.

management and the board useful information about the bank's current position, and changes in the distribution might signal evolving conditions that merit further investigation.

- Metrics derived from probabilities of default and loss given default. Note, however, that PD and LGD values can be difficult to estimate with confidence on the basis of internal data that may be too sparse to generate reliable rating transition matrices and historical recovery rates.

- Borrower/counterparty exposures booked in other business units. The regulators indicate that this reporting, which requires thoroughgoing data aggregation, should consider indirect exposures such as default and total return swaps, collateral exposure through repo transactions, and positions held through structured investment vehicles owned or sponsored by the originating institution and its subsidiaries or affiliates.

On many points, the agencies merely indicate desiderata, and the proposed guidance is sketchy at best. As a practical matter, a financial institution cannot meet the banking regulators' expectations for analyzing and reporting leveraged loan exposures without having developed and implemented a robust risk management framework and built the technological infrastructure to support it. (Regulation is a stimulus for compliance and operational consulting services as well as technology spending.) Nonetheless, the proposed guidance on leveraged lending effectively provides an examiner's checklist that banks can use to evaluate their own internal credit rating systems, processes, and controls. The resulting gap analysis might very well serve as the basis for near-term planning and priority-setting.

# OTC Derivatives and the Real Economy
April 16, 2012

For working purposes, let us broadly differentiate three fairly distinct economic domains and their respective uses of derivative securities.

First, participants in the real economy—roughly, the domain in which non-financial products and services are produced and exchanged—use derivatives to reduce commercial risks due to fluctuations in commodity prices, interest rates, and foreign exchange rates. A cereal company, for example, might use wheat, corn, and sugar futures to attenuate the adverse impact of rising agricultural prices; a real estate developer might enter interest rate futures contracts when starting a major construction project; and a distributor of machine tools might use forex futures to manage currency risk. The list could be extended, but the idea is that non-financial companies make use of derivative securities to mitigate commercial risks that arise in the course of their business but are incidental to their profit-seeking operations. Regulators refer to these market participants as "end-users."

Second, traditional investment managers use derivatives to modify portfolio characteristics. For instance, a firm might wish to equitize cash or reallocate assets quickly without incurring high transaction costs; adjust the duration of a fixed-income portfolio; or manage country and currency risk separately. Using derivative securities to change the risk profile of financial assets could be said to take place in the semi-real economy. An earlier generation might have called it the paper economy, but it's less palpable now.

Third, hedge funds and exchange-traded funds use derivatives to create long and short positions in capital markets, economic sectors, industries, national economies, commodities, interest rates, foreign currencies, the creditworthiness of other companies, and the weather. The speculative use of derivative securities to manage notional exposures, generally on the basis of quantitative methods and models, occurs in what might be called the abstract, symbolic, or unreal economy, an economy of mathematical variables. Trading opportunities arise when $p$ is temporarily out of sync with $q$, or the spread between $r$ and $s$ exceeds the historical average, or a change in the level of $x$ signals a likely adjustment in the level of $y$.

I am reserving "the surreal economy" for future use, possibly in the context of securities regulations.

Of course, the boundaries between the real, semi-real, and unreal economies are vague and, to use a fashionable word, porous. Whether or not they add value in the way skilled labor does, traditional investment managers are compensated in cash that they spend on food and drink, clothing, housing, transportation, luxuries, and, occasionally, leisure. The competitive games alternative asset managers play can have significant effects on traditional managers' investment results as well as producer and consumer prices and the availability of credit for business and household formation. Nonetheless, it seems useful to distinguish among these economies, or sub-economies, however inexactly delineated. Ludwig Wittgenstein wrote, "Frege compares a concept to an area and says that an area with vague boundaries cannot be called an area at all. This presumably means that we cannot do anything with it.—But is it senseless to say: 'Stand roughly there'?"[1]

All this comes to mind because the Canadian Securities Administrators has released a consultation paper, CP 91-405, "Derivatives: End-User Exemption,"[2] the fourth in a series of eight papers building upon the regulatory framework for over-the-counter derivatives that was proposed in November 2010.[3] The consultation paper presents the CSA Derivatives Committee's case for exempting end-users who do not pose systemic risks from proposed regulatory requirements pertaining to registration, trading, clearing, margin, capital, and collateral. Under the CSA proposal, they will be required to notify the regulator of their intention to rely upon the exemption, and, on an ongoing basis, they will have to report transactions to a trade repository.

---

[1] Ludwig Wittgenstein, *Philosophical Investigations*, 2nd ed., trans. G.E.M. Anscombe (New York: Macmillan, 1958), I, 71.
[2] Canadian Securities Administrators, CSA Consultation Paper 91-405, "Derivatives: End-User Exemption," April 13, 2012. Accessed August 3, 2012. http://www.osc.gov.on.ca/documents/en/Securities-Category9/csa_20120413_91-405_end-user-exemption.pdf
[3] Canadian Securities Administrators, CSA Consultation Paper 91-401, "Over-the-Counter Derivatives Regulation in Canada," November 2, 2010. Accessed August 3, 2012. http://www.bcsc.bc.ca/uploadedFiles/securitieslaw/policy9/94-101_Consultation_Paper.pdf

Regulators in other jurisdictions have also addressed the applicability of OTC derivatives regulations to end-users. In the U.S., Section 763(a) of the Dodd-Frank Act states that the otherwise mandatory clearing of security-based swaps is optional if one of the counterparties meets three conditions: it is not a financial entity; it is using security-based swaps to hedge or mitigate commercial risk; and it informs the Securities and Exchange Commission how it generally meets the financial obligations associated with its use of non-cleared security-based swaps. The SEC[4] and the Commodity Futures Trading Commission (CFTC)[5] have formulated extensive rules pertaining, in particular, to the third condition. Last month the U.S. Congress passed and sent to the Senate a bill, H.R. 2682, intended to clarify that end-users of derivatives are not subject to margin and capital requirements.[6]

Under the CSA's recommended eligibility criteria, an end-user:

- trades OTC derivatives for its own account, and is neither a registrant nor an affiliate of a registrant;
- is not a financial institution; and
- conducts trading in OTC derivatives contracts for the purpose of hedging,[7] that is, mitigating a risk related to the operation of the business.

---

[4] Securities and Exchange Commission, Proposed Rule, "End-User Exemption to Mandatory Clearing of Securities-Based Swaps," December 15, 2010. Accessed August 4, 2012. http://www.sec.gov/rules/proposed/2010/34-63556.pdf

[5] Commodity Futures Trading Commission, Proposed Rule, "End-User Exception to Mandatory Clearing of Swaps," 75 FR 80747, December 23, 2010. Accessed August 4, 2012. http://www.cftc.gov/ucm/groups/public/@lrfederalregister/documents/file/2010-31578a.pdf

[6] U.S. House of Representatives, H.R. 2682, July 28, 2011. Accessed August 4, 2012. http://financialservices.house.gov/UploadedFiles/hr2682ai.pdf

[7] The CSA Derivatives Committee recommends adopting the definition formulated by the Committee on Payment and Settlement Systems (CPSS) and the International Organization of Securities Commissions (IOSCO): "the term 'hedge' or 'hedging' generally refers to the taking of a position in a commodity derivative contract opposite to a position held in the physical market to minimize the risk of financial and/or economic loss from an adverse price change, or otherwise for risk management purposes." Technical Committee of IOSCO, Report FR07/11, *Principles for the Regulation and Supervision of Commodity Derivatives Markets: Final Report* (15 September 2011). Accessed August 4, 2012. http://www.iosco.org/library/pubdocs/pdf/IOSCOPD358.pdf

Affiliated legal entities trading with one another will be exempt if they individually satisfy the eligibility criteria. However, "large derivatives participants," summarily defined here as end-users whose default would represent a systemic risk due to the size or significance of their trading relative to the overall market, will not be eligible for the exemption and will have to meet registration requirements. A future consultation paper on registration will contain the specifics for large derivatives participants.

# The Suitability of Complex Products
May 1, 2012

The Financial Industry Regulatory Authority (FINRA)[1] published in January 2012 a notice on complex products which is acquiring momentum as the July 9 effective date for Rule 2111[2]—the new suitability rule—approaches. Regulatory Notice 12-03, "Complex Products," offers guidance on the higher level of internal supervision expected of firms whose offerings include hard-to-understand investments.[3] The present article does not purport to summarize Regulatory Notice 12-03. I will focus here on the special considerations that complex products raise in relation to the reasonable-basis and customer-specific components of Rule 2111, with particular attention to the training implications.

FINRA states that Regulatory Notice 12-03 neither defines a complex product nor provides an exhaustive list of complicating features. The notice does contain the elements of a working definition: "Any product with multiple features that affect its investment returns differently under various scenarios is potentially complex. This is particularly true if it would be unreasonable to expect an average retail investor to discern the existence of these features and to understand the basic manner in which these features interact to produce an investment return." Among the examples FINRA gives are asset-backed securities, unlisted REITS, products that contain embedded derivatives, and products tied to the performance of unfamiliar markets such as VIX futures.

These statements imply that firms are well advised to take a fairly broad, inclusive view of the products to be considered complex. Dividend-paying stocks and coupon-bearing bonds are unquestionably simple instruments, but each arguably has "multiple features that affect its investment returns differently under various scenarios." At the risk of sounding curmudgeonly, I would also say it is most prudent to

[1] FINRA is the U.S. securities industry's self-regulatory organization that oversees brokerage firms and registered representatives serving retail investors.
[2] 2 Rule 2111, FINRA Manual. Accessed August 4, 2012.
http://finra.complinet.com/en/display/display_main.html?rbid=2403&element_id=9859
[3] FINRA, Regulatory Notice 12-03, "Complex Products: Heightened Supervision of Complex Products," January 2012. Accessed August 4, 2012.
http://www.finra.org/web/groups/industry/@ip/@reg/@notice/documents/notices/p125397.pdf

underestimate the average retail investor's grasp of strategies and securities.[4] With that understanding, I would suggest that firms and registered representatives consider a product complex if it would be difficult to explain in such a way that the average customer could realistically evaluate its risk and return characteristics. In other words, rather than asking how hard it is to understand, consider how hard it is to explain to a typical customer.

Under the reasonable-basis component of Rule 2111, registered representatives must have "a reasonable basis to believe, based on reasonable diligence, that the recommendation is suitable for at least some investors." This is a peculiar approach—one hopes no brokerage firm would offer a product that is inappropriate for all investors—but the point is that registered representatives must be qualified to recommend an investment strategy or security by their comprehension of its potential risks and rewards. "The lack of such an understanding when recommending a security or strategy violates the suitability rule."[5]

Rule 2111 effectively obligates financial advisors who recommend complex products to have reached a fairly advanced level of competence. Structured products are one of the examples given in Notice 12-03. Registered representatives should understand the payoff structure— ideally, FINRA states, they should be competent to develop a payoff diagram—as well as the likelihood of a call, any limitations on principal protection, and the characteristics of the reference asset, including its historical performance, volatility, and correlation with other asset classes. If a product contains multiple reference assets, registered representatives should understand their interrelationships.

Further, under the customer-specific component of Rule 2111, registered representatives must "have a reasonable basis to believe that the recommendation is suitable for a particular customer based on that customer's investment profile." Accordingly, they must be qualified by education or training to determine the suitability of a recommendation on the basis of the relationship between the risk/reward profiles of specific strategies and securities, on one hand, and pertinent aspects of customers' investment profiles, on the other. The customers' investment

---

[4] H.L. Mencken is said to have said, "No one in this world, so far as I know— and I have searched the record for years, and employed agents to help me—has ever lost money by underestimating the intelligence of the great masses of the plain people." I do not know the original source of this quotation.
[5] Rule 2111, *op. cit.*, Supplementary Material, .05(a).

experience (and, by implication, knowledge) is a key factor in determining whether a complex product is suitable. In addition, registered representatives are obligated to evaluate individual customers' risk tolerances. This is not a rote exercise because the customers' stated *willingness* to accept risks may, upon examination, prove inconsistent with their *ability* to sustain losses.

Nor can firms merely implement administrative procedures to spare registered representatives from having to demonstrate competence, conduct due diligence, and exercise professional judgment. FINRA encourages firms to adopt the approach that is mandatory for options trading accounts.[6] The regulator observes, however, that such expedients as pre-qualification agreements with customers do not relieve the firm or its registered representatives of the obligation to conduct thorough customer-specific suitability analyses before making investment recommendations.[7]

The suitability rule and FINRA's concerns about complex products may jointly have a significant impact on the design and delivery of brokerage firms' internal training programs (not to mention their record-keeping policies). There may also come about meaningful changes in the larger firms' culture, hiring, social and organizational structure, compliance risk management platform, products and services, and sales practices. Interesting times.

---

[6] Rule 2360(b)(19)(B) states, "No member or person associated with a member shall recommend to a customer an opening transaction in any option contract unless the person making the recommendation has a reasonable basis for believing, at the time of making the recommendation, that the customer has such knowledge and experience in financial matters that he may reasonably be expected to be capable of evaluating the risks of the recommended transaction, and is financially able to bear the risks of the recommended position in the option contract." FINRA Manual. Accessed August 4, 2012. http://finra.complinet.com/en/display/display.html?rbid=2403&record_id=14 208&element_id=6306&highlight=2360#r14208

[7] Speaking at FINRA's 2011 annual conference, Chairman and CEO Richard G. Ketchum said, "Brokers cannot rely on firm approval alone to satisfy their suitability obligations. This is particularly important with the proliferation of increasingly complex financial products, and at a time when certain investors are tempted to chase yield in today's low-interest-rate environment." Accessed August 4, 2012.
http://www.finra.org/Newsroom/Speeches/Ketchum/P123727

## CSA Favors Money-Weighted Returns
June 15, 2012

Yesterday the Canadian Securities Administrators (CSA) issued a notice and second request for comments[1] on regulatory proposals relating to cost disclosure, performance reporting, and client statements. The proposed requirements, which will when finalized be implemented through amendments to National Instrument 31-103 and its companion policy, are intended to provide investors with answers to two basic questions: What did you pay? And how did your investments perform?

The annual investment cost disclosures contemplated in the CSA proposal include the dollar amounts of trailing commissions and of commissions paid on fixed-income transactions. The June 14, 2012 notice also sets forth a market valuation methodology and requirements for expanded client statements. These provisions are highly significant for their potential impact on client relationships. In the present piece, however, I will focus on the CSA's performance-related proposals: the basis for reporting changes in account value, the prescribed rate-of-return calculation methodology, and the recommended presentation of benchmark information.

First, then, the CSA calls for annual client reports to include the account's change in value for the 12-month and since-inception periods.[2] For the 12-month period, the change in value equals $A - B - C + D$, where A is the ending market value of all securities and cash in the account; B is the beginning market value; C is the market value of all deposits and transfers of cash and securities into the account during the period; and D is the market value of all withdrawals and transfers out of

---

[1] Canadian Securities Administrators, "Cost Disclosure, Performance Reporting and Client Statements," Notice and Request for Comment on Proposed Amendments to National Instrument 31-103,*Registration requirements, exemptions and ongoing registrant obligations* and to Companion Policy 31-103CP, *Registration Requirements, Exemptions and Ongoing Registrant Obligations,* June 14, 2012 (2nd Publication). Accessed August 4, 2012.
http://www.bcsc.bc.ca/uploadedFiles/securitieslaw/policyBCN/CSA_Notice_and_Request_for_Comment_NI_31-103.pdf
[2] *Op. cit.*, Appendix C, Sections 14.17(1)g–i. Accessed August 4, 2012.
http://www.bcsc.bc.ca/uploadedFiles/securitieslaw/policyBCN/Blackline_of_Proposed_Amendments_to_National_Instrument_31-103_%28Appendix_C%29.pdf

the account. Similarly, the cumulative change in value since the inception of the account equals $A - E + F$, where E and F are, respectively, the market values of all deposits (withdrawals) and transfers into (out of) the account since opening. If the required since-inception market value information is unavailable, firms are permitted to report the change in value from the implementation date of the new requirements.

The provisionally revised companion policy[3] states, "Generally, the change in value is a reflection of the market performance of the account and includes components such as income (dividends, interest) and distributions, including reinvested income or distributions, realized and unrealized capital gains or losses in the account, and *the effect of operating charges and transaction charges if these are deducted directly from the account.*" (Emphasis added.) In other words, if management fees and other charges[4] are drawn from the investment account, rather than being paid from another account, then the change in value is to be reported after operating and transaction charges. This requirement may have been intended to facilitate reconciliations, but it has consequences for client reporting. We may see Canadian firms start to invoice clients instead of deducting management fees from their accounts.

Secondly, under the CSA proposal, the annual investment performance report must include "the amount of the annualized total percentage return, expressed as a percentage, for the client's account calculated *net of charges*, using a *dollar weighted method.*"[5] (Emphasis added.) Registered firms are permitted to report time-weighted returns in addition to those

---

[3] *Op. cit.*, Appendix D, Proposed Amendments to Companion Policy 31-103 CP, *Registration Requirements, Exemptions and Ongoing Registrant Obligations.* Accessed August 4, 2012.
http://www.bcsc.bc.ca/uploadedFiles/securitieslaw/policyBCN/Proposed_Am endments_to_Companion_Policy_31-103_%28Appendix_D%29.pdf
[4] The revised companion policy gives examples of operating and transaction charges. The former include but are not limited to "service charges, administration fees, safekeeping fees, management fees, transfer fees, account closing fees, annual registered plan fees and any other charges associated with maintaining and using an account that are paid to the registrant." The latter include such items as "commissions, transaction fees, switch or change fees, performance fees, short-term trading fees, sales charges or redemption fees, and foreign exchange spreads that are paid to the registrant." The amended companion policy further clarifies, "Operating and transaction charges include only charges paid to the registered firm. Third-party charges, such as custodian fees that are not paid to the registered firm, are not included in operating charges or transaction charges."
[5] *Op. cit.*, paragraph 14.17(1)j.

calculated on a dollar-weighted basis. At minimum, rates of return must be reported for the previous year, three years, five years, ten years, and since account opening (or, again, if the requisite market values are unavailable, since the implementation date of the amended requirements).[6] In the notice and request for comment, the CSA explain, "We have decided to mandate the dollar-weighted method because it most accurately reflects the actual return of the client's investments." However, they explicitly identify the "benefits and constraints" of this proposal as an issue for comment.

Finally, benchmarks are optional. The amended companion policy confirms, "There is no requirement to provide benchmarks to clients in any of the reports required under NI 31-103." The CSA encourage firms to use relevant benchmarks and also to report an historical five-year GIC rate, described as "a benchmark that represents a very low-risk investment alternative." (That description may tempt the fates.) However, among other specifications, the CSA expect registrants to use benchmarks that are "based on widely recognized and available indices that are credible and not manufactured by the registrant or any of its affiliates using proprietary data." This expectation precludes the use of custom security-based benchmarks. Overall, on the topic of benchmarks, the CSA's conclusions to date are sharply disappointing. In my opinion, valid benchmark returns should be mandatory and custom benchmarks should be permitted with appropriate disclosure.

---

[6] *Ibid.*, paragraph 14.17(2)(a)–(e).

## Basel's Proposal for Monitoring Intraday Liquidity
July 11, 2012

The Basel Committee on Banking Supervision (BCBS) recently released for public comment a consultative document, "Monitoring Indicators for Intraday Liquidity Management,"[1] which describes and explains the types of information that would purportedly enable banking supervisors to watch over banks' ability to meet payment and settlement obligations on a timely basis. The document states that "the proposed indicators are for monitoring purposes only and do not represent the introduction of new standards around intraday liquidity management." Given the regulators' entirely reasonable concern with systemic risk, however, it is realistic to anticipate that, in due time, data gathering and analysis will lead to standard-setting. In addition, if and when adopted, the proposed reporting requirements will entail substantial effort on the banks' part. Accordingly, the consultative document merits the attention of compliance officers, treasury staff, risk managers, and technologists.

The BCBS developed the proposed set of indicators in conference with the Committee on Payment and Settlement Systems (CPSS) and adopts the latter organization's glossary definition of intraday liquidity: "Funds which can be accessed during the business day, usually to enable financial institutions to make payments in real time." The business day is the period in which it is possible for the bank to receive and make payments through the transfer system(s)[2] in which it participates.

As a necessary step in defining the indicators to be monitored, the consultative document lists the sources of and needs for intraday liquidity. The bank's own sources include its reserve balances and collateral pledged with the central bank; unencumbered liquid assets; credit lines that can be drawn down during the business day; and readily available balances with other banks. Sources other than the bank's own include payments received from other payment system participants and from ancillary systems. (Intraday margin reimbursements from clearing

---

[1] Basel Committee on Banking Supervision, "Consultative Document: Monitoring Indicators for Intraday Liquidity Management," July 2012. Accessed August 5, 2012. http://www.bis.org/publ/bcbs225.pdf

[2] "Transfer systems" generically refers to payment and settlement utilities, including clearing and settlement systems (CLS) for securities and derivatives. Central counterparties are counted as CLS.

and settlement systems, including central counterparties, are an example of payments received from ancillary systems.) In addition to payments due other system participants and ancillary systems, the needs for intraday liquidity include contingent payments, for instance, to cover failed trades or customers' withdrawals, and payments related to providing correspondent banking services.

The BCBS proposes eight indicators. (Several have multiple elements.) Here are a few words about each of them:

1. *Daily maximum liquidity requirement.* This indicator is defined as the largest negative net cumulative difference between payments received and payments made during the day.

2. *Available intraday liquidity.* This item includes the amount available at the start of each business day and the lowest amount available during the day.

3. *Total payments.* The total daily gross payments made and received.

4. *Time-specific and other critical obligations.* The volume and value of time-specific and other critical obligations, and the total number and value of time-critical obligations missed during the reporting period.

5. *Value of payments made on behalf of financial institution customers.* This measure, which applies only to correspondent banks, includes the gross value of customer payments made on behalf of financial institutions and the value of payments (including internalized book-entry payments) settled on behalf of each of the bank's five largest financial institution customers.

6. *Intraday credit lines extended to financial institution customers.* Also applicable only to correspondent banks, this indicator includes the total sum of intraday credit lines extended to all financial institution customers; the value of secured, unsecured, committed, and uncommitted credit lines extended to each of the bank's five largest financial institution customers; and those five customers' maximum daily usage of each type of credit line.

7. *Timing of intraday payments.* This indicator, which applies only to direct transfer system participants (*i.e.,* those which do not use

correspondent banks), is defined as the value-weighted average time of day their outgoing payments settle.

8. *Intraday throughput.* This indicator is the proportion, by value, of the bank's outgoing payments that settle by specific times during the day (nine o'clock, ten o'clock, etc.).

The consultative document also describes four proposed stress-testing scenarios: the bank itself is perceived to be under stress; a major counterparty is stressed; a correspondent bank's customer bank suffers a stress event; and a market-wide credit or liquidity stress event occurs. Direct and indirect payment and settlement system participants would be required to report the likely impact of these scenarios on various indicators described above.

In general, the indicators seem to have been well chosen. The last two, for example—those having to do with the pace of outbound payments—may afford supervisors valuable information about the banks' behavior. A bank whose payments shift later in the day may be placing greater reliance on receipts from other system participants as a cost-free funding source. Such a trend may be symptomatic of the bank's declining creditworthiness. In addition, given the extent to which financial institutions are entangled with one another, delayed payments might lead to inadequate system-wide liquidity and increase the risk of an operational crunch at the close of business.

The BCBS envisions monthly reporting of the indicators and, in many cases, their values at the 95th percentile. (A sample reporting form accompanies the consultative document.) To meet the proposed reporting requirements, banks will have to capture and record all the indicator measures at least daily and many of them throughout the day. Clearly, the data collection will have to be automated; it is to be hoped that the information thus provided will not only enable the bank to file monthly regulatory reports but also assist the treasurer in centrally managing the bank's intraday positions. If so, the very fact that there are reporting requirements might contribute to reducing systemic risk. However, my optimism varies with my intraday blood sugar level.

## Friendly Fire
August 16, 2012

The Battle of Antietam, one of the worst in the American civil war, took place 150 years ago next month. Both sides suffered terrible losses; neither achieved a decisive victory. Including those killed, wounded, and missing in action, total casualties at day's end may have been undercounted at approximately 23,000. Twice in the chaos and carnage of the 12-hour battle inexperienced Union troops opened fire on their own men. Engaged in the northeastern portion of the battlefield the morning of September 17, 1862, soldiers in the Twelfth Corps inadvertently shot their comrades in the back; later, in the West Woods, troops in the 59th New York fired through the 15th Massachusetts. Ironically, Gen. Joseph Mansfield, who was in command of the Twelfth Corps, was mortally wounded when he rode to the front and tried to stop another regiment from firing on what he mistakenly believed to be Union forces. After Antietam, Gen. Robert E. Lee called a halt to the Maryland campaign and led the exhausted Confederate army back to Virginia.[1]

This month Knight Capital Group, Inc. primarily inflicted losses on itself when a high-speed trading algorithm spun out of control. The event was contained; although it gravely threatened Knight's viability, it did not massively affect the capital markets or the financial system as it conceivably might have done. Instructively, it appears to have been an exemplar of operational risk. The misfiring reportedly occurred because the firm did not uniformly upgrade software across all its trading platforms. When the new program went live the morning of August 1st, surviving code from an older system launched a spate of spurious buy and sell orders.[2] The offending software was removed from the company's systems, and within a week of the event Knight announced that a $400 million equity infusion from other firms would allow it to resume normal operations.[3]

---

[1] Ted Alexander, *The Battle of Antietam: The Bloodiest Day* (The History Press, 2011), Kindle version.

[2] Scott Patterson, Jenny Strasburg, and Jacob Bunge, "Knight Upgrade Triggered Old Trading System, Big Losses," *Wall Street Journal*, August 14, 2012.

[3] Knight Capital Group, Inc., Press Release, "Knight Capital Group Completes $400 Million Equity Financing Agreement," August 6, 2012. Accessed August 16, 2012.

Managing investment systems is inherently challenging, and successfully installing an upgrade or a new program in a complex organization is especially fraught. Moreover, without knowing the details one cannot say whether Knight's misadventure resulted from a flawed project plan or a lapse in the execution of a well defined and properly documented process. I assume the company has conducted an internal investigation, determined the failure point(s), and initiated remedial action. But would tighter regulations on algorithmic trading have mitigated the risk?

Regulatory authorities in Hong Kong and Australia have come forward with proposals, and in the U.K. the Financial Services Authority is said to have stiffer rules under consideration.[4] The Canadian Securities Authority (CSA) published a proposal on electronic trading for comment last year and recently issued the final requirements, which will become effective on March 1, 2013.[5] Canada's NI 23-103, *Electronic Trading*, sets out provisions applying to market participants generally; the use of automated order systems in particular; and marketplaces.[6] I will limit myself to a few remarks about the requirements surrounding the use of an automated order system, defined as "a system used to automatically generate or electronically transmit orders on a pre-determined basis." This definition includes smart order routers and trading algorithms.

The CSA states, "…the Instrument requires marketplace participants to take all reasonable steps to ensure that the use of these automated order systems, by itself or any client, does not interfere with fair and orderly markets." Firms are specifically directed to have "a general understanding" of their own and their clients' automated order systems. In addition, they must ensure that each automated order system is tested

---

http://www.knight.com/investorRelations/pressReleases.asp?compid=105070&releaseID=1722658

[4] Geoffrey Rogow, "Foreign Regulators Take Lead on High-Frequency Trading," *MarketBeat*, August 15, 2012. Accessed August 16, 2012. http://blogs.wsj.com/marketbeat/2012/08/15/foreign-regulators-take-lead-on-high-frequency-trading/

[5] Canadian Securities Administrators, Notice of National Instrument 23-103 *Electronic Trading*, June 28, 2012. Accessed August 16, 2012. http://www.bcsc.bc.ca/uploadedFiles/securitieslaw/policyBCN/CSA%20Notice%282%29.pdf

[6] NI 23-103 does not include provisions related to dealers granting clients direct electronic access, a topic area which figured in the 2011 proposal. The CSA and the Investment Industry Regulatory Authority of Canada (IIROC) have a revised proposal in the works.

before its first use and at least annually once it has been deployed. "We expect these provisions will help to support the fair and orderly functioning of our markets upon the deployment of a smart order router, trading algorithm or any other aspect of an automated order system." Thus NI 23-103 makes sound managerial practice a regulatory obligation.

Under a further provision, firms must be able to disable the system and "to immediately prevent orders generated from such a system from reaching a marketplace." The CSA sees this as an essential risk mitigant, but engineering this control logically entails adding a step to the process. How else might market participants have a chance to thwart a machine in blinding motion? Low latency traders in Canada will have to anticipate speed bumps.

The SEC has scheduled a market technology roundtable for September 14th.[7] My position? Rules intelligently written by regulators who understand investment operations might reduce risk if the penalties for non-compliance are truly dreadful. But, in the interest of public safety, I'd sooner see assault rifles, extended magazines, and high-speed trading banned.

---

[7] Securities and Exchange Commission, Press Release, "SEC to Host Market Technology Roundtable," August 8, 2012. Accessed August 16, 2012. http://www.sec.gov/news/press/2012/2012-153.htm

# Part Four: Risk Management

# Anatomy of a Calamity, Stage 4: "Recovery"

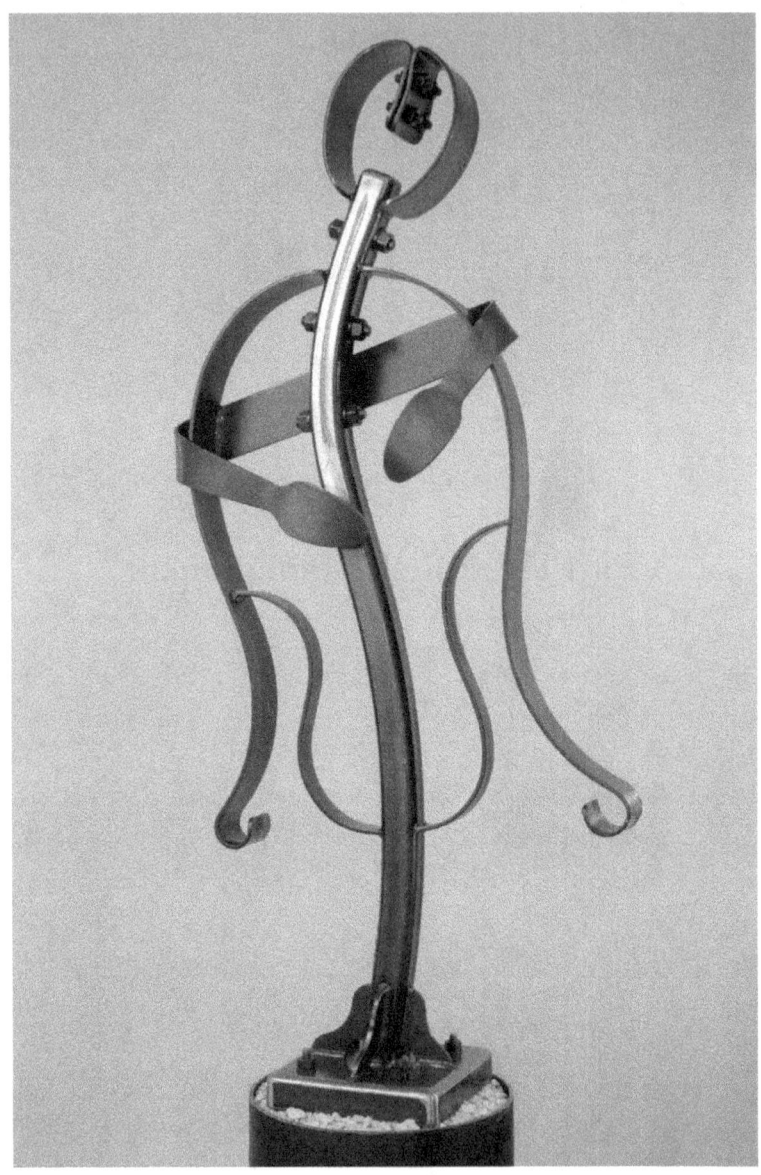

*Their recovery involves many forms of therapy. The physical part of the incident may require medical attention while the psychological and spiritual needs require more personal and human interaction.*

# Real Risk
September 17, 2012

The probability-based risk measures of conventional financial theory might be termed "idealized," suggest David Tuckett and Richard J. Taffler. "They may even be viewed on one level as *pseudo-defences against uncertainty*, or *real* risk." Moreover, the definitions of risk employed for analytical purposes do not reflect the actual experience of fund managers who are on "the emotional front line of the asset management industry." Real risk, say Tuckett and Taffler, is the risk of losing clients, bonuses, and ultimately one's job due to underperformance in a conflict-ridden role and an inherently unpredictable environment.[1]

Soldiers, sailors, combat pilots, firefighters, police officers, spies, drug dealers, racecar drivers, coal miners, and roughnecks on offshore oil rigs might very well offer another point of view on the true meaning of risk. Nonetheless, within the domain of financial services, Tuckett and Taffler insightfully present risk as a lived experience with significant implications for individual investment professionals as well as asset management firms and the investment industry as a whole. Their description and analysis of fund managers' anxieties and coping mechanisms appreciably deepen our understanding of the investment profession.

Taffler and Tuckett are leading theoreticians and researchers in the domain of emotional finance, an emerging discipline that differs in provenance[2] and content from the more established field of behavioral finance. Rather than focusing on cognitive biases, emotional finance explores the affective consequences of making decisions whose outcomes cannot be known in advance and take time to materialize. The emotions triggered by decision-making under conditions of uncertainty have a dynamic impact on the individual's thought processes. Because others in the same situation have similar experiences, certain ways of feeling and thinking become normal across the industry. "Emotional finance seeks to incorporate such understanding within a formal theoretical framework that has direct practical relevance to all financial market participants and is close to their personal experience."[3]

---

[1] David Tuckett and Richard J. Taffler, *Fund Management: An Emotional Finance Perspective* (Research Foundation of CFA Institute, 2012), 34, 69, 81-82.
[2] Tuckett and Taffler trace key concepts of emotional finance to Sigmund Freud, Melanie Klein, and Wilfred Bion.
[3] *Op. cit.*, 1.

On the basis of in-depth qualitative interviews,[4] Tuckett and Taffler discern recurrent features of fund managers' professional experience. Given the relentless pressure to outperform the market and their peers, asset managers must be exceptional. (We will return to the social value of their stardom.) They have to make decisions on the basis of incomplete and ambiguous information. They know that asset valuations rest upon their own and their colleagues' perceptions and beliefs, and they know, too, that the assumptions behind their claims about portfolio holdings are doubtful. Finally, the investment relationships they have with their assets are highly emotional; in fact, Tuckett and Taffler characterize holdings as phantastic[5] objects—"powerful psychological attractors acting beneath consciousness"[6]—with which fund managers more or less stand in a love-hate relationship. The authors state that, in combination, these themes "have the potential to lead to problematic states of mind and dysfunctional outcomes for investors and society generally."[7]

Tuckett and Taffler identify specific areas of concern arising from the unpredictability of investment results. These areas notably include information asymmetry, business risk, and career risk.[8] Fund managers are uneasy about the quality of the information on which they base decisions, and, sometimes, about the trustworthiness of the issuing companies' executives. They are also apprehensive that clients, including those who say they are long-term investors, will withdraw funds and the firm will penalize or terminate them if their short-term results are disappointing.

The fund managers' coping strategies include selective interpretation (e.g., "A benchmark is only a reference point") and denial through the divided-mind mechanism of knowing-but-not-knowing. In addition, storytelling is one of the most important ways fund managers deal with

---

[4] The authors expound their research methodology and defend its validity in Chapter 2. (See especially pages 20-22.) They also note that interviews conducted after "meaning saturation" occurs generally do not produce new insights; rather, they tend to reinforce points that participants have already expressed. Meaning saturation conventionally occurs after as few as 15 to 25 interviews, but the authors interviewed 52 qualified participants for this study.
[5] The spelling matters; unconscious phantasies are distinct from conscious fantasies in the sense of daydreams or wishful thinking. *Op. cit.*, 85, footnote 48.
[6] *Ibid.*, 86.
[7] *Ibid.*, 3-4.
[8] *Ibid.*, 70.

anxiety. Firms and fund managers construct meta-narratives to describe their fundamental investment philosophy, strategy, or process,[9] and managers tell stories to explain their successes and failures. Tuckett and Taffler do not say that fund managers invariably confabulate, but, quoting Yiannis Gabriel, they indicate that the plausibility and coherence of these narratives may be valued more than their accuracy.[10] In other words, beauty stands above truth. Stories about successful investments generally fall into the epic genre, sometimes with a romantic subtext: through perseverance and insight, the fund manager prevailed in a noble quest to find an undervalued security, championed buying it, and held it through many tribulations until the market acknowledged its inherent value. Stories about failed investments tend to evoke the tragic genre, recounting the protagonists's undeserved misfortune at the hands of villains or malevolent fate. After providing examples, Tuckett and Taffler write,

> "It is significant and interesting that because of the way the interviewees explained their failures through plausible stories, the failures do not appear to threaten the interviewees' meta-narratives or underlying investment *credos*....This conclusion has an important implication: The market as a whole, fund managers, their investment houses, and their clients may have problems learning from experience. Storytelling, in the sense we have described, is a wonderfully flexible way of explaining misfortune and managing anxiety without threatening underlying beliefs."[11]

Tuckett and Taffler state that the investment industry transforms superior fund managers themselves into phantastic objects. "They *are* the phantastic objects that their clients, employers, consultants, financial advisers, and the media unconsciously need to be superior to alleviate the anxiety they experience because of the future being unknowable." And, they argue, "An industry that expects its foot soldiers to be phantastic objects clearly rests on problematic foundations...."[12]

I strongly recommend Tuckett and Taffler's fascinating monograph to investment, risk, and human resource professionals. Note, however, that

---

[9] *Ibid.*, 52.

[10] *Ibid.*, 48. See also Yiannis Gabriel, *Storytelling in Organizations: Facts, Fictions, and Fantasies* (New York: Oxford University Press, 2000), 4.

[11] *Op. cit.*, 67.

[12] *Ibid.*, 91-92.

recognizing the incidental psychological utility of quantitative risk measures most emphatically does *not* mean they are superfluous. Those who think an investment firm can be effectively managed without rigorous risk measurement and robust risk management should have their heads examined.

# When Default-Free Assets Don't Pay
July 18, 2011

At this writing, the U.S. government has not raised the country's $14.3 trillion debt limit. Continued inaction over the next two weeks will trigger a default by preventing the government from rolling over its debt, almost one-third of which is held by foreign investors.[1] Reinhart and Rogoff point out that *willingness* rather than *ability* to pay has historically proven to be the main determinant of country default.[2] In my reading, then, there is typically a thin line between sovereign debt default and repudiation. Such an event in this country would once have been unthinkable, but the cavalier brinksmanship we are currently witnessing means that financial risk managers must attend to the possible consequences, insofar as they can be foreseen. That the leaders of the U.S. government would actually allow the effective deadline to pass without having raised the ceiling is practically beyond belief—but what if they did?

Although exceedingly difficult to quantify, certain social, political, and economic effects can reasonably be anticipated. Wealth would immediately evaporate with the decline in the market value of Treasurys. Interest rates would rise, extending the recession and, of course, adding to the federal debt burden. Over time, inflation would rise. (Inflation is not a desirable way to pay down the debt.) Banks, which hold large quantities of public debt, would probably fall into crisis again. With the economy stalled and borrowing more expensive, publicly traded companies would falter and the stock market would decline. Liquidity would probably shrink across asset classes and, in some instruments, disappear entirely. Unemployment, already high, would rise further, and individuals who rely upon transfer payments, including unemployment insurance, would have a hard time. The dollar would weaken and relations with trading partners who are also creditors would be strained. Fragile international defense arrangements might be disrupted....

The foregoing consequences of a U.S. default are those, more or less probable, that occur to me. I offer them, however, with two reservations. First, the list is undoubtedly incomplete. Studying economic

---

[1] Foreign individuals, corporations, and governments hold 31.6% of the outstanding U.S. national debt. (*The Washington Post*, July 17, 2011, p. G1.)
[2] Carmen M. Reinhart and Kenneth S. Rogoff, *This Time Is Different: Eight Centuries of Financial Folly* (Princeton University Press, 2009), p. 49.

history (for example, the Russian default of 1998) might help us identify further possibilities, but credit risk has not been associated with Treasurys, and there is no precedent for default on the part of the U.S. government. Second, the above list is limited to first-order consequences. It takes into account neither the impact of derivative securities such as credit default swaps nor, more importantly, the aggressive or defensive behavior of other participants in the densely integrated global markets. It is to be assumed that a default on the part of the U.S. government would lead to unobvious outcomes.

Chances are the politicians will come to an agreement and raise the debt limit. All the same, the exercise in these paragraphs will have been worthwhile if it brings home one key fact: we cannot grasp, much less manage away, all the risks to which our firm and our clients might be exposed. What we *can* do is try to imagine potential states of the world, consider how our holdings might be affected, identify the obvious risks, suss out their ramifications, restructure our portfolios (or not), and recognize that in some cases the best result we can achieve is to lose less than we might have lost.

# What You Don't Know
July 23, 2011

There are many examples of questionable advice implicit in popular sayings, but one of the worst is, "what you don't know can't hurt you." Discretion has its place in interpersonal relationships; there are circumstances where thoughtful consideration would support less-than-full disclosure. My gratuitously telling a friend what somebody else thinks of him might not increase the total amount of happiness in the world. In business, however, and particularly in the business of investment management, information risk—what you don't know—can be catastrophic.

Information risk is a pervasive form of operational risk. To establish the context, let's define these terms. Operational risk is "the risk of loss resulting from inadequate or failed internal processes, people and systems, or from external events."[1] Information risk is the risk that business managers will not have pertinent, accurate, and meaningful facts readily available when critically needed.

Setting aside instances where no information is available anywhere, the more or less controllable sorts of information risk arise in the processes of identifying, gathering, processing, and disseminating information that exists somewhere in the capital markets or somewhere in the organization. Aggregating counterparty credit exposures is a case in point.

Challenging in small and mid-size firms, monitoring credit risk can be a Herculean task in large organizations—especially those with multiple product lines, investment strategies, geographical locations, and legacy portfolio accounting systems and risk models. If a trader in the Singapore office executes a forward contract with Nirgendwo Forex Australia (NFA) and a trader in London enters an interest rate swap with Irgendwo UK International (IUK), the firm may be ill-equipped to capture its combined exposure to the two entities' common parent, Woher Holdings (WH). Even if the Augean stable that is the firm's securities master file has been thoroughly mucked, NFA and IUK's

---

[1] Now generally accepted, this definition was originally formulated by the Basel Committee on Banking Supervision in BCBS Working Papers No. 8, "Regulatory Treatment of Operational Risk," September 2001, p. 8. Accessed August 5, 2012. http://www.bis.org/publ/bcbs_wp8.htm

kinship via WH might not be registered or passed along to the risk management system.

Many providers collect reference data, typically including an issuer's direct and/or ultimate parent.[2] Ironically, their very number may render data management more complex. The Office of Financial Research (OFR), established by the Dodd-Frank Act to support the Financial Stability Oversight Council, recognizes the problem: "because there is no industry-wide legal entity identification standard, tracking counterparties and calculating exposures across multiple data systems is complicated, expensive, and can result in costly errors."[3] The Legal Entity Identifier (LEI) project initiated by OFR last year has great potential to help firms manage this kind of information risk.

There is much, much more to say about information risk, but I'll close for now with a comment on another dubious aphorism. In my experience, ignorance generally isn't bliss very long.

---

[2] Linda F. Powell, Mark Montoya, and Elena Shuvalov list a number of providers in "Legal Entity Identifier: What Else Do You Need to Know?", Finance and Economics Discussion Series (FEDS) 2011-31, 12–14. Accessed August 5, 2012.
www.federalreserve.gov/pubs/feds/2011/201131/201131pap.pdf
[3] Office of Financial Research, Department of the Treasury, "Statement on Legal Entity Identification for Financial Contracts," p. 4. Accessed August 5, 2012. www.treasury.gov/initiatives/Documents/OFR-LEI_Policy_Statement-FINAL.PDF

# Summer Reading—Risk Management
August 17, 2011

Marcus Aurelius wrote, "And give up your thirst for books, so that you do not die a grouch…." (*Meditations* 2.2.) But I am unconcerned. Here are a few recommendations.

Thomas S. Coleman's book, *A Practical Guide to Risk Management* (Research Foundation of CFA Institute, 2011), is a thoughtful, engaging work that board members and senior managers, in particular, will find most instructive. Coleman argues that, while risk measurement is a specialized technical discipline that should often be housed in a separate department, risk management is the responsibility of the board, the CEO, and every line manager in the firm. One chapter presents fundamental concepts of risk management, including a lucid explanation of frequency-based and belief-based probability. Another, devoted to managing risk, incorporates a superb essay comparing a firm's financial exposures to small-group ski mountaineering in avalanche country. The author also surveys historic trading losses and comments on specific cases of fraud and "normal business activity gone wrong." In addition, there is a full-length primer on measuring risk and a brief consideration of the uses and limitations of quantitative techniques. Valuable for motivated generalists and experienced risk professionals alike, Coleman's work fully meets the standards of excellence in writing and editing we have come to expect from CFA Institute.

Christina I. Ray's *Extreme Risk Management: Revolutionary Approaches to Evaluating and Measuring Risk* (McGraw-Hill, 2010) is a revelatory work. Ray, who specializes in analyzing the risk of low-frequency, high-severity events, helped create the field of MARKINT ("the systematic collection and analysis of open-source information from the global capital and commodities markets") for the mutual benefit of the financial and intelligence communities. The author sets the stage by contrasting the approaches of financial analysts, who employ quantitative models based upon statistical correlations, and intelligence analysts, who develop causal models to assess the likelihood and consequences of events that have not previously occurred. The early part of the book, presumably intended to introduce intelligence analysts to the probabilistic approach, makes for pleasant reading, but the material will be familiar to most financial risk professionals. The later part, however, crucially introduces the discipline and surveys the techniques of structured causal modeling, including directed acyclic graphs, connectivism, and risk inference networks—

hence its inestimable value to financial risk managers. Ray cogently advocates combining the best methodologies of both worlds: "The financial community might more explicitly include cause and effect and expert opinion in its models, while the intelligence community might likewise include more mathematical models, automated sensemaking tools, and open-source market data." This book is fascinating and important.

Finally, the August–September 2011 issue of *The Journal of Risk Management in Financial Institutions* (vol. 4 no. 3) is a special issue on the financial crisis. Two articles stand out. The first is Giorgio Szegö's account of the causes of the crisis, most interestingly including regulatory and financial accounting decisions such as mandatory risk-adjusted capital requirements and fair value accounting for untraded assets. The second is "Credit Models and the Crisis: An Overview," by Damiano Brigo, Andrea Pallavicini, and Roberto Torresetti. The authors recount the history of quantitative methods for pricing credit derivatives and collateralized debt obligations, and they explain the pricing models' deficiencies, particularly in the treatment of correlations. Although somewhat polemical, this paper is a case study in a key technical aspect of model risk.

# Credit Quality
September 7, 2011

Investors' interests were subordinated to corporate revenue targets, and presumably independent, objective research proved to be biased and unreliable. Firms' public opinions were sharply at variance with their own analysts' private views. When the bubble burst and the failure of internal controls came to light, the firms were charged with issuing reports that were fraudulent or contained unwarranted claims and unsupported opinions. The SEC extracted massive penalties and imposed new rules.

Can our experience with conflicts of interest in dot-com equity research help us deal with credit rating agencies today?

In April 2003, the SEC announced its global settlement[1] with ten Wall Street firms and two individuals. The firms paid $875 million in disgorged profits and civil penalties, $432.5 million to fund independent research, and $80 million to fund investor education. They also agreed to structural reforms, physically and organizationally separating research from investment banking as well as placing a firewall between them, and to enhanced conflict-of-interest disclosures.

Today, more than eight years later, it appears that the combination of staggering monetary penalties and common-sense structural reforms succeeded in restoring the integrity of sell-side research. In addition, there are alternatives: independent research boutiques have stepped up to serve the buy side.

In view of the role inflated credit ratings on structured products ostensibly played in the financial crisis, the SEC is in the process of formulating new rules[2] to govern the Nationally Recognized Statistical Rating Agencies' internal controls. This seems a reasonable approach; it worked the last time. However, the NRSROs are significantly different from the Wall Street firms in at least two ways.

---

[1] Securities and Exchange Commission, "SEC Fact Sheet on Global Analyst Research Settlements," April 28, 2003. Accessed August 5, 2012. http://www.sec.gov/news/speech/factsheet.htm
[2] Securities and Exchange Commission, "Proposed Rules for Nationally Recognized Statistical Rating Organizations," May 18, 2011. Accessed August 5, 2012. http://www.sec.gov/rules/proposed/2011/34-64514.pdf

First, while the investment firms gave away their equity research reports, the credit rating agencies' core revenue-generating product is issuer-paid credit ratings. Section 932 of the Dodd-Frank Act calls upon the SEC to issue rules preventing sales and marketing considerations from influencing ratings. That's a sound principle. However, the conflicts of interest—analytical independence vs. customer satisfaction, due diligence vs. efficiency, and deliberative process vs. foregone conclusion—are not incidental; on the contrary, these conflicts are inherent and insidious in the credit rating business. Moreover, it is doubtful that the credit rating agencies could produce adequate income from impartial sources.

The second difference seems equally inalterable. While large organizations can do their own analysis (as the insurance companies always have done), many managers have no practical alternative to the credit rating agencies. Independent fixed-income research boutiques are unlikely to emerge because the NRSRO oligopoly is operationally entrenched in the U.S. investment industry.

For example, the summary prospectus for a PIMCO bond fund reads, "The Fund may invest in…high yield securities ("junk bonds") subject to a maximum of 10% of its total assets in securities rated below B by Moody's Investors Service, Inc. ("Moody's"), or equivalently rated by Standard & Poor's Rating Services ("S&P") or Fitch, Inc. ("Fitch"), or, if unrated, determined by PIMCO to be of comparable quality."

The NRSROs are similarly written into countless investment policy statements and investment management agreements. Their ratings are employed in fixed-income investment strategies that factor spreads into the security selection and portfolio construction processes. They are encoded in security master files' reference data, compliance monitoring systems' constraints, and credit risk models' transition matrices. Replacing the existing providers would be a whopping legal, clerical, and technological challenge.

NRSROs found to have misrepresented the credit quality of structured securities will probably be fined and subjected to appreciably more stringent regulatory oversight. Fitch may gain market share. But the conflicts of interest are embedded in the rating agencies, the rating agencies are entrenched in the investment industry, and there will be no fundamental change in the business model or the competitive environment. Risk managers take note: along with credit risk there is ineluctable credit rating agency risk.

# Dependence

September 14, 2011

The notion of causal dependence is philosophically rich, scientifically stimulative, and emotionally resonant. "Nothing is more curiously enquired after by the mind of man," wrote David Hume, "than the causes of every phenomenon."[1]

Many financial institutions rely upon expert judgment to identify dependencies for the purpose of estimating the severity of low frequency, high impact (LFHI) events. A brief survey of the types of dependence may provide a framework for eliciting and organizing business line managers' expert opinions. A useful typology distinguishes between path-dependent, common-factor, and antecedent-condition risks. Within the category of common-factor risks, it is also helpful to differentiate external events from internal episodes that are specific to the firm's people, processes, and systems.

First, then, path-dependent risks. A commuter driving to Richmond swerves to avoid a squirrel and causes a highway accident. Long after the roadway has been cleared, traffic continues to slow and compress at the scene of the accident, almost as if the road remembered the crash. Traffic engineers call this the pinch effect.

Market, credit, liquidity, and operational risks are not perfectly distinct; sometimes, for instance, market events have consequences for investment operations as well as asset valuations. (In another context, Arthur O. Lovejoy spoke of "the universal overlappingness of the real world.")[2] That said, the failure of Northern Rock in 2007 may broadly be considered a path-dependent outcome: the market's revaluation of structured investment vehicles, coupled with Northern Rock's securitization-based business strategy and reliance upon short-term wholesale funding, led to a run on deposits.

---

[1] David Hume, *A Treatise of Human Nature*, Bk. I, Pt. IV, Sec. VII. In scenario analysis, of course, the objective is to deduce consequences, not to infer causes; Hume's statement would apply more directly to reverse stress-testing. However, the connection is still dependence.

[2] Arthur O. Lovejoy, *The Great Chain of Being* (Harvard University Press, 1936), p. 57.

Second, external common-factor risks. Patch.com, the provider of hyper-local online news in many communities, reported last month that a squirrel in Manassas attempted to cross power lines designed to trip and shut down a nearby electrical substation. Erin Gibson wrote, "Traffic lights along busy Liberia Avenue were affected, and City Hall was reportedly without power for nearly a half hour. The Giant Food store located on Centreville Road at the Manassas Junction Shopping Center was without power as well, but the use of a generator allowed them to remain open."[3]

In investment management, a business interruption at a major exchange or clearing facility would be an external common-factor event, not only because it would affect many managers but also—more pertinently—because it would embroil multiple business processes at each firm: portfolio management, trading, settlement, accounting, and compliance.

Third, internal common-factor risks. A man injures himself while hunting in the Blue Ridge Mountains. (Squirrel season opened September 3rd in Virginia.) Unfortunately, he is the only portfolio accountant at a small firm, and he has always been too busy to document the daily system-updating and monthly closing processes. His extended absence will bring firm-wide operations to a halt.

Similarly, a system that is out of commission may affect multiple processes. For example, the investment accounting system may interface with the order management, portfolio management, trade matching, and performance measurement systems.

Finally, antecedent condition risks. I cannot come up with a plausible example involving squirrels, but an operational failure will generally have downstream effects within a single business process. For instance, a transaction that is incorrectly entered to the accounting system and not timely corrected will lead to a mismatch at settlement. The result is a failed trade (usually not an LFHI event).

Before closing, a few tips and resources:

1. Because dependence relationships are directional, arrow diagrams are apt representations. There are many examples of

---

[3] Erin Gibson, "Squirrel Cuts Power in Manassas," ManassasPatch, August 15, 2011. Accessed August 5, 2012. http://manassas.patch.com/articles/squirrel-cuts-power-in-manassas

visual aids to discovery and understanding in Christina Ray's book, *Extreme Risk Management: Revolutionary Approaches to Evaluating and Measuring Risk* (McGraw-Hill, 2010).

2. In "Principles for the Sound Management of Operational Risk," Basel II identifies business process mapping as a tool for identifying and assessing operational risk.[4] System diagrams and "swim-lane" workflow charts are particularly helpful in identifying the impact of failures at any point. There are examples in Holly H. Miller and Philip Lawton, *The Top Ten Operational Risks: A Survival Guide for Investment Management Firms and Hedge Funds* (Stone House Consulting, 2010).

3. "A robust governance framework surrounding the scenario process is essential to ensure the integrity and consistency of the estimates produced." The Basel II publication, *Operational Risk—Supervisory Guidelines for the Advanced Measurement Approaches*, sets forth the elements of well-managed scenario forecasting processes.[5]

The errant squirrel in Manassas perished on the power lines, but a solid understanding of dependences may help investment organizations recover from operational shocks.

---

[4] Basel Committee on Banking Supervision, "Principles for the Sound Management of Operational Risk," June 2011, Section 38(e). Accessed August 5, 2012. http://www.bis.org/publ/bcbs195.htm

[5] Basel Committee on Banking Supervision, *Operational Risk—Supervisory Guidelines for the Advanced Measurement Approaches,* June 2011, Section 254. Accessed August 5, 2012. http://www.bis.org/publ/bcbs196.htm

## War Games
September 19, 2011

Kweku Adoboli's father said that his son was "elated" when he left an operational unit at UBS and became a trader on the bank's Global Synthetic Equity desk.[1]

Well, of course he was thrilled.

If UBS is like other financial services companies, Adoboli moved from a support area, where staff are most likely to be noticed for their mistakes, to a trading desk where he could be a star. He transferred from a cost center, where merit increases are slim and bonus participation is limited, to a revenue-generating position with potential for a high level of total compensation. He was admitted to membership in the club.

Once seated, he undoubtedly found that trading is the most competitive arena on the planet. He'd have to engage all his resources to distinguish himself. All his energy. ("Sometimes I would call before I went to bed and he would say: 'Daddy, I'm still at work.'") Both sides of his brain. Everything he knew about quantitative modeling and index futures. But he would soon have discovered that all Delta One traders are vigorous, smart, and knowledgeable. In this dog-eat-dog, winner-take-all environment, Adoboli had a rare advantage: he understood back-office operations.

It was an edge he had in common with another infamous miscreant, Jérôme Kerviel, whose unauthorized trading cost SocGen €4.9 billion three years ago. Kerviel also had back-office experience.[2] The Wall Street Journal reports, "Mr. Kerviel's case and others prompted Société Générale and some other banks, including HSBC Holdings PLC, to prohibit or tightly restrict the shift of back-office and technical personnel to client-trading desks, because the risk of a such a person being able to manipulate trades is seen as too high, said some bankers."[3]

---

[1] Peter Wonacott, "UBS Trader's Arrest Stuns Family," *The Wall Street Journal*, 17 September 2011.
[2] Carrick Mollenkamp, "Links Between UBS, SocGen Trading Scandals," *The Wall Street Journal*, 15 September 2011.
[3] Alastair MacDonald and Deborah Ball, "Questions Arise About UBS Risk Controls," *The Wall Street Journal*, 16 September 2011.

Given the apparent failure of other risk controls, it is hard to argue that UBS was justified in allowing capable employees to transfer from operations to trading.[4] But implementing this rule puts companies in the awkward position of foreclosing an attractive career path to certain employees. Operational staff are disqualified as a class.

Wanted: Delta One trader. Back-office personnel need not apply.

I'd like to suggest another possibility. Risk management departments should actively recruit the strongest individuals in the organization's investment operations area, notably including trade support, and offer them an office rather than a cubicle.

Then, and only then, can scenario analysis become a two-team, zero-sum war game within the risk management group. The Red Team, comprised of the best former ops specialists, would try to discern and exploit flaws in the company's systems and processes; the Blue Team would use their entire arsenal of risk management techniques and operational controls to frustrate and repel them. The common ground is that both sides have to work with the organization's *actual* systems, processes, and controls, not the documented standards. Kerviel's fraud was facilitated, in part, by SocGen's neglecting to update system access privileges.

Operational risk management is a war—make no mistake about it—and investment management organizations are under assault by fiercely intelligent, highly motivated criminals, possibly including employees. Simulating agent behavior through realistic war games may prove a powerful means to find system and process vulnerabilities and fix them before appalling loss events occur.

And, by opening an alternate avenue to advancement for operational staff, senior management can communicate that the organization recognizes and rewards talent throughout its ranks. In other words, they can be discriminating in the archaic sense of making fine distinctions and selecting the best.

---

[4] "UBS had no rule banning back-office employees from taking client-facing positions." Dana Cimilluca, Deborah Ball, and Carrick Mollenkamp, "UBS Raises Tally on Losses," *The Wall Street Journal*, 19 September 2011.

# ISO 31000

## Designing a Risk Management Framework
October 5, 2011

Large financial institutions generally have well-established policies and procedures for managing market, credit, operational, and liquidity risk. The principal challenge they currently face at the enterprise level is execution—compiling, analyzing, and presenting timely, accurate, and meaningful information derived from multiple sources and systems. Firm-wide execution on a large scale involves a complex set of inter-related managerial and technological issues which are more easily unpacked in theory than resolved in practice.

Today, however, let us turn our attention to another domain. The capital markets vitally depend upon the reliability of non-financial organizations such as reference data providers, exchanges and clearinghouses, safekeepers, and regulatory agencies, including self-regulatory organizations. If risk is "the effect of uncertainty on objectives," then service providers also stand in need of robust risk management.

Released two years ago next month, ISO 31000 is one of the best resources available to *any* organization seeking to design and implement a sound risk management program. The standard (which is subtitled "Risk Management—Principles and Guidelines") is not intended for certification purposes, but it represents the international standard-setting organization's best thinking about a framework for managing risk. The principles and guidelines articulated in this 26-page document will help the project team design a risk management program that is appropriate to the organization's mission and fully integrated into its operations. I will limit this post to highlights of the design process.

ISO 31000 sets forth eleven principles, expressed as descriptive statements, that apply at all levels of an organization. For example, risk management is "an integral part of all organizational processes"; "systematic, structured, and timely"; and "based on the best available information." However platitudinous these statements may seem, they reflect value propositions to which the project team can usefully refer when evaluating alternatives. Indeed, one of the principles explicitly addresses the likelihood of disagreements. By taking cultural and human factors into account, risk management "recognizes the capabilities, perceptions and intentions of external and internal people that can facilitate or hinder achievement of the organization's objectives."

The standard rightly emphasizes the importance of management's "strong and sustained commitment." An emphatic message from the board and the CEO should be backed by convincing resource allocations. Senior management must ensure that the organization's culture, objectives, strategies, and risk management policy are properly aligned, and at the outset the project team should identify contextual factors that might affect the framework's architecture. Among other considerations, evaluating the external context entails surveying the social, political, legal, regulatory, technological, and economic environment as well as taking industry trends and business drivers into account. Similarly, evaluating the internal context means objectively reviewing the organization's structure, governance, and capabilities (resources and knowledge).

The risk management policy typically contains such elements as accountabilities, protocols for dealing with conflicting interests, risk measures, escalation guidelines, and provisions for internal and external reporting. Far from being a separate function, risk management should be embedded in all the organization's decision-making processes.

Clearly, getting off to a good start requires assembling people who know both the business and the organization under the leadership of a credible and effective project manager. The organization's own staff almost certainly have the requisite knowledge. However, they also have ongoing managerial and technical responsibilities which may restrict their availability. It makes sense to consider engaging an experienced consultant to facilitate designing and implementing the risk management framework. Operational consultants' familiarity with the investment industry enables them to challenge assumptions and encourage critical thinking; their expertise in risk management equips them to guide the organization toward sound policies and effective practices; and their project management skills keep the initiative on track while respecting the internal participants' time.

I'm all too aware that the treatment of framework design in this essay is sketchy. My modest hope is that it will encourage you to download ISO 31000 and think about how it applies to your organization. It is available from ANSI at www.ansi.org and ISO at www.iso.org.

## The Risk Management Process: Context and Assessment

October 12, 2011

Last week I introduced ISO 31000, "Risk Management—Principles and Guidelines," as a valuable resource for any organization, and I highlighted some of its recommendations for designing a risk management framework. ISO 31000 goes on to describe the attributes of a well-managed process. This further part of the standard also merits commentary.

According to ISO 31000, risk management comprises these activities: ongoing communication and consultation; establishing the context (that is, examining the internal and external environments in greater depth, delimiting the scope of risk management, and defining evaluative criteria); risk assessment; risk treatment; and continual monitoring and review. The present post will take us through the assessment phase.

Communicating the organization's risk management objectives, and ensuring that the interests of internal and external stakeholders are understood and respected, are vital steps in creating a culture of compliance. In my experience with internal stakeholders, topmost management should not only make a company-wide announcement but also schedule and lead kick-off meetings and periodic feedback sessions with key people. Career employees, notably including overstretched line managers, decide for themselves which corporate initiatives they will back, must endure, and can politely disregard. They are most likely to attend to messages delivered in person by C-level executives. In all interactions with stakeholders, of course, risk management staff should watch for signs of the Karmarkar gambit.[1]

When establishing the internal context, a key objective is articulating the organization's culture. For expediency, let us follow Jim Ware's usage and define culture as "the values, behaviors, and beliefs that distinguish the people of one organization from those [of] another."[2] The

---

[1] In 1984, while seeking to patent some applications, Bell Labs withheld critical steps in the published proof of Narendra Karmarkar's algorithm for solving complex linear programming problems. See Holly H. Miller and Philip Lawton, *The Top Ten Operational Risks: A Survival Guide for Investment Management Firms and Hedge Funds* (Stone House Consulting, 2010), 66.

[2] Jim Ware with Beth Michaels and Dale Primer, *Investment Leadership: Building a*

organization's culture—which finds expression not only in speeches and press releases but also in the employee evaluation process and the compensation scheme—may profoundly affect individuals' attitudes toward risk. Ware suggests, "Another way to define culture is to ask employees, 'What does it take to succeed in this organization?'"[3]

ISO 31000 also calls for establishing the context of the process itself: defining the goals, responsibilities, scope, and methodologies, as well as determining how to evaluate the effectiveness of risk management. These are significant governance issues and, although I am merely mentioning them here, they mustn't be given short shrift in actuality. Clear thinking now may head off confusion and conflict later.[4]

The project team should additionally reach agreement on risk criteria reflecting the organization's values, objectives, and resources. The standard recommends considering such factors as the types of causes and consequences that can occur, how they will be measured, how likelihood will be defined, and how the level of risk will be determined. As a practical matter, the project team should expect to revisit the risk criteria as issues come to light during the initial assessment phase.

There are, unsurprisingly, three steps in risk assessment: identification, analysis, and evaluation. The project team should catalog all plausible changes or events that might in any way affect the achievement of the organization's objectives. Any risks overlooked at this stage will not be analyzed and evaluated later. Section 5.4.2 of ISO 31000 also states, "People with appropriate knowledge should be involved in identifying risks." In my reading, this recommendation refers to seasoned people throughout the organization.

Analysis essentially means estimating the probability and impact of events affecting the achievement of objectives. ISO 31000 usefully points out that the analysis should be accompanied by a statement about the team's level of confidence, explicitly mentioning such factors as differences of opinion, the quality of information, and limits on modeling. (Operational risks are especially difficult to model

---

*Winning Culture for Long-Term Success* (Wiley, 2004), p. 63.
[3] *Ibid.*, p. 18.
[4] Leslie Rahl offers excellent advice in her paper, "Advances in Risk Management and Risk Governance," *CFA Institute Conference Proceedings Quarterly (September, 2011)*, 74-79. Accessed August 12, 2012. http://www.cfapubs.org/doi/pdf/10.2469/cp.v28.n3.7

satisfactorily.) Evaluation involves comparing the level of risk found through analysis with the team's risk criteria; its purpose is to prioritize risks for treatment.—That's all for now. I will wrap up my notes on ISO 31000 with a discussion of risk treatment options next week.

## The Risk Management Process: Treatment
October 19, 2011

This is the third and last *Middle Office* piece on ISO 31000, "Risk Management—Principles and Guidelines," a document I have recommended as an excellent non-technical resource for any organization seeking to implement a sound risk management program. The present post focuses on the standard's approach to selecting risk "treatment" options. ISO 31000 calls for an iterative process of evaluating a risk treatment, determining whether the residual risk is tolerable, and, if necessary, selecting another treatment for evaluation, until the project team settles on a solution.

One of ISO 31000's qualities is the common sense its authors bring to practical risk management issues. The treatment alternatives they consider range from avoiding the risk by discontinuing an activity to increasing the risk in pursuit of an opportunity. These extremes should, of course, be seen in light of the organization's risk criteria. In some cases a particular risk could be entirely avoided only at the sacrifice of a key objective, while increasing a risk might entail committing inordinate resources to inessential activities. But sometimes avoidance is the best course of action, and sometimes it is appropriate to go all-out for the upside.

Another treatment that may occasionally be possible is to remove the source of the risk. Take the case of a state regulatory agency whose managers are worried about low morale due to the staff's overcrowded working conditions in a very old building. Management knows that the agency cannot relocate to more commodious quarters in the near term; that many midsize firms will have to be registered for the first time next year; and that qualified compliance, examination, and enforcement professionals are hard to find in the local labor market. In this situation, the organization might well consider instituting flexible hours and equipping employees to work from home in order to eliminate dissatisfaction with the office environment. I do not, however, suppose there are many situations where the source of risk can be removed.

The classical treatments are changing the likelihood of a risk; changing its consequences; and sharing it. In manufacturing and distribution, for instance, the probability of a sole supplier's going out of business could be reduced by using multiple suppliers with adequate financial resources. The consequences of a supplier's failing to make timely deliveries could be attenuated by holding a larger inventory. Alternately, the financial impact of late deliveries could be shared by buying insurance coverage for business interruptions. Raising inventory levels and purchasing insurance, however, are expensive solutions. As a rule, cost/benefit analysis is a necessary step in selecting risk treatments.

There remains one other option. After evaluating the alternatives, an organization may make the conscious, deliberate decision to accept a risk. Although the outcome is the same, this decision is qualitatively different from disregarding a risk or, what is worse, being unaware of it. It is especially important to document the evaluation process when management chooses to live with a risk.

Whatever risk treatment is recommended, the organization should take stakeholders' perceptions and interests into account—they may have preferences when more than one solution is available—and decide how to communicate with them.

Risk treatments are, themselves, risky. Because they may prove more or less ineffective, they must be monitored. In addition, they may introduce secondary risks. For example, by entering an interest rate swap, an organization can exchange a fixed rate for a floating rate, more nearly matching its cash flow requirements and/or reducing mark-to-market risk in the event rates rise. By so doing, however, the organization accepts counterparty credit risk whenever it is in a net positive position. The ISO standard states that secondary risks should be incorporated into the same treatment plan as the original risk.

Allow me to close by restating a few key points from this three-part series:

1.  All organizations are subject to risk defined as the effect of uncertainty on objectives.

2.  The risk management policy should be aligned with the organization's culture, and the framework should reflect its internal and external context.

3.  Stakeholders should be informed and consulted during all stages of the risk management process.

4. Risk management should be embedded in the organization's practices and decision-making processes.

Finally, it bears repeating that these *Middle Office* commentaries are not intended to replace ISO 31000; they merely highlight certain aspects of the recommended approach. ISO 31000 is available from the American National Standards Institute and the International Organization for Standardization.

## Two Standards of Risk Assessment
March 19, 2012

Open for public comment until March 31st, the revised COSO framework for internal control includes significant changes in the treatment of risk assessment. The modified COSO standards invite comparison with those set out in ISO 31000, *Risk Management—Principles and Guidelines*. Are they consistent with one another? To what extent do they overlap? Is there a need for two international standards?

For background, the Committee of Sponsoring Organizations of the Treadway Commission (COSO)[1] was formed in 1985 to support the work of the National Commission on Fraudulent Financial Reporting, an independent initiative of the accounting industry originally chaired by James C. Treadway, Jr. The members of COSO are the American Accounting Association, the American Institute of CPAs, Financial Executives International, the Institute of Management Accountants, and the Institute of Internal Auditors. The Treadway Commission issued its report in 1987,[2] and COSO published the first version of *Internal Control—Integrated Framework* in 1992. COSO has continued to provide thought leadership, most notably including the publication in 2004 of *Enterprise Risk Management—Integrated Framework* (sometimes informally called COSO II).[3] But the current exposure draft[4] is the first revision of the internal control framework since its initial appearance 20 years ago. The update was written by PwC.

The COSO internal control framework and ISO 31000 agree in defining risk in relation to the achievement of objectives.[5] ISO 31000 presents a

---

[1] The website address is www.coso.org. Accessed August 8, 2012.
[2] *Report of the National Commission on Fraudulent Financial Reporting*, October 1987. Accessed August 8, 2012.
http://www.coso.org/Publications/NCFFR.pdf
[3] *COSO Enterprise Risk Management -- Integrated Framework* (2004) is available from the American Institute of Certified Public Accountants (AICPA). Accessed August 8, 2012.
http://www.cpa2biz.com/AST/Main/CPA2BIZ_Primary/InternalControls/C OSO/PRDOVR~PC-990015/PC-990015.jsp. Juxtaposing COSO's ERM framework and the ISO 31000 standard is a topic for another day.
[4] COSO, *Exposure Draft: Internal Control Integrated Framework*. Accessed August 8, 2012. http://www.ic.coso.org/default.aspx
[5] ISO 31000 defines risk as "the effect of uncertainty on objectives," allows that effects can be positive and/or negative, and presents objective-setting as an

comprehensive plan for developing and implementing a risk management program in support of any objectives, while the COSO internal control framework is principally concerned with objectives promoting effective and efficient operations, reliable reporting, and compliance with applicable laws and regulations. In the revised framework, the reporting objective includes internal and non-financial reporting as well as external financial reporting.

Although the pertinent standards in the revised COSO framework fall under the heading of risk *assessment*, the scope of risk management activities they address—at least summarily—is roughly comparable to that of ISO 31000. For example, COSO considers the organization's risk tolerance, and includes a reasonably substantive section on "risk response." ISO 31000 is, however, considerably more process-oriented than the COSO document. Among other things, it emphasizes the importance of consulting and communicating with stakeholders at every stage of designing and implementing a risk management framework.

ISO 31000 is principles-based; COSO's original framework remains structurally intact, but the revised version strengthens the foundation by newly incorporating principles and attributes. In the risk assessment component of the COSO internal control framework, there are four principles and, by my count, 23 attributes. Informally paraphrased, the principles state that the organization specifies pertinent objectives clearly enough to enable risk assessment; identifies and analyzes risks to the achievement of its objectives; considers, in particular, the potential for fraud; and assesses changes that could significantly affect the system of internal control.

The attributes express characteristics of the principles. Many attributes seem to have broad applicability (e.g., "Risk identification considers both internal and external factors and their impact on the achievement of objectives"), but some apply specifically to the reporting of results (e.g., "Management considers materiality in financial statement presentation") or the safeguarding of assets (e.g., "The assessment of fraud risk considers incentives and pressures").

---

iterative process. COSO defines risk as "the possibility that an event will occur and adversely affect the achievement of objectives." In the course of identifying and analyzing risks, an organization may also discover opportunities that should be communicated to strategists. "However," COSO states, "identifying and assessing potential opportunities is not a part of internal control."

The two voluntary standards address many of the same issues, then, and they generally appear to be consistent. ISO 31000 is unrestricted to a functional domain, while COSO's risk assessment component is valuable to financial and accounting managers, in particular, because it can be explained and implemented in the context of a broader initiative to strengthen internal controls. Nonetheless, in my opinion, ISO 31000 offers appreciably more useful guidance on the process of putting a risk management framework in place. Managers who are charged with implementing or upgrading an organization's COSO regime might find additionally consulting ISO 31000 most helpful.

# Fire Drill
October 17, 2011

Traffic was momentarily interrupted but the New York Stock Exchange was not shut down by a distributed or directed denial of service (DDoS) attack last week.

Reputable news agencies had reported a threat, said to have originated with Anonymous, to disrupt NYSE operations on October 10th in solidarity with the Occupy Wall Street movement. The Federal Bureau of Investigation (FBI) started looking into the matter. The news services also reported, somewhat less prominently, that Anonymous called the announcement a hoax; that placed all of us in the position of second-guessing a clandestine activist organization known to be a credible menace. Hackers collaborating to isolate the NYSE on a trading day seemed a plausible scenario.

But Monday, October 10, 2011 came, and went, and nothing happened.

This time 12 years ago, in the fourth quarter of 1999, financial services companies–indeed, most industries and many households–were feverishly preparing for the new year. It was widely feared that computers' clocks would be stymied by a calendar year starting with the number 2. Corporations formed interdepartmental Y2K committees to devise and test business continuity plans. But Sunday, January 1, 2000 came, and went, and nothing happened. Clocks ticked on, calendars rolled over, businesses reopened on schedule, and families started to consume their stores of canned goods and bottled water.

Fast forward. My office on the 20th floor of the Deutsche Bank building at 130 Liberty Street had a window facing north by northeast. The last time I enjoyed that view was Monday, September 10, 2001. However, my department was up and running in new quarters at Exchange Place, Jersey City, within days of the deadly Al Qaeda attack. Not all New York-based custodians resumed operations so quickly. My manager at the time had served on the bank's Y2K committee and took disaster preparedness seriously. She kept the business continuity plan current, and at her direction we periodically repaired to the contingency site for practice runs. Y2K proved a false alarm, but we regrouped and went back to work not long after 9/11. It was a lesson in managing operations I shall never forget.

There will probably be more hoaxes and, from time to time, there will be real catastrophes, whether they result from acts of God, acts of war, simple accidents, or some combination of causes. The fact that the October 10 DDoS was a non-event arguably makes it just a little more likely that the next reported threat will also be empty. But nothing beats good planning to mitigate operational risk.

# Reputational Risk
November 2, 2011

Reputational risk seems high these days, and I think I know why.

Basel II defines reputational risk as "the risk arising from negative perceptions on the part of customers, counterparties, shareholders, investors or regulators that can adversely affect a bank's ability to maintain existing, or establish new, business relationships and continued access to sources of funding (e.g., through the interbank or securitization markets)."[1] Unwieldy though it may be, this definition recognizes that reputational risk events belong to a chain of causes and effects.

Here's how it might go.

1. Doubts emerge about the viability of a firm's strategy or the strength of its internal controls.
2. Journalists hear the gossip and make telephone calls to investigate, thereby giving the rumors greater credibility and currency.
3. Investors start to withdraw funds.
4. Counterparties require more collateral.
5. Credit rating agencies downgrade the firm.
6. The firm privately attempts to reassure investors and creditors.
7. Withdrawals accelerate.
8. News services report on the firm's efforts to secure short-term funding.
9. The authorities take an interest in the firm's compliance with pertinent regulations.
10. In-depth feature stories start to appear....

The central mechanism is a "cascade of availability." In *Thinking, Fast and Slow*, Daniel Kahneman explains, "An availability cascade is a self-sustaining chain of events, which may start from media reports of a relatively minor event and lead up to public panic and large-scale government action."[2] We saw this progression with LTCM in 1998 and

---

[1] Basel Committee on Banking Supervision, "Enhancements to the Basel II Framework," July 2009, Section 47. Accessed August 6, 2012. http://www.bis.org/publ/bcbs157.pdf
[2] Daniel Kahneman, *Thinking, Fast and Slow* (Farrar, Strauss and Giroux, 2011), p. 142. Kahneman attributes the name, "the availability cascade," to Cass

Northern Rock in 2007. Lately we've been watching MF Global snowball through the media.

A few observations:

- Reputational risk—broadly defined as the risk of negative perceptions on the part of stakeholders—is not limited to ethical lapses such as a conflict of interest at the SEC or the falsification of documents at FINRA, nor to the kind of slippage in governance and process that allegedly enabled credit rating agencies to stamp questionable mortgage-backed securities as safe as houses.

- Reputational risk is typically entangled with other kinds of risk. For instance, it might result from a hapless business plan (strategic risk) or a failure of internal controls (operational risk) and result in a funding crisis (liquidity risk).

- Reputational risk doesn't merely mean embarrassment on the cocktail circuit; it is serious business with potentially devastating consequences. LTCM and Northern Rock were bailed out; MF Global has filed for bankruptcy. The SEC and FINRA may have impaired their political capital at a critical moment. U.S. and European regulatory authorities[3] are reconsidering the rules to which credit rating agencies are subject.

Reputational risk may be lower in firms which take professional ethics seriously, align the compensation structure with organizational values, and continually remind employees that the company's good name is in their keeping. But the complex of related risks must also be managed. For example, implementing a robust, evidence-based business planning process may diminish strategic risk. Ensuring that internal controls are well-designed and consistently applied tends to reduce operational risk. And monitoring asset-liability mismatches may attenuate funding liquidity risk. Every organization needs and deserves a risk management program that is sound, comprehensive, and embedded in its processes.

---

Sunstein and Timur Kuran.

[3] Huw Jones, "Rating Agencies Face Shake-Up Under EU Plan," Reuters, October 28, 2011. Accessed August 6, 2012. http://uk.reuters.com/article/2011/10/28/uk-eu-ratingsagencies-idUKTRE79R4PP20111028

So why does reputational risk seem elevated of late?

It's easy to come up with a coherent story. We've understood rumor since Vergil described it, but online news services and social media have increased the flow of information fantastically. Moreover, investors and regulators are more vigilant in the aftermath of the financial crisis. It makes sense that there would be more occurrences now than in the past....

But the *real* reason is that, indolent as I am, I didn't come up with an empirically grounded estimate of the baseline or normal incidence of reputational risk events; rather, I uncritically used what Tversky and Kahneman called the availability heuristic—"the process of judging frequency by 'the ease with which instances come to mind'"[4]—and reckoned the current rate is pretty high. This is, for me, a cautionary insight. I strongly recommend Kahneman's new book to anyone whose work requires critical thinking.

---

[4] Ibid., p. 129; Kahneman is paraphrasing the celebrated article he co-authored with Amos Tversky, "Judgment Under Uncertainty: Heuristics and Biases," which originally appeared in *Science* (1974) and is reprinted as Appendix A in *Thinking, Fast and Slow*.

# Cybersecurity
December 2, 2011

The Securities and Exchange Commission recently released CF Disclosure Guidance: Topic No. 2,[1] presenting the Division of Corporate Finance's views on registrants' obligations to disclose cybersecurity[2] risks and cyber events in regulatory filings and offering prospectuses.[3] The document is written for issuers rather than investment managers. Nonetheless, the underlying problems mentioned in Topic No. 2—the facts and circumstances that make disclosure necessary—are germane to buy-side operational risk management.

The SEC acknowledges that cyber incidents can be unintentional but focuses on deliberate attacks. One kind of assault on a firm requires social engineering skills rather than unauthorized access to the target system; such is an orchestrated denial-of-service campaign. In another kind of strike against a firm, insiders or third parties attempt to infiltrate a system in order to filch intellectual property, misappropriate sensitive information, corrupt data, or disrupt operations.

Topic No. 2 lists the potential consequences of attacks that achieve their objectives. Firms that fall victim may incur damages including the cost of remediation and stronger information security, lost revenues, litigation, and reputational harm affecting customer or investor confidence. Remediation costs may include system repairs, make-whole expenses, and incentives offered to maintain business relationships with customers or partners.

---

[1] U.S. Securities and Exchange Commission, "CF Disclosure Guidance: Topic No. 2, Cybersecurity," October 13, 2011. Accessed August 6, 2012. http://www.sec.gov/divisions/corpfin/guidance/cfguidance-topic2.htm#_ednref6

[2] The SEC uses the What Is definition: "Cybersecurity is the body of technologies, processes and practices designed to protect networks, computers, programs and data from attack, damage or unauthorized access." (CISOs may wish to request updated titles and higher compensation.) Accessed August 6, 2012. http://whatis.techtarget.com/definition/cybersecurity

[3] For instance, significant cybersecurity risks should be included among the risk factors described in accordance with Item 503(cd) of Regulation S-K and Item 3.D of Form 20-F.

To my knowledge, apart from maintaining excess capacity and a favorable public image, there's not much the firm can do to defend itself against distributed denial-of-service attacks. There *are* proactive measures the firm can take to improve the way it authenticates users' identities and, where applicable, authorizes online transactions. Risk managers and IT professionals at investment organizations might look to the banking and payment industries for advice because they have had to strengthen controls in an increasingly hostile environment. The Federal Financial Institutions Examination Council (FFIEC) published especially useful guidance this year under the prosaic title, "Supplement to *Authentication in an Internet Banking Environment*."[4]

The FFIEC calls for layered security, a set or series of controls which compensate for one another's weaknesses. "Layered security can substantially strengthen the overall security of Internet-based services and be effective in protecting sensitive customer information, preventing identity theft, and reducing account takeovers and the resulting financial losses." Minimally, a financial institution's layered security program will include measures to detect and respond to suspicious or anomalous activity and enhanced controls for systems administrators who have privileges to set up or change configurations and access permissions.

In addition to describing layered security requirements, the Supplement evaluates the effectiveness of certain authentication techniques. For example, simple device identification by means of cookies, usernames, and passwords is more vulnerable than complex techniques using one-time cookies and digital fingerprints that additionally take into account the customer's PC configuration, IP address, geo-location, and other factors. "Institutions should no longer consider simple device identification, as a primary control, to be an effective risk mitigation technique." Similarly, FFIEC recommends using several sophisticated "out-of-pocket" challenge questions which do not rely on information that is publicly available on social networking sites. "Although no challenge question method can mitigate all threats…the use of sophisticated questions as described above can be an effective component of a layered security program." FFIEC also defines minimal standards for a financial institution's customer awareness and education efforts.

---

[4] Federal Financial Institutions Examination Council, "Supplement to *Authentication in an Internet Banking Environment,"* June 22, 2011. Accessed August 6, 2012. http://www.ffiec.gov/pdf/Auth-ITS-Final%206-22-11%20%28FFIEC%20Formated%29.pdf

An appendix to the Supplement addresses malware threats such as keylogging, Man in the Middle (MIM), and Man in the Browser (MIB) attacks. Potential countermeasures include anti-malware software, transaction monitoring/anomaly detection software, "out-of-band" authentication techniques such as telephone calls to verify transactions, and the use of USB devices to enable secure links independently of the customer's operating system and applications. None of these methods offers absolute assurance, but incorporating one or more of them in a layered security program may increase the likelihood of preventing or detecting successful cyber attacks.

In my opinion, a firm with significant online exposures should include cyber attacks among the operational risks it manages. Depending upon the firm's internal and external contexts (including its access controls), it may, for example, be appropriate to model cyber events as a low frequency, high impact risk. The responsibility for cybersecurity should remain with the IT organization—they alone have the requisite technological expertise—but, given that the firm's response affects customers' perceptions and involves legal as well as operational issues, it is important for technology professionals to confer with other stakeholders.

# The Idea of Europe
December 29, 2011

With illness in the family, this month has gone by in a strange loop of reading, caregiving, writing, and housekeeping. Christmas was a quiet interlude, as it should be, and we may celebrate New Year's Eve merely by giving Wyatt the "speak" command at midnight. (He's an accomplished hound dog with a strong, vibrant voice.) At odd moments, these weeks passing, I've thought about money, time, and the menace of European disunity.

The Czech philosopher Jan Patočka said, "Europe is a concept which rests upon spiritual foundations."[1] In his understanding, the "specificity" of European life is the heritage of caring for the soul[2] and the primacy of intuition, the unflinching "look into things,"[3] which "accords a determinant role to the intellectual view in all the essential questions of life, whether it has to do with knowledge or practical affairs."[4] Patočka believed that this spiritual and rational Europe—his conception was "neither geographical nor purely political"[5]—had already perished by the early 1970s. What most worried him was "the destiny of Europe beyond nihilism,"[6] and he called for a certain "solidarity of the shaken"[7] to overcome differences without war.

Patočka did not survive to learn about the Maastricht Treaty, participate in the Velvet Revolution, witness the new Czech Republic's entry into the E.U., or travel and put a euro in his pocket. Regrettably, in a stressful economic and political environment, bankers are now planning for a possible disintegration of the eurozone. A breakup could prove disastrous for the global banking system and capital markets.

---

[1] Jan Patočka, *Platon et l'Europe*, trad. du tchèque par. E. Abrams (Éditions Verdier, 1983), 191.
[2] *Ibid.*, 79 and 117.
[3] *Ibid.*, 98-99, 159, and 235.
[4] Jan Patočka, "L'Europe et l'héritage européen jusqu'à la fin du XIX<sup>e</sup> siècle," in *Essais hérétiques sur la philosophie de l'histoire*, trad. du tchèque par. E. Abrams; Préface de Paul Ricoeur; Postface par Roman Jakobson (Éditions Verdier, 1999), 110. Patočka attributes the concept and phrasing to Edmund Husserl.
[5] *Platon et l'Europe, op.cit.*, 191.
[6] Paul Ricoeur, Préface, *Essais hérétiques sur la philosophie de l'histoire, op. cit.*, 15.
[7] Jan Patočka, "Les guerres du XX<sup>e</sup> siècle et le XX<sup>e</sup> siècle en tant que guerre," in *Essais hérétiques sur la philosophie de l'histoire, op. cit.*, 167.

Determining the relative value of putative national currencies is, nonetheless, a fascinating theoretical problem. Interest rates are observable, and it is to be hoped that *The Economist* will contribute empirical data on purchasing power by recompiling the Big Mac Index[8] and publishing local prices within the euro area. In the interim, hedge fund managers are undoubtedly eager to test their quantitative valuation models against the banks' in actual foreign exchange trades. Should they come back, the French, Belgian, and Luxembourgeois francs, the lira, Deutschemark, peseta, and drachma, all the former currencies of the 17 euro nations will quickly find their market level.

Foreign exchange rates can be mathematically modeled in terms of interest-rate and purchasing-power parity, but money, like thought itself, has a biological substratum. As a store of value and a medium of exchange, it is the principal means by which we convert physical and mental effort into life-sustaining or death-postponing resources. Money is, moreover, fraught with symbolic value; in the social and corporate world, it constitutes the primary basis for competitive scorekeeping.

But money is also, and essentially, time; work is a way of providing not only for today but also for the future. Had my spendthrift generation borrowed less, fiercely prevented wants from becoming needs, and saved more, many of my contemporaries would be free to live less strenuously and use their remaining time on earth however they wish. Throughout our working lives, far too many of us—at least in the U.S.—grievously miscalculated the present value of money and the future value of time.

Patočka asked, "Is there, in what one could call the European heritage, something capable of finding credence among us, too, capable of working for us, too, of working on us in such a way as to make us conceive of new hopes [and] not despair of the future, without our abandoning ourselves to illusory dreams or underestimating the hardness and seriousness of our situation?"[9]

In the new year, let's carve out time to care for our souls.

---

[8] *The Economist*, "Currency Comparisons, To Go," July 28, 2011. Accessed August 6, 2012. http://www.economist.com/blogs/dailychart/2011/07/big-mac-index

[9] Jan Patočka, *Platon et l'Europe, op.cit.*, 19-20.

## Intraday Liquidity Risk
February 12, 2012

Early in my career, when I worked in the treasurer's department at a large multiline insurer, our principal concerns were to stay fully invested in short-term instruments while reaching day-weighted compensating balance targets and avoiding daylight overdrafts. Given the rise of the shadow banking system,[1] and the corollary need to monitor counterparty exposures and collateral positions, liquidity management is far more challenging today. Financial institutions must actively control liquidity— and manage collateral—across and within legal entities, business lines, and currencies. Emerging regulatory requirements augment the pressure to strengthen risk management policies, streamline processes, integrate systems, and make sense of new information as it arrives.

For context, risk managers distinguish between *transaction* and *funding* liquidity. Malz introduces the former as "the property of an asset being easy to exchange for other assets" and the latter as "the ability to finance assets continuously at an acceptable borrowing rate."[2] Transaction liquidity has to do with asset valuations; funding liquidity is partially dependent upon the creditworthiness of the firm and its counterparties; cash flow forecasting and collateral monitoring involve people, processes, and systems. Accordingly, I would situate a financial institution's liquidity risk at the intersection of its market, credit, and operational risks.

From the perspective of central banks and regulators, liquidity is a key factor in appraising a financial institution's contribution to systemic risk.[3]

---

[1] The Financial Stability Board, an international coordinating body, broadly defines the shadow banking system as "the system of credit intermediation that involves entities and activities outside the regular banking system" and estimates that in 2010 its assets totaled $60 trillion, representing 25% to 30% of the total financial system. See *Shadow Banking: Strengthening Oversight and Regulation. Recommendations of the Financial Stability Board*, October 27, 2011. Accessed August 6, 2012. http://www.financialstabilityboard.org/publications/r_111027a.pdf

[2] Allan M. Malz, *Financial Risk Management: Models, History, and Institutions* (Wiley, 2011), 421. This work should figure prominently in every risk manager's library.

[3] In the U.S., for example, the Financial Stability Oversight Council proposes to use the following six factors in the designation of non-bank financial institutions as "systemically important": (1) size, (2) interconnectedness, (3) substitutability, (4) leverage, (5) liquidity risk and maturity mismatch, and (6) existing regulatory scrutiny.

Recognizing how quickly financial systems can seize, regulatory authorities are turning their attention to intraday liquidity risk.

- *Principles for Sound Liquidity Risk Management and Supervision*, issued by the Basel Committee on Banking Supervision (BCBS) in September 2008, explicitly states in Principle 8 that banks should actively manage their intraday liquidity positions and risks.[4]

- In the United Kingdom, the *Prudential Sourcebook for Banks, Building Societies and Investment Firms* (BIPRU) contains Rule 12.3.4, stating in pertinent part, "A firm must have in place robust strategies, policies, processes and systems that enable it to identify, measure, manage and monitor liquidity risk over an appropriate set of time horizons, including intra-day, so as to ensure that it maintains adequate levels of liquidity buffers."[5]

- In the United States, Section 24 of the *Interagency Policy Statement on Funding and Liquidity Risk Management* states that "institutions with material payment, settlement and clearing activities should actively manage their intraday liquidity positions and risks to meet payment and settlement obligations on a timely basis under both normal and stressed conditions."[6] U.S. regulators will give further attention to rulemaking on liquidity this year (2012).[7]

---

[4] Basel Committee on Banking Supervision (BCBS), *Principles for Sound Liquidity Risk Management and Supervision*, September 2008. Accessed August 6, 2012. http://www.bis.org/publ/bcbs144.pdf Admittedly, BCBS has not yet taken regulatory action on the basis of this principle. For example, liquidity coverage ratio (LCR) stress testing does not cover intraday liquidity needs. However, BCBS is "currently reviewing if and how intraday liquidity risk should be addressed." BCBS, *Basel III: International Framework for Liquidity Risk, Risk Measurement, Standards, and Monitoring*, December 2010, 31. Accessed August 6, 2012. http://www.bis.org/publ/bcbs188.pdf In addition, the foundational Basel III document says, "One area in particular where more work on monitoring tools will be conducted relates to intraday liquidity risk." BCBS, *Basel III: A Global Regulatory Framework for More Resilient Banks and Banking Systems*, December 2010, 43. Accessed August 6, 2012. http://www.bis.org/publ/bcbs189.pdf
[5] Financial Services Authority, *Prudential Sourcebook for Banks, Building Societies and Investment Firms*, Rule 12.3, Liquidity Risk Management. Accessed August 6, 2012. http://fsahandbook.info/FSA/html/handbook/BIPRU/12/3. Note that the FSA's Policy Statement 09/16, *Strengthening Liquidity Standards*, October 2009, sets out the new liquidity regime in full. Accessed August 6, 2012. http://www.fsa.gov.uk/pubs/policy/ps09_16.pdf
[6] Office of the Comptroller of the Currency, Federal Reserve System, Federal

All financial intermediaries (not only depository institutions) are vulnerable to fast-breaking liquidity risk events. The Lehman Brothers case is an object lesson. In the period immediately preceding its bankruptcy, Lehman's correspondent banks changed the terms under which they were willing to provide intraday liquidity. Meeting their rising demands for pre-funding and collateralization depleted Lehman's pool of unencumbered liquid assets to the point where the firm could not support projected outflows.[8] Similarly, MF Global was overwhelmed by customers' withdrawals and counterparties' margin calls in the firm's last days. The trustee's February 6, 2012 status report charts the day-by-day increase in margin calls.[9]

As Lehman and MF Global demonstrate, firms that are perceived to be in distress (a reputational risk event) face a hard, fast liquidity squeeze on both sides: depositors withdraw assets just as funding becomes scarcer and more expensive. But even strong firms with ample liquidity buffers may have to act quickly if, for instance, an operational shock affects a

---

Deposit Insurance Corporation, Office of Thrift Supervision, and National Credit Union Administration, *Interagency Policy Statement on Funding and Liquidity Risk Management,* March 2010, Section 24. Accessed August 6, 2012. http://www.gpo.gov/fdsys/pkg/FR-2010-03-22/pdf/2010-6137.pdf
[7] Speaking as Chair of the Financial Stability Oversight Council, Timothy Geithner said, "In 2012, we will focus on defining the new liquidity standards...." U.S. Department of the Treasury, "Remarks by Treasury Secretary Tim Geithner on the State of Financial Reform," February 2, 2012. Accessed August 6, 2012. http://www.treasury.gov/press-center/press-releases/Pages/tg1408.aspx#.TzGj90GLcOY.email
A press release from the Federal Reserve Board on December 20, 2011, indicates that the liquidity requirements will be implemented in two phases. "Federal Reserve Board proposes steps to strengthen regulation and supervision of large bank holding companies and systemically important nonbank financial firms." Accessed August 6, 2012.
http://www.federalreserve.gov/newsevents/press/bcreg/20111220a.htm
[8] Alan Ball, Edward Denbee, Mark Manning and Anne Wetherilt, Bank of England Financial Stability Paper No. 11, *Intraday Liquidity: Risk and Regulation,* June 2011, 12-13. An excellent resource, this paper explains intraday liquidity risk in the context of large-value payment and settlement systems. Accessed August 6, 2012.
http://www.bankofengland.co.uk/publications/Documents/fsr/fs_paper11.pdf
[9] See "Trustee Press Release: February 6, 2012" and "Slides: February 6, 2012," both regarding a status update on the investigation conducted by James W. Giddens, Trustee for the SIPA Liquidation of MF Global Inc. Accessed August 6, 2012. http://dm.epiq11.com/MFG/Project

major counterparty or a change in market conditions suddenly throws a particular asset class into disfavor. In a crisis, treasurers can mobilize resources efficiently only if they have accurate, up-to-date, and meaningfully integrated information about the firm's cash, near-cash, and collateral positions.

# Risk and Uncertainty
May 9, 2012

More than 90 years ago Frank H. Knight famously distinguished between measurable, insurable risk and unmeasurable, non-insurable uncertainty. Frequently cited in the risk management literature of today, the distinction seems useful—I'll have more to say about that—but Knight himself was an economist (he was, in fact, one of the founders of the Chicago school of economics), not a businessman and certainly not a risk manager. It is interesting to explore his motivation for emphasizing the difference between risk and uncertainty as he used the terms. Knight was highly critical of his discipline's traditionally simplistic view of human psychology and behavior, and he would, I think, approve of our squandering a few minutes this way. "Man's chief interest in life," he wrote, "is after all to find life interesting, which is a very different thing from merely consuming a maximum amount of wealth."[1]

Knight's concern in *Risk, Uncertainty, and Profit* (1921) was to resolve the problem of profit in distributive theory. In the perfect competition of classical economic thought, the values of goods and the costs of productive factors tend to reach an equilibrium point at which there is neither profit nor loss. In other words, "the tendency is toward a remainderless distribution of products among the agencies contributing to their production."[2] In *actual* competition, however, there are usually profits and losses. It is in the context of explaining "pure profit," defined as "a distributive share different from the returns to the productive services of land, labor, and capital,"[3] that Knight distinguishes between risk and uncertainty. "The only 'risk' which leads to a profit," he wrote, "is a unique uncertainty resulting from an exercise of ultimate [entrepreneurial] responsibility which in its very nature cannot be insured nor capitalized nor salaried."[4]

Pure profit is bound up with economic change, but change, in itself, does not create potentially profitable opportunities. Rather, change is "a necessary condition of our being ignorant of the future," and that very ignorance—that uncertainty—accounts for the possibility of profit, understood, again, not as net income but as the residual share after

---

[1] Frank H. Knight, *Risk, Uncertainty, and Profit* (Boston and New York: Houghton Mifflin Company, 1921), Kindle version, Part III, Chapter XII.
[2] *Ibid.*, Part I, Chapter I.
[3] *Ibid.*, Part I, Chapter I, footnote 12.
[4] *Ibid.*, Part III, Chapter X.

imputed rents, wages, and interest. "Dynamic change gives rise to a peculiar form of income only in so far as the changes and their consequences are unpredictable in character." In fact, any surprise, including the failure of expected changes to materialize, may induce uncertainty. "It is not dynamic change, nor any change, as such, which causes profit, but the divergence of actual conditions from those which have been expected and on the basis of which business arrangements have been made."[5]

In addition to the uncertainty occasioned by rapid economic change, there is the uncertainty associated with differences in business ability, differences, Schumpeter remarks, that are "are much more obviously relevant to the explanation of profits and losses in conditions of rapid economic change than they would be otherwise."[6] Knight demonstrates at considerable length that the functions of making decisions and taking responsibility for them are inseparable even in large shareholder-owned corporations with hired managers. The owners whose capital is at risk have "indirect knowledge" and exercise "indirect control" by selecting managers in whom they have confidence. "In the field of organization, the knowledge on which what we call responsible control depends is not knowledge of situations and problems and of means for effecting changes, but is knowledge of other men's knowledge of these things." In other words, the owners make judgments about the managers' powers of judgment. "Like a large proportion of the practical problems of business life, as of all life, this one of selecting human capacities for dealing with unforeseeable situations involves paradox and apparent theoretical impossibility of solution. But like a host of impossible things in life, it is constantly being done."[7]

In summary, then, profit arises not from known risks but "out of the inherent, absolute unpredictability of things, out of the sheer brute fact that the results of human activity cannot be anticipated and then only in so far as even a probability calculation in regard to them is impossible and meaningless."[8] Not from calculable risks but from uncertainty about the future and about our capacity to evaluate others' abilities, our "faculty of judging faculties," especially in times of change. It is, Knight argues, "uncertainty in this sense which explains profit in the proper use

---

[5] *Ibid.*, Part I, Chapter II.
[6] Joseph A. Schumpeter, *History of Economic Analysis* (New York: Oxford University Press, 1954), p. 894.
[7] Frank H. Knight, *op. cit.*, Part III, Chapter X.
[8] *Ibid.*, Part III, Chapter X.

of the term, the sense toward which economic usage has been groping, that of a pure residual income, unimputable by the mechanism of competition to any agent concerned in its creation."[9]

It is hard to convey the richness of Knight's thought in a short piece like this. Not impossible—Peter L. Bernstein explained Knight's concepts of risk and uncertainty admirably[10]—but, nonetheless, hard. In addition to elaborating the profit theory recapitulated here, *Risk, Uncertainty, and Profit* presents, almost incidentally, a view on the relationship between theoretical and empirical economics, a theory of knowledge, a discussion of the social basis for private property, and observations on the psychology of risk-taking, the impact of technological advances, and the nature of leadership, among many other things. But 90 years, while not a long time in the history of thought, is an abyss when we consider the practice of risk management. What meaning does Knight's distinction between risk and uncertainty have for risk professionals now?

High-frequency, low-impact risk events, such as credit card fraud, retail pilferage, and grocery coupon redemptions, can be fully modeled and confidently reflected in product pricing. Low-frequency, high-impact risk events, such as operational failures, can be modeled only with difficulty, and the value of stochastic forecasts is conditional on the analyst's skill in identifying dependencies and estimating probabilities. And some risk events cannot be modeled because they are unimaginable; such might be the sudden appearance of a radically new substitute that irremediably changes the competitive environment. Risk and uncertainty, as Knight defined them, are the extremes of a continuum. When we attempt to quantify the impact of risk events, it is salutary to ask ourselves where a given scenario falls on that gamut.

---

[9] *Loc. cit.*

[10] Peter L. Bernstein, *Against the Gods: The Remarkable Story of Risk* (John Wiley & Sons, 1996), pp. 218-223.

## Messmore's Duration of Surplus
May 21, 2012

Sooner or later interest rates will rise and the market value of fixed-income portfolios will fall. This is not necessarily bad news: it's not *news* because, as **Figure 1** illustrates, rates have been low for years, and it's not necessarily *bad*—or at least as not as bad as it may seem—for financial institutions whose assets and liabilities are interest-rate sensitive. The concept of surplus duration,[1] introduced by Thomas E. Messmore in 1990,[2] offers an intriguing approach to estimating the impact of interest rate changes on institutions that are broadly engaged in asset-liability management.

Messmore defines the duration of surplus as the term $D_S$ that satisfies the equation:

$$(A \times D_A) - (L \times D_L) = S \times D_S$$

Equation 1

where A is the fair value of assets, $D_A$ is the duration of assets, L is the present value of liabilities, $D_L$ is the duration of liabilities, and S is surplus, i.e., the difference between assets and liabilities.

On the basis of this definition, Messmore observes that the duration of surplus equals the duration of liabilities plus leverage times mismatch (Equation 2) or the duration of liabilities plus mismatch divided by the surplus cushion (Equation 3).

$$D_S = D_L + \frac{A}{S}(D_A - D_L)$$

Equation 2

$$D_S = D_L + \frac{D_A - D_L}{\dfrac{S}{A}}$$

Equation 3

---

[1] For the purpose of this discussion, duration may be described as the approximate percentage change in the price of a bond for a 1% change in interest rates.

[2] Thomas E. Messmore, "The Duration of Surplus," *The Journal of Portfolio Management*, Vol. 16, No. 2 (Winter, 1990), 19-22.

**Figure 1.** Intermediate Treasury Rates

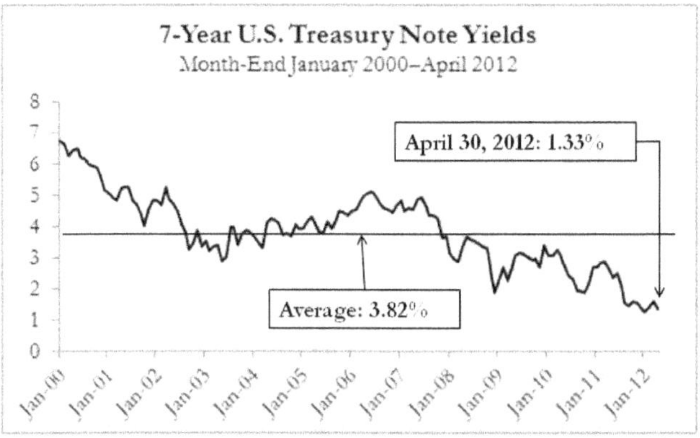

Data Source: U.S. Department of the Treasury—Daily Yield Curve Rates

Without attempting to relay all of Messmore's insights, we can use the Rivanna District Retirement System (RDRS), a fictitious public defined-benefit pension plan, to explore some implications for tactical market risk management in financial institutions. RDRS provides retirement benefits to District employees, including administrative staff, teachers, sheriffs, and firefighters. The system has assets fair-valued at $51.3 million, including debt securities of $19.7 million representing 38% of total assets. The debt securities' asset-weighted average effective duration is 3.73. RDSS has actuarial accrued liabilities present-valued at $72.8 million; therefore, it is about 70.5% funded. On the basis of a very rough estimate, the duration of the system's liabilities is 13.13.

Let's first consider the potential impact of a 100-basis point increase in interest rates on the system's debt and liability portfolios. The fair value of the debt portfolio would decline by approximately 3.73%, or $735,000, from $19.7 million to about $19.0 million, while the present value of the liabilities would decline by approximately 13.1%, or $9.6 million, from $72.8 million to about $63.2 million. The net effect is to reduce the surplus deficit by roughly $8.8 million. Thus, assuming the system's non-debt assets are unaffected, the increase in interest rates would boost the funded status to approximately 80%. That would, indeed, be good news for Rivanna District taxpayers.

In the absence of duration estimates for the system's other investments, we might further assume that the average fixed-income asset duration of 3.73 applies to total assets. In that case, for RDRS as a whole:

- Leverage $(A/S)$ = –2.39
- Surplus Cushion (S/A) = –0.42
- Mismatch $(D_A– D_L)$ = –9.4
- Duration of surplus $(D_S)$ = 35.5

And, mathematically, a 100-basis point increase in interest rates would raise the system's funded status to roughly 78%. Were rates to rise, then, RDRS would benefit from both components of surplus duration: its negative cushion and its short mismatch.

To be clear, in a more usual interest rate environment, RDRS's volatile negative surplus would make it dicey to follow the seemingly risk-averse policy of holding the duration of assets substantially shorter than the duration of liabilities. But these are not normal times. Interest rates have little room to fall and ample room to rise.

## Managing Central Counterparty Credit Risk
August 1, 2012

In 1957 Heinz Haber famously demonstrated the dynamics of nuclear fission by tossing a ping-pong ball into a field of spring-loaded mousetraps, each of which was set to launch two ping-pong balls. The first ball, representing a neutron bullet, tripped a mousetrap, representing the nucleus of an atom of uranium; the mousetrap shot out two neutron-balls; they hit two more mousetrap-nuclei; and a lively chain reaction ensued. Haber gave his memorable demonstration in "Our Friend the Atom," an episode of Disneyland that promoted nuclear energy as a power source.

If we were to take Haber's uncontrolled chain reaction as a simplified image of a systemic risk event in the world of bilateral OTC derivative contracts, then, without pushing the analogy too far, a nuclear power plant might stand for a central counterparty: a socially beneficial utility that contains risk in the flow of financial transactions. The new danger, as everyone knows, is the risk of the ultimate low-frequency, high-impact event—a core meltdown. In a CCP, a catastrophic failure might result, for example, from defaults that exceed the utility's financial resources.[1]

In short, CCPs have to manage their credit risk exposure to participants, and vice-versa.

Regulators are well aware of the fact that, while CCPs mitigate systemic or chain-reaction risk, they are in themselves a source of highly concentrated and potentially explosive risk. Accordingly, regulatory authorities in various jurisdictions have proposed or enacted tighter prudential standards for CCP risk management. Most recently, the Canadian Securities Administrators (CSA) released a consultation paper on central counterparty clearing for over-the-counter (OTC) derivatives,[2]

---

[1] It should be evident that credit risk, the narrow topic of this blog entry, is not the only kind of risk that CCPs have to manage. Other types notably include legal, liquidity, and operational risk.

[2] Canadian Securities Administrators, CP 91-406, "Derivatives: OTC Central Counterparty Clearing," June 20, 2012. Accessed August 7, 2012. http://www.bcsc.bc.ca/uploadedFiles/securitieslaw/policy9/91-406_June_20_2012.pdf. As we have come to expect, this consultation paper provides a cogent summary of the issues and a useful update on pertinent international regulatory developments.

and the Board of Governors of the U.S. Federal Reserve System issued a final rule, Regulation HH, on financial market utilities.[3] Both the CSA's proposal and the Fed's final rule set out standards governing CCPs' internal risk management capabilities.[4] For example, among many other requirements, Regulation HH includes certain provisions specifically related to a CCP's management of credit risk. Without venturing to comment on the overall adequacy of Regulation HH, I would mention, in particular, the credit-related provisions paraphrased here:

- The CCP must maintain sufficient financial resources to withstand, at a minimum, a default by the participant to which it

---

[3] Federal Reserve System, "Financial Market Utilities," July 27, 2012. Accessed August 7, 2012.
http://www.federalreserve.gov/newsevents/press/bcreg/bcreg20120730a1.pdf.
Regulation HH, which becomes effective September 14, 2012, applies to financial market utilities (FMUs), including payment systems, central securities depositories, and central counterparties, that are designated systemically important by the Financial Stability Oversight Council (FSOC). The present blog piece considers only the risk-management standards applicable to central counterparties (CCPs). On July 18, 2012, the FSOC designated eight FMSs as systematically important:: Clearing House Interbank Payments System; Chicago Mercantile Exchange; Depository Trust Company; Fixed Income Clearing Corporation; ICE Clear Credit LLC; National Securities Clearing Corporation; and The Options Clearing Corporation. U.S. Department of the Treasury, "Financial Stability Oversight Council Makes First Designations in Effort to Protect Against Future Financial Crises," July 18, 2012. Accessed August 7, 2012. http://www.treasury.gov/press-center/press-releases/Pages/tg1645.aspx
[4] For international context, in April, 2012, the Committee on Payment and Settlement Systems (CPSS) and the Technical Committee of International Organization of Securities Commissions (IOSCO) presented updated risk management standards, reflecting in part the lessons of the financial crisis, in their joint publication, *Principles for Financial Market Infrastructure*. Accessed August 7, 2012. http://www.bis.org/publ/cpss101a.pdf. The CSA states that Consultation Paper 91-406 "incorporates and requires compliance with CPSS-IOSCO's *Principles for Financial Market Infrastructures* (the 'FMI Principles') particularly in the areas of governance, CCPs' fees, access, risk management and systems and technology." The Board of Governors of the Federal Reserve thought it "more suitable" to use principles and recommendations developed by CPSS and IOSCO between 2001 and 2004 as the basis for the initial risk management standards defined in Regulation HH. "[The] Board anticipates that it will review the new international standards, consult with other appropriate agencies and the Council, and seek public comment on the adoption of revised standards for designated FMUs based on the new international standards."

has the largest exposure[5] in extreme but plausible market conditions. [Section 234.4(a)(18).]

- While permitting fair and open access, the CCP must require participants, on an ongoing basis, to have sufficient financial resources and operational capacity to meet their obligations. [Section 234.4(a)(2).]

- The CCP must measure its credit exposures to its participants at least once a day, and limit its exposures to losses from participants' defaults in normal market conditions so that its operations would not be disrupted and non-defaulting participants would not be exposed to unforeseeable or uncontrollable losses. [Section 234.4(a)(16).]

- The CCP must use risk-based models and parameters to set margin requirements limiting its credit exposures to participants in normal market conditions; review and back-test models and parameters at least quarterly; and provide for annual model validation by a qualified person who neither performs other model-related functions nor reports to someone who does. [Section 234.4(a)(17).]

These are, to be sure, minimum requirements, and the Federal Reserve asserts the right to raise them in specific cases. Regulation HH states, "The Board, by order, may apply heightened risk-management standards to a particular designated financial market utility in accordance with the risks presented by that designated financial market utility."[6] [Section 234.4(b).]

Finally, as a matter of sound risk management, clearing members should also be concerned to manage their own exposures to the CCPs in which

---

[5] In the 2012 CPSS-IOSCO document, Principle 4 states, "In addition, a CCP that is involved in activities with a more-complex risk profile or that is systemically important in multiple jurisdictions should maintain additional financial resources sufficient to cover a wide range of potential stress scenarios that should include, but not be limited to, the default of the *two* participants and their affiliates that would potentially cause the largest aggregate credit exposure to the CCP in extreme but plausible market conditions." (Emphasis added.)

[6] Admittedly, the same section also states that the Board may waive the application of one or more standards to a particular designated financial market utility.

they participate. Matthias Arnsdorf has developed a methodology for quantifying participants' exposures to the loss of their initial margin and their contribution to the mutualized collateral pool that constitutes the CCP's guarantee fund.[7] Arnsdorf's approach models the CCP's risk waterfall—the order in which financial resources are tapped—and uses the fact that initial margin levels are risk-based to estimate the distribution of losses across clearing members. Because a given participant's overall exposure equals the sum of its exposures to other clearing members, its CCP-related credit risk can be hedged with a set of single-name credit default swaps. Given the regulators' interest in channeling OTC derivatives to CCPs, Arnsdorf's work is a significant contribution to the practice of risk management.

---

[7] Matthias Arnsdorf, "Quantification of Central Counterparty Risk," *Journal of Risk Management in Financial Institutions*, Vol. 5 No. 3 (April-June 2012), 273-287. This number of the *Journal* is a special issue on "Systemic Connectedness: Measuring and Managing Counterparty Risk."

## The Biology of Financial Crises
August 26, 2012

Writing in *Nature* in 1879, W. Stanley Jevons braved "inconsiderate ridicule" to advance his theory that business cycles are indirectly but ultimately caused by solar activity.[1] In the 1960s Edgar Lawrence Smith and Charles J. Collins took up a similar idea, gracing the pages of the *Financial Analysts Journal* with articles postulating that sunspots affect the stock market. Without quite coming out and saying it, Smith intimated that the sunspot minimum predicted for 1964 might very well depress equity prices.[2] Collins reviewed equity index levels over the eight complete sunspot cycles observed between 1871 and 1964, and soberly pointed out "an apparent relationship between a recurrent phase of each sunspot cycle and an important stock market peak."[3]

Admittedly, a solar storm on the order of the Carrington event would probably disable the electrical grid for months, devastating the economy and the capital markets. But the pseudoscientific notion that stock market cycles are predictably influenced by sunspots verges on lunacy.[4]

---

[1] Specifically, Jevons hypothesized that economic collapses often occur at intervals of ten or eleven years because of "the cessation of demand from India and China occasioned by the failure of harvests there, ultimately due to changes of solar activity." He acknowledged that "they who theorize about the relations of sun-spots, rainfall, famines, and commercial crises are supposed to be jesting, or at best romancing," but, he wrote, "I beg leave to affirm that I never was more in earnest." W. Stanley Jevons, "Sun-Spots and Commercial Crises," Nature 19, 588-590. doi:10.1038/019588a0. Accessed August 25, 2012. http://www.nature.com/nature/journal/v19/n495/pdf/019588a0.pdf

[2] Edgar Lawrence Smith, "Low Tide in Sunspots—1964," *Financial Analysts Journal*, July/August 1963, Vol. 19, No. 4: 91-92. doi: 10.2469/faj.v19.n4.91. In fact, the Dow Jones Industrial Average rose 14.6% from 762.95 on December 31, 1963 to 874.13 a year later; imagine how high it might have gone had more sunspots been observed. (Source: Dow Jones Averages. Accessed August 25, 2012. https://www.djaverages.com/) On the testimony of Collins, cited below, Smith was not as reticent elsewhere: "...Edgar Lawrence Smith has been one of the more prominent protagonists in the further development of sunspot-economic theory." Collins mentions in particular two of Smith's publications, *Tides in the Affairs of Men* (1939) and *Common Stocks and Business Cycles* (1959).

[3] Charles J. Collins, "An Inquiry into the Effect of Sunspot Activity on the Stock Market," *Financial Analysts Journal*, November/December 1965, Vol. 21, No. 6: 45-56. doi: 10.2469/faj.v21.n6.45.

[4] To be sure, the idea that phases of the moon affect the behavior of sensitive individuals is also delusional. Scott O. Lilienfeld and Hal Arkowitz state that

John Coates, formerly a derivatives trader and now a senior research fellow in neuroscience and finance at Cambridge, has a better idea, one that's *not* daft. In *The Hour Between Dog and Wolf*, he hypothesizes that steroid hormones tend to amplify market swings. Given that most traders are young men,[5] testosterone levels are likely to spike and stay high in bull markets, leading to ebullient self-confidence and irrational risk-taking; and in bear markets cortisol levels are apt to rise, eventuating in profound self-doubt and unreasoning risk aversion. "Steroid hormones building up in the bodies of traders and investors may thus shift risk preferences systematically across the business cycle, destabilizing it."[6]

In the interest of respectability, I will have little to say about testosterone.[7] The subject is principally cortisol, "the molecule of irrational pessimism,"[8] a primary hormone of the stress response.

Short-term infusions of cortisol are bracing, but an elevated level over an extended period provokes "feelings of anxiety, a selective recall of disturbing memories and a tendency to find danger where none exists."[9] Cortisol secretions are produced most abundantly in situations characterized by novelty, uncertainty, and uncontrollability[10]—the very conditions traders and investors experience when markets collapse. Persistently high cortisol is physically and psychologically damaging. It tends to make us continually, even obsessively, revisit bad memories, falling into a mental pattern that keeps stress hormones in circulation and contributes over time to pathological risk aversion, depression, viral

---

there is no scientific evidence for the lunar lunacy effect and seek alternate explanations for this myth in "Lunacy and the Full Moon," *Scientific American Mind*, February 9, 2009. Accessed August 25, 2012.
https://www.scientificamerican.com/article.cfm?id=lunacy-and-the-full-moon
[5] Coates asserts, "Women make up at most 5 percent of the traders in the financial world," but does not back up the estimate. *The Hour Between Dog and Wolf: Risk Taking, Gut Feelings, and the Biology of Boom and Bust* (New York: The Penguin Press, 2012), Kindle edition, 271.
[6] *Ibid.*, 30.
[7] Coates acknowledges, "It can be difficult to view testosterone as…a subject fit for serious scientific and medical research, because it comes shrouded in myth and cliché. The mere mention of the word seems enough to dispel any air of scientific objectivity." *Ibid.*, 163-164.
[8] *Ibid.*, 29, 234.
[9] *Ibid.*, 29.
[10] *Ibid.*, 217.

infections, gastric ulcers, abdominal fat deposits—"A year into the financial crisis, the testosterone-ripped iron men of the bull market start to look decidedly puffy"[11]—and high blood pressure.[12]

The adverse health effects are serious—hypertension is associated with heart attacks and strokes—but from the perspective of central bank policy the key factor is the paralyzing risk aversion of what soon becomes "a clinical population." Coates argues, "Once stress in the financial world has reached this pathological state, governments must step in, as they did in 2008-9, and do the job that traders can no longer perform—buy risky assets, reduce credit risk, lead the traders, now reduced to a shell-shocked state, out of the slough of despond."[13]

Coates also comes forward with ideas for attenuating the biochemical swings. A bank's management might, for instance, mitigate the testosterone feedback effect by setting fixed risk limits rather than raising the ceiling for traders who are on a winning streak, and compensating them on the basis of their results over a market cycle. Management might additionally bring more women and older men to the trading desk; stabilize traders' careers by hiring fewer and making a long-term commitment to them; and build on-site gyms, ideally staffed with personal trainers, physiologists, and medical doctors.[14] Most intriguing is his suggestion that mental toughening regimes, developed on the model of sports science, might reduce traders' vulnerability to chronic stress.[15]

Jevons wrote, "The history of many bubbles shows that there is no proportion between the stimulating cause and the height of folly to which the inflation of credit and prices may be carried. A mania is, in short, a kind of explosion of commercial folly followed by the natural collapse."[16] Coates teaches us that the stimulating cause is not in the stars but in ourselves—not in the solar system but in our bloodstream. *The Hour Between Dog and Wolf* is a fascinating book with an important message.

---

[11] *Ibid.*, 232.
[12] Coates lists these afflictions on pages 3-4.
[13] *Ibid.*,229-230.
[14] Coates, *op. cit.*, 265.
[15] *Ibid.*, 241-242.
[16] W. Stanley Jevons, *op. cit.*, 590.

# Part Five: Performance Measurement and Client Reporting

# Anatomy of a Calamity, Stage 5: "Serenity"

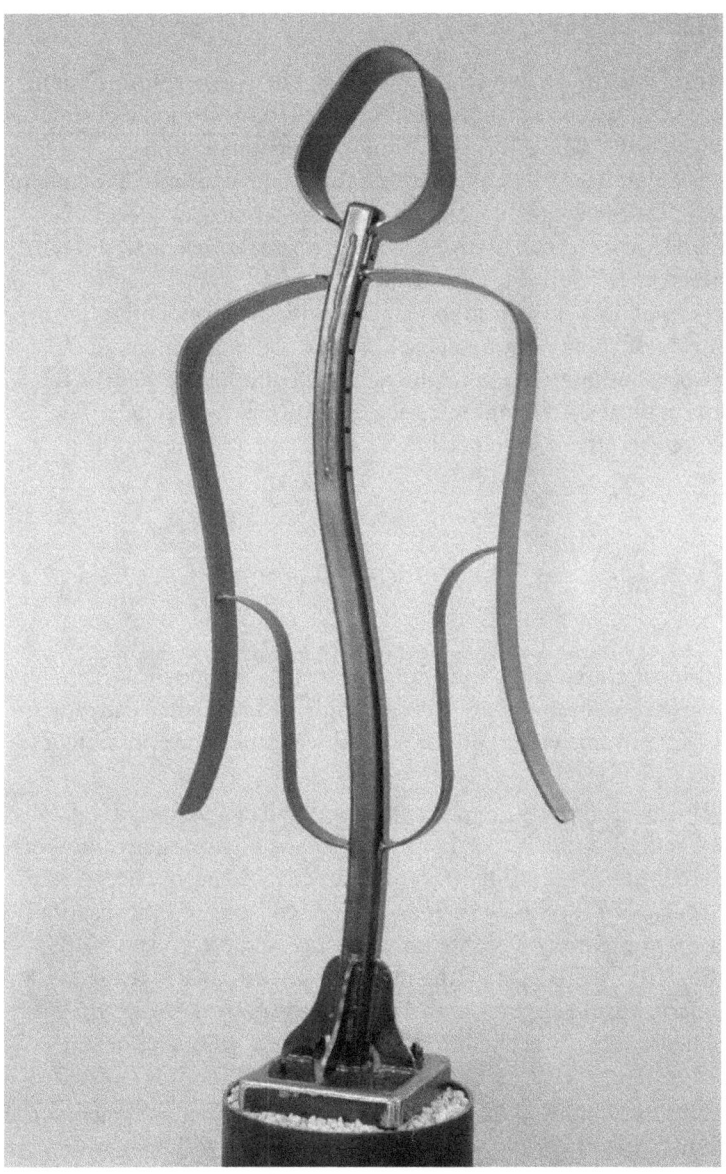

*Finally they evolve into a new self. They are often stronger, more realistic and self-confident. The incident becomes part of the person's history and no longer controls their day-to-day existence.*

## On a Clear Day
July 22, 2011

Imagine this. You are an investment professional whose responsibilities include presenting and explaining performance to institutional clients, and you have just wrapped up a 15-minute presentation to the investment committee of an endowment fund. The committee members are reasonably knowledgeable and the portfolio's return is acceptable. Your remarks covered the portfolio's quarterly results compared to a valid benchmark; the economic and capital market environment over the measurement period; an attribution analysis intended to identify the major sources of value-added return; key portfolio and benchmark characteristics; and how the portfolio is now positioned in view of the relative attractiveness of economic sectors, industries, or issuers. The investment committee's agenda allows for another 15 minutes of discussion.

Are there any questions?

No?

It is possible, of course, that your firm's reports and your own explanations are so limpid that all conceivable questions have already been satisfactorily answered. But let's consider some other possibilities.

- The client reports are not conducive to dialogue because they contain too much strictly quantitative data—too many numbers. There are pages of digits. A few of the tables have numerically designated footnotes such as, "weighted average P/E excludes negative earnings" and "totals may not add due to rounding," but that's just about all the narrative provided. There are a few charts but they are busy and unattractive; one surmises that Microsoft® Excel® selected the data series' colors by default.

- Your presentation discouraged dialogue because it contained too much information. It was overwhelming. In addition, your highly professional demeanor and fluent use of terms such as "stochastic" and "optionality" might have made asking a question seem too risky, especially in the presence of other investment committee members. Nobody wants to sound stupid or ignorant.

These are not insoluble problems. Graphic designers might collaborate with performance analysts to improve the effectiveness of your firm's client reporting. (Explore the possibilities with your firm's marketing department.) Colleagues might help you develop new ways to explain complex matters, and a speaking coach might guide you toward a style that conveys, not only self-assurance and expertise, but also a reassuring openness to questions.

Assuming no change in asset allocation, clients de-select managers because they lose confidence in them. Effective client reporting and communications do not guarantee that the manager will retain a client's confidence; the manager may very well have deviated from the firm's mandate or discipline. But, over time, ill-designed reports and poorly delivered explanations may damage relationships and erode trust. Client reporting and communications are so important, and they can go wrong so many ways, that we will undoubtedly return to these topics time and again, focusing, in the future, on how the middle office can help the firm get it right.

## The Harmonic Mean
July 29, 2011

It's a Friday afternoon in July, and work is a little tedious. Let's have some fun exploring the difference between arithmetic and harmonic means in equity portfolio characteristics analysis. We'll use an example.

At the end of last month, a portfolio held two energy stocks, Anadarko (APC) and Chevron (CVX). According to Bloomberg News, APC has a market capitalization of $40,924.9 million, 497.809 million shares outstanding, and 12-month earnings of $1,120.07 million. CVX has a market cap of $209,882.3 million, 2,010.27 million shares outstanding, and 12-month earnings of $22,756.26 million. These data are summarized in Figure 1. (The share price is the market capitalization divided by the number of shares outstanding.)

Figure 1: Input Data

| | Market Capitalization (US$ Millions) | 12-Month Earnings (US$ Millions) | Shares Outstanding (Millions) | Share Price | Earnings Per Share (EPS) |
|---|---|---|---|---|---|
| APC | 40,924.9 | 1,120.07 | 497.809 | 82.21 | 2.25 |
| CVX | 209,882.3 | 22,756.26 | 2,010.27 | 104.41 | 11.32 |
| Total | 250,807.2 | | | | |

The portfolio assets are allocated between the two stocks in proportion to their market capitalizations. Thus, the portfolio is invested 16.32% in APC, whose price-to-earnings ratio (P/E) is 36.54, and 83.68% in CVX, whose P/E is 9.22.

What is the portfolio's weighted P/E ratio? The weighted arithmetic mean P/E is 13.68. Is that a solid value to use in analyzing portfolio characteristics? APC and CVX are both held in the Standard and Poors 500 Index, and in June the average P/E of the energy sector of the S&P 500 was 11.47. Can we conclude that, despite being heavily invested in CVX, a low-P/E stock, this energy portfolio seems more growth-oriented than the corresponding index sector?

In fact, the weighted harmonic mean is a demonstrably superior measure of the portfolio's P/E ratio. Let's review how it is calculated and why it is the preferred method for averaging ratios. In practice, the weighted harmonic mean can be found by taking the inverse of the portfolio's weighted earnings-to-price ratio. In these terms, the portfolio is invested 16.32% in APC, whose E/P ratio is 0.0274, and 83.68% in CVX, whose E/P ratio is 0.1084. Accordingly, the portfolio's weighted E/P ratio is 0.0952, and its P/E ratio, calculated as a weighted harmonic mean, is the inverse, or 10.5. These calculations are displayed in Figure 2.

Figure 2: Harmonic Mean Calculation

|  | Weight in Portfolio | P/E Ratio | E/P Ratio |
|---|---|---|---|
| APC | 16.32% | 36.54 | 0.0274 |
| CVX | 83.68% | 9.22 | 0.1084 |
| Weighted Average Ratios |  | 13.68 | 0.0952 |
| Harmonic Mean P/E Ratio (1/0.0952) |  |  | 10.50 |

This result can be validated—and, more importantly, its meaningfulness demonstrated—by calculating the portfolio's P/E as the sum of its holdings' market capitalizations divided by the sum of their earnings. In addition, the portfolio's weighted harmonic mean P/E is directly comparable to the benchmark. Standard and Poors explains, "The price-earnings (PE) ratio for the index is simply the ratio of the index level (or price) to the index EPS. For a cap-weighted index, this can also be calculated directly from the stock level data by dividing the total market cap of the index by total earnings of all companies in the index."[1]

What's the difference? It's a matter of getting the comparison right. The arithmetic approach produced a higher-than-index P/E, misleading us to think that the portfolio is growth-oriented. The harmonic approach rightly shows the portfolio to have a lower-than-index P/E ratio. For greater confidence we'd want to calculate the dividend yield and price-to-book ratios, but at this point it appears the portfolio is value-oriented.

---

[1] Standard and Poors, *Index Mathematics Methodology*, January 2012, p. 33. Accessed August 7, 2012. http://us.spindices.com/documents/index-policies/methodology-index-math.pdf

## The ATV Approach to After-Tax Performance Measurement
August 3, 2011

In my experience, managers who offer tax-aware or tax-efficient strategies have two things in common: they generally seek to earn competitive returns while limiting investment income and realized capital gains,[1] and they do not—because they cannot—report their results on an after-tax basis. In this week's piece I will discuss why it is has proven so difficult for firms to calculate after-tax portfolio and benchmark rates of return, and I will call a practical solution to your attention. My previous attempts to display formulas in this blog have been unsuccessful, so the following exposition will be delightfully math-free.

The data requirements for tax-aware investing and performance measurement are not trivial. Each client has a particular tax situation, anticipated tax rates, and planning horizon. Managers who have a presence in international markets have to take multiple tax codes into account. Even if the firm only manages portfolios whose owners fall under a single tax regime, the portfolio accounting system must capture and maintain each client's cost basis in every holding, and, when securities are sold, the system must classify each client's gains or losses as short-term or long-term. Data management on this scale is all the more difficult in organizations whose infrastructure is not fully integrated.

In addition, creating and maintaining customized after-tax benchmarks to reflect each client's situation is expensive and technologically challenging. For instance, it might be appealing to adjust the before-tax returns of a capital market index on the simplifying assumption that the client's aggregate cost basis can be uniformly applied to all the securities held in the index. However, it remains to capture taxable turnover within the index, as well as corporate actions and dividend payments, and to calculate all the effects with client-specific tax rates. The firm may have to construct, monitor, and repeatedly adjust as many after-tax variants of a single before-tax index as it has tax-efficient portfolios.

---

[1] On occasion, of course, clients will instruct their managers to realize losses to offset capital gains realized within the portfolio or in other assets held outside the portfolio. Lee Price describes how to calculate the benefit of tax loss harvesting in "Calculation and Reporting of After-Tax Performance," *Journal of Performance Measurement*, vol. 1, no. 2 (1996).

Conceptually, one of the thorniest issues is the treatment of net unrealized gains held in the portfolio at the close of a measurement period. There are two established approaches to the calculation of after-tax returns, and they have complementary deficiencies. The pre-liquidation method takes into account only tax liabilities incurred during the period. It disregards unrealized capital gains as though they are untaxed. The post-liquidation method, on the other hand, recognizes the tax liability on unrealized gains immediately. It disregards the time value of money. In short, the pre-liquidation technique overstates the after-tax return and the post-liquidation technique understates it.

Relatively unknown among practitioners, the after-tax value (ATV) method pioneered by Stephen Horan[2] reduces the required data to a set of client-specific factors, offers a reasonable treatment of embedded tax liabilities, and lays the foundation for customized benchmarks. It additionally has the unique merit of accounting for tax-induced risk differentials. (By taxing investment returns, the government effectively absorbs some of the investor's risk; consequently, after-tax risk is lower than pre-tax risk.) In addition to the client's marginal tax rates and planning period, the factors include the portfolio's before-tax return for the measurement period; its cost basis as a percentage of market value; its normal dividend and capital gain realization rates; its beta; the default-free rate; and the expected market return over the planning period. Unlike most of the other factors, the expected market return is, of course, unobservable. Clients are more likely to buy into the ATV method if the manager has a robust asset allocation process.

Once the input data have been entered, the ATV approach estimates the impact of taxation on embedded gains by projecting the portfolio to the terminus of the client's planning period, recognizing taxes on unrealized gains at that time, and applying a tax- and risk-adjusted discount rate to estimate the present after-tax value. (As a simple proof of concept, the calculations can be replicated in a spreadsheet.) For consistency, an indexed portfolio with the same cost basis and investment characteristics will serve well as a benchmark. After-tax performance, then, is reflected by the change in ATV from one measurement period to another.

Finally, Dr. Horan recently found what appears to be a theoretically consistent and mathematically elegant way to extend the ATV method to

[2] Stephen M. Horan, Philip N. Lawton, and Robert R. Johnson, "After-Tax Performance Measurement," *The Journal of Wealth Management*, vol. 11 no. 1 (Summer 2008).

fixed-income portfolios. To my knowledge, however, this insight has not yet been validated and published.

# On Fair Value Accounting
August 24, 2011

The debate over fair value accounting has exhibited characteristics one would normally associate with the theological disputes of yore—dogmatic pronouncements, appeals to first principles and higher values, and prophesies of doom. Before and during the financial crisis, proponents of amortized cost or book value accounting argued that fair value accounting would jeopardize banks' viability by excessively exposing their capital to market-induced volatility. When certain types of structured instrument disappeared, the sheer difficulty of estimating the fair value of illiquid or untraded assets became starkly evident. It seemed there might be reasonable grounds for considering fair value accounting both irresponsible and unrealistic.

Nonetheless, the financial accounting standard-setting bodies are firmly committed to fair value. In May, the Financial Accounting Standards Board (FASB) issued Accounting Standards Update (ASU) 2011-04,[1] and the International Accounting Standards Board (IASB) simultaneously issued International Financial Reporting Standard (IFRS) 13.[2] The two releases are the result of the boards' joint effort to develop common fair value measurement and disclosure requirements. Fair value accounting is an exceedingly complex topic; for expediency, I will limit my remarks to the fair valuation of financial instruments as set forth in ASU 2011-04.

For background, FASB defines fair value as "the price that would be received to sell an asset or paid to transfer a liability in an orderly transaction between market participants at the measurement date." At all levels of the fair value hierarchy, the objective remains the same, that is, to reflect an exit price at the measurement date from the perspective of a market participant that holds the asset or owes the liability. The levels are

---

[1] FASB Accounting Standards Update No. 2011-04, *Fair Value Measurement (Topic 820)*, May 2011. Accessed August 7, 2012.http://www.fasb.org/cs/BlobServer?blobcol=urldata&blobtable=Mungo Blobs&blobkey=id&blobwhere=1175822486936&blobheader=application%2F pdf

[2] IASB provides a Project Summary and Feedback Statement on IFRS 13, Fair Value Measurement, May 2011. Accessed August 7, 2012. http://www.ifrs.org/NR/rdonlyres/04E9F096-B1F8-410A-B1E9-2E61003BADFA/0/FairValueMeasurementFeedbackstatement_May2011.pdf

determined with reference to the inputs upon which the valuations are based:

- Level 1 inputs, the most reliable, are unadjusted quoted prices for identical assets or liabilities in active markets that the reporting entity can access at the measurement date.

- Level 2 inputs are other directly or indirectly observable inputs, such as quoted prices for similar assets or liabilities, interest rates or yield curves, and credit spreads.

- Level 3 inputs, the least reliable, are unobservable. They are "inputs for which market data are not available and that are developed using the best information available about the assumptions that market participants would use when pricing the asset or liability"—in other words, assumptions about assumptions.

The amendments set forth in ASU 2011-04 clarify that a reporting entity should disclose quantitative information about the unobservable inputs used in a Level 3 fair value measurement (see Section 820-10-50-2.bbb). They also contain a new exception: If a reporting entity manages a group of financial assets and liabilities on the basis of its net exposure to market or credit risk, it is permitted to measure the fair value of such financial assets and liabilities at the price that would be received to sell a net asset position or transfer a net liability position for a particular risk. (Section 820-10-35-18D.) In granting this exception, FASB recognizes a fundamental risk management practice.

I cannot claim to have been an impartial observer of the debate. In my view, fair valuation has always had an ethical dimension—we are obligated not to misrepresent investment results or mislead the users of financial statements—and, while I acknowledged that valuing illiquid assets is not easy, I did not suffer gladly those who preferred the fiction of book value accounting. I still maintain that tough-minded, realistic thinking requires us to make investment decisions, manage risks, and report results based on good-faith estimates of current asset values. Moreover, SEC staff analyzed 2008 bank failures and concluded that fair value accounting was *not* a primary underlying cause of their demise.[3] All

---

[3] U.S. Securities and Exchange Commission, *Report and Recommendations Pursuant to Section 133 of the Emergency Economic Stabilization Act of 2008: Study on Mark-To-*

the same, the interaction between fair value accounting and risk-adjusted capital requirements undeniably influences banks' competitiveness and profitability. In other words, I've kept the faith, but I'm a little more tolerant now. And I've learned (again) that non-physical things such as principles, purposes, and rules—what Karl Popper memorably called "the universe of abstract meanings"[4]—can have very tangible, and lasting, effects.

---

*Market Accounting*, n.d., p. 97. Accessed August 7, 2012.
http://www.sec.gov/news/studies/2008/marktomarket123008.pdf
[4] Karl Popper, *Of Clouds and Clocks: An Approach to the Problem of Rationality and the Freedom of Man* (Washington University in St. Louis, 1965), Section XII.

## The Interquartile Range
October 7, 2011

Some, but not all, philosophers are mathematicians. Among modern French-speaking philosophers, for instance, René Descartes (1596–1650) was a mathematician of the first order, whereas Jean-Jacques Rousseau (1712–1778) was in his thirties before he picked up some books and taught himself elementary arithmetic. However, what he learned evidently stayed with him. Two decades later, he wrote: "The first quarter of life has been lived before one knows the use of it. The last quarter is lived when one has ceased to enjoy it...."[1] In Rousseau's view, only the middle 50 percent of the human lifespan is truly meaningful. This brings us to our topic.

Firms that claim to comply with the GIPS® standards must include in each compliant presentation a measure of internal dispersion of portfolio returns for each annual period presented. (Provision 5.A.1.i.) The Standards do not specify a methodology (except in the case of real estate composites, where, under provision 6.A.16, the high and low returns must be shown). Firms are, however, required to disclose which measure of internal dispersion is presented. (Provision 4.A.8.) In the 2010 edition of the GIPS standards, the Glossary entry for "internal dispersion" states, "Measures may include, but are not limited to, high/low, range, or standard deviation (asset weighted or equal weighted) of portfolio returns." Not mentioned in this edition is another permissible, and arguably superior, measure.

The interquartile range (IQR) is the difference between the returns in the first and third quartiles of an ordered distribution. It represents the length of the interval containing the middle 50 percent of the data. By definition, therefore, IQR excludes any possible outliers that might cause high/low and standard deviation to overstate the internal dispersion. I suspect IQR isn't used very often only because it's hard to explain.

For ease of exposition, let's use a simplified example. Consider a composite that includes 25 portfolios arrayed in ascending order by their respective rates of return. The portfolio with the lowest rate of return earned 1.75%, and there is a constant spread of 3 basis points from the

---

[1] Jean-Jacques Rousseau, *Emile, or On Education*. Introduction, Translation, and Notes by Allan Bloom (Basic Books, 1979), p. 211.

return of one portfolio to that of the next. Thus the series runs 1.75%, 1.78%, 1.81%...2.47%.

The formula for locating a percentile, $y$, in a distribution of returns arrayed from lowest to highest is

$$L_y = (n + 1) \times \frac{y}{100}$$

In our example, the 25th percentile falls at 6.5, that is, halfway between the sixth and seventh observations. The value of the sixth observation is 1.9% and the value of the seventh is 1.93%. The interpolated value of the 25th percentile return is, therefore, 1.915%. Similarly, we determine that the interpolated value of the return at the 75th percentile is 2.305%. The IQR for this distribution—this composite—is the difference between these returns, or 39 basis points.

Incidentally, in Excel® the quartile function can be used to find the IQR. (It is the difference between the results for the first and third quartiles.) Applying this formula to our example, however, the IQR turns out to be 36 basis points. The variance of 3 basis points is due to the fact that the underlying percentiles in Excel are not interpolated.

Rousseau said, "At first we do not know how to live; soon we can no longer live; and in the interval which separates these two useless extremities, three-quarters of the time remaining to us is consumed by sleep, work, pain, constraint, and efforts of all kinds." But I don't know about that. I had a great day today, and I can't wait for tomorrow. Life is good.

## Fair's Fair
November 10, 2011

Last month, major banks publicly granted the consensus view that their own credit quality declined in the third quarter. The evidence was clear—credit spreads on their debt had widened—and the banks did not attempt to dispute the market's judgment. On the contrary, they acknowledged their weakened position by…well, by recognizing additional non-interest revenue. And in substantial amounts: Bank of America, $1.7 billion. Citigroup, $1.9 billion. Morgan Stanley, $3.4 billion. JP Morgan Chase booked a third-quarter gain of $1.9 billion, partially offset by a loss of $0.7 billion on derivative assets due to the simultaneous widening of credit spreads for the bank's counterparties.

Paradoxes like this generally don't trouble me very much. I've long believed that irony governs human affairs. But the financial press raised a ruckus about the banks' deriving an economic benefit from the deterioration of their own credit, and the topic came up again in an exceptionally worthwhile PRMIA conference I attended yesterday. So let's take a look at credit risk-related valuation adjustments.

A quick note on terminology. In the Basel II framework, a credit valuation adjustment (CVA) is defined as "an adjustment to the mid-market valuation of the portfolio of trades with a counterparty." A one-sided CVA reflects the market value of the credit risk of the counterparty. However, CVA adjustments may reflect the non-performance risk of both the bank and the counterparty.[1] In practice, firms sometimes distinguish between credit valuation adjustments and debit valuation adjustments (DVAs), or use one or the other phrase to describe the net amount. For clarity in this piece, I will maintain the distinction between credit and debit valuation adjustments.

JPMorgan Chase's press release quotes chairman and CEO Jamie Dimon: "The DVA gain reflects an adjustment for the widening of the Firm's credit spreads which could reverse in future periods and does not relate to the underlying operations of the company."[2] His statement is

---

[1] Basel Committee on Banking Supervision, International Convergence of Capital Measurement and Capital Standards, Annex 4, "Treatment of Counterparty Credit Risk and Cross-Product Netting," June 2006, p. 256. Accessed August 7, 2012. http://www.bis.org/publ/bcbs128.pdf

[2] "JPMorgan Chase Reports Third-Quarter 2011 Net Income of $4.3 Billion, or

entirely true. Narrowing credit spreads in future periods would generate negative entries. Although JP Morgan Chase "actively manages its exposure to CVA," and flowing the adjustments through the income statement is technically correct, the periodic accounting entries are far removed from operations.

Moreover, the banks patently disclosed the impact of the third quarter adjustments. JP Morgan Chase said that after-tax earnings per share were increased by $0.29 and reduced by $0.11 by the DVA and CVA, respectively. Citigroup's press release stated, "CVA increased reported third quarter earnings by $0.39 per share."[3] There is no need to pore over the footnotes or back into these numbers.

However, security analysts rightly focus on income from operations when they evaluate the quality of a company's earnings. They look right through debit valuation adjustments. Why should banks report them?

Conceptually, DVAs arise in the context of fair value accounting, whose objective, we have seen, is to reflect "exit prices" from the perspective of market participants. If financial assets are shown at fair value on the bank's balance sheet, then it is logically consistent and equally meaningful so to report financial liabilities. The FASB and the IASB agree that "the fair value of a liability equals the fair value of a properly defined corresponding asset (that is, an asset whose features mirror those of the liability), assuming an exit from both positions in the same market."[4] When interest rates rise, the prices of fixed-income assets fall. Accordingly, when an issuer's credit spread widens, the price of its debt declines. In principle, then, the issuer could extinguish its debt by repurchasing it at a favorable price. The DVA recognizes a gain in the amount by which the fair value of eligible liabilities is reduced.

---

$1.02 Per Share, on Revenue[1] of $24.4 Billion," October 13, 2011. Accessed August 7, 2012.
http://investor.shareholder.com/jpmorganchase/releasedetail.cfm?ReleaseID=614601
[3] "Citigroup Reports Third Quarter 2011 Net Income of $3.8 Billion, Compared to $2.2 Billion in Third Quarter 2010," October 17, 2011. Accessed August 7, 2012. http://www.citigroup.com/citi/news/2011/111017a.htm
[4] FASB Accounting Standards Update No. 2011-04, *Fair Value Measurement (Topic 820)*, May 2011. Accessed August 7, 2012,BC33.http://www.fasb.org/cs/BlobServer?blobcol=urldata&blobtable=MungoBlobs&blobkey=id&blobwhere=1175822486936&blobheader=application%2Fpdf

Thus, by lessening what the IASB calls "accounting mismatches,"[5] DVAs contribute to the integrity of financial reporting.

This is not to deny that the DVAs reported last month mightily boosted headline EPS in the third calendar quarter of 2011. But what goes around comes around. Let's hope the banks' credit quality improves and spreads narrow. Lower earnings per share next time would be a reasonable price to pay for less credit risk in the banking system.

---

[5] IASB, International Financial Reporting Standard 9, Financial Instruments, Appendix B: Application Guidance, B4.1.29. Accessed August 7, 2012. http://eifrs.ifrs.org/eifrs/bnstandards/en/2012/ifrs9.pdf

## Back to the Basics: Benchmarks
November 15, 2011

Ten years ago I heard a relationship manager at a regional bank tell a municipal pension plan's investment committee, "You can't spend relative returns." The other day I read much the same message on the website of a well-known wealth management organization. "Successful portfolios are built around, and measured against, each client's individual goals–not the financial markets."[1] In other words, what matters to clients is not whether the market is up or down but how much they themselves earned on their actively managed assets. Why, then, do most investment management firms include pertinent capital market index returns in client reports?

Benchmarks enable clients to appraise the contribution of the firm's active management to investment results. (I will write about the internal role of performance measurement in a future article.) By comparing actual portfolio returns with the returns of a valid benchmark over the same measurement period, clients can evaluate the benefit they derive from their investment manager's execution of the strategy they have chosen. They can see how much they gained from the manager's decisions. They can also estimate whether they would have done better to invest in a low-cost passive alternative.

This explains why benchmark information is valuable, or potentially valuable, to investors. It doesn't explain the widespread industry practice of inviting comparison by putting benchmark returns right there alongside portfolio returns in client reports. It is reasonable to surmise that advisors who choose *not* to provide benchmark returns prefer to dispense with clients' pesky questions about past results. Regrettably, however, they also deprive themselves of an opportunity to discuss capital market conditions and explain how they add value.

Here is an example. Napper Tandy, a hate-to-lose investor,[2] has a small cap equity account with Messbar Capital Management. At the beginning of the year his portfolio was valued at $250,000. His most recent monthly statement shows these rates of return:

---

[1] PSA Financial. Accessed August 12, 2012.
http://www.psafinancial.com/Wealth%20Management/Investments.html
[2] Nicholas Dunbar distinguishes between love-to-win and hate-to-lose investors in *The Devil's Derivatives* (Harvard Business School Press, 2011), pp. xi–xii.

October        +14.27%
Year-to-Date   −4.02%

Tandy is more displeased by Messbar's year-to-date performance than he is gratified by the turnaround in October. He has lost over $10,000 this year. However, as he picks up the telephone, he notices the returns of the portfolio's benchmark, the Russell 2000® Index:

October        +15.14%
Year-to-Date   −4.46%

In the context of the benchmark returns, Messbar's return for October isn't as impressive as it first appeared—but over the ten-month period the manager outperformed the benchmark by 44 basis points (0.44%). Not so bad after all! Thacker's pretax loss before fees would have been approximately $1,100 worse if he had chosen an index fund over Messbar's active management. Because the government shares the risk, the effect of taxation substantially offsets the investment management fees in a losing year. And his advisor has a story to tell: the portfolio's benchmark-relative return for the month of October reflects the cost of downside protection she put in place for her hate-to-lose client. They go on to discuss how the portfolio is positioned for developing opportunities and risks....

Of course, it isn't hard to imagine other, more difficult scenarios with less favorable outcomes, but it is generally more satisfactory to explain investment results in the context of benchmark returns than solely in comparison with the client's financial objectives.

I apologize if all this seems stupefyingly self-evident. That managers will make benchmark returns conveniently available simply goes without saying in the institutional marketplace. However, the rationale may not be equally obvious to all the firms serving high net worth and mass market investors. As financial advisors increasingly resemble portfolio managers, I think it is worthwhile to reach agreement on the fundamentals.

# Switching Benchmarks
November 16, 2011

In my experience, when investment management firms devise new strategies, design new products, or enter new client relationships, the front office rarely consults the performance measurement staff about which capital market index, or combination of indexes,[1] to select or recommend as the bogey. Accordingly, we needn't review the well-established criteria of benchmark validity or the tests of benchmark quality.[2] It might be useful, however, to consider the circumstances under which it is appropriate to switch from one benchmark to another.

Firms which claim to comply with the Global Investment Performance Standards (GIPS®)[3] are required to disclose the reasons for changing a composite's benchmark in a compliant performance presentation.[4] The GIPS standards do not, however, state when composite benchmark changes are permissible, nor do they address firms' performance reporting for individual existing clients. It is up to each firm to decide upon its own approach.

In my opinion, investment management organizations should have written internal policies governing benchmark changes. The policy statements should list the conditions under which changes are allowed, describe the required documentation, and prescribe an approval process (including client approvals where appropriate). For example, it might be suitable for both the Chief Investment Officer and the Chief Operating Officer, or their lieutenants, to authorize a change. In the absence of such firm-wide policies, *ad hoc* changes might be unduly influenced by interested parties such as portfolio managers and asset-gathering staff. As

---

[1] I made it my practice to use "indexes" as the plural after hearing clients and colleagues transmogrify the singular form of "indices" [in'dǐ-sēz] into the hyperurbanism "indice" [in'dǐ-sē]. One might ungenerously suppose this reflects a sort of inverted snobbery on my part, but I see it as making everyone comfortable.

[2] See Jeffery V. Bailey, Thomas M. Richards, and David E. Tierney, "Evaluating Portfolio Performance," Chapter 1 in Philip Lawton and Todd Jankowski, eds., *Investment Performance Measurement: Evaluating and Presenting Results* (Wiley, 2009), pp. 24–36.

[3] Global Investment Performance Standards. Accessed August 11, 2012. www.gipsstandards.org

[4] GIPS Provision 4.A.30 states, "If the firm changes the benchmark, the firm must disclose the date of, description of, and reason for the change."

always, it is advisable to consult stakeholders and communicate the final procedures.

It is, of course, necessary to switch benchmarks if the provider discontinues an index the firm is currently using or an institutional client with a separately managed portfolio directs the firm to use another index. Here are some possible guidelines for other situations.

- Discretionary benchmark changes should be infrequent, fully justified, properly approved, and documented.

- It may be appropriate to change benchmarks if the way a strategy is executed changes. For example, expanded reference data feeds may lead to adjustments in the firm's portfolio construction and security selection processes. If the manager's research universe becomes substantially broader, or significantly varies from the existing index in some other respect, there may be a better benchmark.

- It is appropriate to switch benchmarks if an alternative is *shown* to be a more valid representation of the portfolio's existing strategy. The relative merits of the existing and the proposed index should be explained, and the new one tested, if possible, for systematic biases vis-à-vis the portfolio.

- Benchmarks should not be changed retroactively; for historical periods, the benchmark in use at the time should be presented.

The last point merits discussion. Consider the case of a portfolio that was managed against Benchmark A until fifteen months ago, when the client instructed the manager to switch to Benchmark B. The one-year portfolio return should, of course, be shown in comparison with Benchmark B. However, in my opinion the three-year portfolio return should be shown in comparison with a combined benchmark return calculated by linking 21 months of Benchmark A returns to 15 months of Benchmark B returns. A reasonable firm-wide policy might state that Benchmark B returns for the entire period may be presented in addition to but not instead of the historical series.

The GIPS standards offer somewhat more liberal guidance on retroactive benchmark changes. A GIPS Q&A database entry dated March, 2001 states, in part, "Because benchmarks are continually evolving, if the firm deems the new [composite] benchmark is a more representative test of the effective implementation of an investment strategy, the firm may consider changing the benchmark retroactively. In most cases, however, it may be most appropriate to change the benchmark starting in the current period.... In addition, firms are encouraged to continue to present the old benchmark."[5]

Managing the performance measurement function is always tough and sometimes contentious. Having sound governance policies in place makes it easier. Defining when and how the firm will change benchmarks is a step in the right direction.

---

[5] Global Investment Performance Standards, Q&A Database. Accessed August 7, 2012. http://www.gipsstandards.org/programs/faqs/gipsresults.asp?Id=2

## Controlling Spreadsheets
November 28, 2011

I have based a varied and moderately successful career on an intuitive understanding of present value and a working knowledge of spreadsheet software.

It was my good fortune to be a financial analyst at a manufacturing company whose Chief Financial Officer brought in Apple® computers in 1979, the year the first spreadsheet program, VisiCalc, was introduced. We took corporate financial planning and analysis seriously, and I soon acquired respectable VisiCalc skills. Over the years, personal circumstances, business combinations, and a low tolerance for boredom carried me to other cities, companies, and disciplines. I moved on to PCs and, after a brief dalliance with Lotus 1-2-3®, settled down with Excel®. I'm gravitating towards Apple products again—phase three, by my reckoning, of an extended midlife crisis—so I may have to learn to use Numbers®.

With these bona fides, let me say it clearly: I respect the power and flexibility of electronic spreadsheet applications. But hard experience has taught me that what seems attractive and is readily available may not be the best choice in life or work.

It is worrisome that many investment performance measurement departments evidently make extensive use of Excel spreadsheets. Not only are they employed for the occasional ad hoc analysis or speaking engagement; they are often embedded in routine operations such as conducting attribution analysis or maintaining GIPS® composites.

Spreadsheets are not well suited for production purposes because, in addition to the problems cited below, they are not scalable. Moreover, results-oriented business units usually turn to spreadsheet solutions because they cannot go on waiting for IT resources to become available, and the IT organization invariably has a hard-and-fast policy of disavowing the business lines' spreadsheets. They are, consequently, a hidden source of risk. It is each department manager's unstated responsibility to police the unit's use of them.

Although the author doesn't mention spreadsheets, an *Intelligent Risk* article entitled "IT Risk Evaluation"[1] helps identify their deficiencies.

Setting forth an internal audit methodology, John Kyriazoglou lists major systems-related risks to any organization. Among others, they include:

- computer systems and software not properly supported;
- lack of security of computer systems;
- inadequate documentation for information systems;
- incomplete IT standards, procedures and policies;
- inadequate back-up of software and data;
- lack of contingency and fall-back procedures; and
- no audit trail.

Some firms or departments may, more or less, address some of these risks. For example, mission-critical spreadsheets may be encrypted, stored on dedicated, non-networked PCs with password protection, and backed up every night. And it might be said that spreadsheets are self-documenting because the macros and formulas are visible and the functions are vendor-defined. As a practical matter, however, only the analyst who initially developed a spreadsheet fully understands it. When she leaves, and other analysts add embellishments—possibly with new names for existing variables—the spreadsheet becomes more difficult to troubleshoot.

A manager who suspects the proliferation of spreadsheets has created unacceptable operational risks might consider taking a few steps towards remediation. Here are some suggestions.[2]

1. Inventory all the spreadsheets in use throughout the department. Analysts should be directed to list their spreadsheets—not always easy, given the lack of naming conventions—and to state how, and how often, each is used.

2. Confirm that every time a spreadsheet enters a workflow, it is identified as such. Cross-check the workflow documentation and

---

[1] John Kyriazoglou, "IT Risk Evaluation," Intelligent Risk, October 2011, 14-19. Accessed August 8, 2012.
http://www.prmia.org/Weblogs/General/PRMIA_docs/IRisk3Oct11Rev4FINAL.pdf
[2] I returned to this topic in a 2017 piece that I co-authored with Dominic Pazzula for the Financial Risk Group blog. Please see "Spreadsheet Risk Is Career Risk" at https://www.frgrisk.com/spreadsheet-risk-is-career-risk/

swim lane diagrams against the spreadsheet inventory and revise
them wherever necessary.

3.  Tell the analysts to document every non-trivial spreadsheet,
    minimally including its purpose; the data input sources; the
    unique spreadsheet formulas and underlying mathematical
    equations; and any procedural tips. Attach a copy of the
    spreadsheet.

4.  Let users know they are expected to back up their work and
    document new spreadsheets as well as changes to existing ones.
    Include these items in their annual goals and corroborate their
    performance.

5.  Select the operationally embedded spreadsheets whose failure
    would be most injurious to departmental objectives, downstream
    processes, or client relations, and look for long-term solutions
    with proper internal controls.

Overseeing the use of spreadsheets means acceding to yet another
demand on the manager's and analysts' time. However, it is better to
inventory and examine the department's spreadsheets before a problem
comes to light because a key person leaves the organization, the internal
auditors take an untoward interest, a client discovers a mistake, or a
snafu halts reporting. Resolving a crisis takes time, too, and it's never
convenient.

# GIPS® for Pension Plan Sponsors
December 14, 2011

Investment firms have always been eligible to implement and claim compliance with the Global Investment Performance Standards (GIPS®). A Questions and Answers item posted on the GIPS website this year also invites pension plan sponsors, among others, to claim compliance with the Standards.

This is a welcome development; sponsors have every reason to reassure plan participants that performance presentations meet the investment industry's highest standards. However, implementation raises some practical issues we'll broach here.

Dated June 2011, the pertinent Q&A uses the word "organization" where we might previously have seen "investment firm." It reads, in part, "An organization that manages actual assets may claim compliance with the GIPS standards. This includes plan sponsors, foundations, endowments, and similar entities that manage discretionary assets either internally and/or via third party sub-advisors."[1]

There are several provisos. The organization must have discretion over the selection of external managers or "sub-advisors" (GIPS Provision 0.A.14) and must disclose the use of sub-advisors and the periods they were used (4.A.25). And, of course, the organization must adhere to all the requirements of the GIPS standards. The requirements notably include capturing and maintaining all data and information necessary to support all items included in a compliant presentation (1.A.1).[2]

In the case of plan sponsors and other institutional investors, the recordkeeping requirements introduce some complexities. If the organization calculates returns for internally managed assets, then the portfolio accounting and/or performance measurement system will capture the input data. However, for externally managed assets, plan sponsors who claim to comply with the Standards must not only ensure

---

[1] Global Invesstment Performance Standards, Q&A Database. Accessed August 8, 2011. http://www.gipsstandards.org/programs/faqs/gipsresults.asp?Id=318
[2] See also the *Guidance Statement on Recordkeeping Requirements* (2010). Accessed August 8, 2012.
http://www.gipsstandards.org/standards/guidance/develop/pdf/gs_recordkee ping_requirements_clean.pdf

they can produce all the supporting data; they must additionally ascertain that the returns were properly calculated for inclusion in a GIPS-compliant performance presentation.

A comparable situation arises for sub-advisors to wrap-fee sponsors. The *Guidance Statement on Wrap Fee/Separately Managed Account (SMA) Portfolios* says that, in the absence of the data necessary to substantiate portfolio-level performance, sub-advisors may choose to rely upon the performance calculated and reported by the wrap-fee/SMA sponsor.[3] "When relying on information provided by a third party (in this instance, the wrap fee/SMA sponsor), the firm claiming compliance with the GIPS standards must take the necessary steps to be satisfied that the information provided by the wrap fee/SMA sponsor can be relied on to meet the requirements of the GIPS standards."[4]

Presumably, then, plan sponsors can depend upon their external managers for returns as long as they are calculated in accordance with an acceptable methodology on the basis of input data that also meets the requirements of the GIPS standards. Optimally, the external managers themselves claim to comply with the Standards and have been verified.

Can plan sponsors similarly choose to rely upon performance calculated by their custodian? Their investment consultant?

These questions are not so easily answered. Custodians and consultants cannot claim compliance (nor, perforce, be verified) because they don't have actual assets under management. In addition, they are prohibited from describing their methodology as GIPS-compliant. (GIPS Provision 0.A.7.)

In my view—this is not an authoritative opinion—plan sponsors can rely upon third-party service providers provided they take "the necessary steps" to be confident the information supports GIPS-compliant performance presentations. No matter who calculates the rates of return, the plan sponsor is answerable for the claim to comply with the GIPS

---

[3] An alternative is to engage in "shadow accounting" and independently produce the requisite data. This does not seem like a practical choice for small and midsize plan sponsors.

[4] Global Investment Performance Standards, *Guidance Statement on Wrap Fee/Separately Managed Account (SMA) Portfolios*, 5. Accessed August 8, 2012. http://www.gipsstandards.org/standards/guidance/develop/pdf/gs_wrap_fee_clean.pdf

standards and for all the information included in a purportedly GIPS-compliant performance presentation.

The GIPS Executive Committee's strategic plan dated October 2011 includes developing guidance on applying the GIPS standards to pension plans and other institutions.[5] The projected timeline is 2012, and the U.S. Investment Performance Committee and the Canadian Investment Performance Committee are reportedly engaged in writing a paper on the subject. This is a meritorious project; the USIPC and CIPC are to be warmly congratulated for accepting the assignment. Their efforts will undoubtedly lead, in due time, to useful *ex cathedra* direction for plan sponsors.

---

[5] Global Investment Performance Standards (GIPS®) Executive Committee Strategic Plan, October 2011, Item 1.13. Accessed August 8, 2012. http://www.gipsstandards.org/about/governance/pdf/gips_strategic_plan.pdf

## KIID Performance Scenarios
January 26, 2012

U.S. investors have read the obligatory disclaimer, "Past performance does not guarantee future results,"[1] so many times that the words may no longer register with them. The E.U. has decided that the Key Investor Information Document (KIID) for structured UCITS[2] should not include historical performance at all.

The UCITS IV Directive issued in 2009 requires instead the use of "prospective scenarios" for structured UCITS. The scenarios, which are to be called "illustrative examples," must minimally exemplify low, medium, and high returns. The low example should show an unfavorable outcome; if there is no guarantee of capital, the scenario will show that investors may suffer a loss. The medium example should illustrate a moderate growth of capital. The high example should show a positive return but mustn't be premised upon unduly optimistic assumptions. If a structured UCITS has special features, such as a capital guarantee with a conditional floor, then a fourth scenario may be required.

For context, structured UCITS are defined as "UCITS which provide investors, at certain predetermined dates, with algorithm-based payoffs that are linked to the performance or to the realization of price changes or other conditions, of financial assets, indices or reference portfolios or UCITS with similar features." In December 2010, the Committee of European Securities Regulators (CESR) published guidelines for the selection and presentation of performance scenarios.[3] (CESR was the predecessor of ESMA, the European Securities and Markets Authority.) In the simplest example CESR provided, a fund that is indexed to the average performance of a benchmark will require scenarios illustrating

---

[1] Under Rule 482, advertisements that present performance data of a U.S.-registered open-end management investment company must include this and other disclosures. See 17 CFR 230.482(b)(3)(i). Accessed August 8, 2012. http://www.gpo.gov/fdsys/pkg/CFR-2012-title17-vol2/pdf/CFR-2012-title17-vol2-sec230-482.pdf

[2] UCITS: Undertakings for Collective Investments in Transferable Securities, *i.e.*, open-end funds.

[3] Committee of European Securities Regulators, *Guidelines: Selection and Presentation of Performance Scenarios in the Key Investor Information Document (KII) for Structured UCITS*, 20 December 2010. Ref.: CESR/10-1318. Accessed August 8, 2012. http://www.esma.europa.eu/system/files/10_1318.pdf

the payout under favorable conditions; the positive impact of the formula if the benchmark declines at the end of the fund's life (where, having grown at the average index return over the entire period, the portfolio's ending value exceeds the final index level); and the negative impact if the benchmark performs strongly near the end date.

In conformity with the CESR guidelines, each scenario must be presented by means of tables or graphs. Firms should choose whichever format is the clearer way to demonstrate the characteristics of each structured UCITS. Certain restrictions apply to graphs. The presentation must, whenever possible, avoid double scales, that is, primary (left) and secondary (right) vertical axes. Nonlinear scales are also to be avoided, as are different scales for different scenarios. The guidelines also state, "the [graphical] presentation shall avoid artificially magnifying the positive aspects of the fund payout."

Low, medium, high: it sounds fairly straightforward. However, the phrase "scenario selection" skates over the hard part. Building defensible prospective scenarios—especially for medium and high returns—is not an entirely mechanical exercise. "Medium" does not necessarily mean "most likely;" indeed, the CESR guidelines state, "The narrative shall make it clear that [the scenarios] are not forecasts and that they are not equally probable." Nonetheless, it seems reasonable to suppose that regulators don't want ridiculous illustrations, and realistic to anticipate that they will second-guess the fund companies.

The construction of justifiable scenarios would appear, then, to presuppose informed views about reasonable outcomes, or, better, about outcomes that are not unreasonable, over the projected life of the structured fund. Accordingly, product managers or performance analysts charged with ginning up illustrative data confront, on a reduced scale, some of the same scenario forecasting and stress testing issues that are familiar to risk managers. In the simplistic case mentioned above, what's the "right" way to project "medium" index returns? How should more complex structures be modeled?

Regulators may have to be persuaded that the illustrative examples presented in the KIID of a given structured UCITS meaningfully convey important performance characteristics of the fund. Risk managers have the training, tools, and experience to help the firm do a credible job.

## Provisional Principles of Client Reporting
February 6, 2012

In *Discourse on the Method*, René Descartes concisely set out the systematic rules that guided him in an effort to place his knowledge on solid footing. He would accept as true only that which presented itself to his mind so clearly and distinctly that he could have no occasion to doubt it; and he would proceed by dividing each difficulty into the smallest possible parts, progressively advancing from the simplest to the most complex, and reviewing each step to ensure he hadn't omitted anything. But Descartes recognized that, while he was engaged in demolishing and rebuilding his conceptual house, he would need temporary lodging. Accordingly, he formulated a "provisional morality"—three or four maxims to live by while rehabilitation was in progress.[1]

At present the investment industry does not have generally accepted client reporting standards. Developing global standards, as Stefan J. Illmer and Dmitri Senik have urged,[2] will require organizational sponsorship and the active participation of many knowledgeable practitioners. Until the project is undertaken, however, and the industry reaches agreement on client reporting standards, a small set of provisional principles might be useful. Here are some common-sense ideas.[3]

1.  *The purpose of client reporting is to communicate portfolio and performance information.*

In other words, the purpose is not, say, to retain and grow assets under management, nor to demonstrate the firm's cleverness. In application, Provisional Principle 1 means that client reports should be formatted to convey portfolio and performance information effectively, and commentaries should be written in plain language. By writing *Discourse on the Method* in French, rather than Latin, Descartes sought to reach literate

---

[1] Descartes introduced his provisional moral system with this housing metaphor in the third part of *Discours de la method* (1637). *Oeuvres de Descartes*, ed. Charles Adam and Paul Tannery (Paris: Vrin, 1996), vol. VI, 22.
[2] Stefan J. Illmer and Dmitri Senik, "Client Investment Reporting: The Need for a Global Standard," *Investment Performance Measurement Newsletter* (CFA Institute), August 2009. Unfortunately, Illmer and Senik's article is not available on the CFA Institute website.
[3] The principles have been reordered in the version presented here.

people outside the scholarly community. The simplicity and directness of his style are also exemplary. *A propos*, an earlier version of this first principle read, "The purpose of client reporting is to communicate portfolio and performance information enabling the client to evaluate the manager's execution of the investment strategy in light of market conditions during the measurement period." The revised version represents a considerable gain in economy for a small loss in content.

2. *Client reporting policies should be developed in consultation with internal stakeholders, documented, and kept up to date.*

Descartes devised his methodology with a specific project in mind, but he clearly intended it to apply to any intellectual endeavor. Breaking things down, moving from the simpler elements to the more complex, and continually reviewing the work for completeness are generally good rules for thinking. Similarly, establishing a consultative process, documenting policies, and keeping them current are sound managerial practices in any organization and any function. The internal process of setting, memorializing, and refreshing policies is especially important in the present case because client reporting directly affects how the firm is perceived by those who have entrusted it with their wealth.

3. *Portfolio performance should be presented fairly, accurately, and completely.*

This wording, borrowed from the CFA Institute *Standards of Professional Conduct*,[4] is somewhat less exigent than a similar provision in the *Asset Manager Code of Professional Conduct*,[5] which states that managers must present performance information that is "fair, accurate, relevant, timely, and complete." It doesn't seem necessary to mention relevance and timeliness; the one is implicit in communicating effectively, and the other is a competitive requirement. In practice, fairness means using standard measurement periods such as the month, quarter, or year; presenting the performance of a valid benchmark for the same period(s); and ensuring that all charts are straightforward. Accuracy means calculating results correctly on the basis of the firm's best estimate of asset values. Completeness means providing sufficient pertinent information for the

---

[4] CFA Institute, *Code of Ethics and Standards of Professional Conduct*, 2010, Section III.D. Accessed August 8, 2012.
http://www.cfapubs.org/doi/pdf/10.2469/ccb.v2010.n14.1
[5] CFA Institute, *Asset Manager Code of Professional Conduct*, 2nd ed., 2010, Section E.1. Accessed August 8, 2012.
http://www.cfapubs.org/doi/pdf/10.2469/ccb.v2009.n8.1

client to evaluate investment results, possibly including market commentaries, portfolio and benchmark characteristics, *ex post* risk measures, and/or attribution analyses.

4. *Clients should be informed of revised portfolio and performance information when material errors are discovered.*

This is a tough one. Everybody knows that people who actually work occasionally make mistakes, but nobody likes admitting them. Owning up to an error may be especially painful for people in operational roles who have few offsetting opportunities to gain more favorable attention from senior management. All the same, firms should formulate and consistently adhere to well-defined policies for evaluating materiality, correcting errors, and disseminating revised information. (The *GIPS Guidance Statement on Error Correction*[6] is a valuable resource.) For supervisors, the key is never to squander a good mistake, nor, for that matter, a near miss. Figure out how it happened and strengthen internal controls to safeguard against a recurrence.

---

[6] Global Investment Performance Standards, *Guidance Statement on Error Correction*, 2010. Accessed August 8, 2012.
http://www.gipsstandards.org/standards/guidance/develop/pdf/gs_error_corr ection_clean.pdf

## Money-Weighted Benchmark Returns
March 5, 2012

An apparent advantage of reporting the time-weighted total return of a client's portfolio is its comparability to the return of the capital market index that serves as the benchmark. However, the portfolio's money-weighted return is also comparable to the benchmark's calculated money-weighted return.

The approach I have in mind consists in generalizing the private equity concept of a public market equivalent (PME). The GIPS® Glossary defines PME as the "performance of a public market index expressed in terms of an internal rate of return (IRR), using the same cash flows and timing as those of the composite over the same time period." Reading "portfolio" in place of "composite," I'll use an example to demonstrate the method.

James "Napper" Tandy IV opened an account at Canard Capital Management with an initial deposit of $105,250 on February 28, 2011. His assets were to be invested immediately in U.S. large-cap stocks, and the portfolio was benchmarked against the S&P 500® index. Tandy contributed additional amounts of $31,500 on April 19th and $12,250 on May 18th. He withdrew $14,425 on August 31st and $9,950 on November 18th. His account was valued at $126,885.71 on February 29, 2012.

Tandy's time-weighted rate of return (TWR) for the year ended February 29, 2012, was 3.19%. The S&P 500 index level was 1327.22 on February 28, 2011, the day he opened his brokerage account, and 1365.68 on February 29, 2012, so the benchmark's TWR for the 12-month period was 2.90%. On a time-weighted basis, Tandy's account outperformed the benchmark by 29 basis points. These calculations are shown in Figures 1 and 2. (In Figure 2, the pro forma end-of-day index value is not needed for calculating the benchmark's time-weighted return, but we will use it later.)

**Figure 1.** Time-Weighted Portfolio Return

| Date | Beginning-of-Day Contribution (Withdrawal) (US$) | End-of-Day Portfolio Value (US$) | Subperiod Portfolio Return (%) |
|---|---|---|---|
| February 28 | | 105,250.00 | |
| April 18 | | 102,860.83 | −2.27 |
| April 19 | 31,500 | | |
| May 17 | | 137,752.28 | 2.52 |
| May 18 | 12,250 | | |
| August 30 | | 135,579.86 | −9.61 |
| August 31 | (14,425) | | |
| November 17 | | 123,057.48 | 1.57 |
| November 18 | (9,950) | | |
| February 29 | | 126,885.71 | 12.18 |
| Time-Weighted Return for the 12 Month Period | | | 3.19 |

**Figure 2.** Time-Weighted Benchmark Return

| Date | Beginning-of-Day Contribution (Withdrawal) (US$) | Index Level | Pro Forma End-of-Day Portfolio Value (US$) | Subperiod Portfolio Return (%) |
|---|---|---|---|---|
| February 28 | | 1,327.22 | 105,250.00 | |
| April 18 | | 1,305.14 | 103,499.03 | −1.66 |
| April 19 | 31,500 | | | |
| May 17 | | 1,328.98 | 137,464.96 | 1.83 |
| May 18 | 12,250 | | | |
| August 30 | | 1,212.92 | 136,640.33 | −8.73 |
| August 31 | (14,425) | | | |
| November 17 | | 1,216.13 | 122,739.30 | 0.26 |
| November 18 | (9,950) | | | |
| February 29 | | 1,365.58 | 126,659.23 | 12.30 |
| Time-Weighted Return for the 12 Month Period | | | | 2.90 |

It is Tandy's strong preference, however, to evaluate his portfolio's performance on the basis of money-weighted returns which more nearly represent what he actually earned. Canard reported that his portfolio's money-weighted return (MWR) for the year ended February 29, 2012, was 1.71%. See Figure 3, where the portfolio MWR is calculated using the Excel® XIRR function, which is accurate enough for the present purpose.

**Figure 3.** Money-Weighted Portfolio Return

| Date | Cash Flow To (From) Tandy |
|---|---|
| February 28 | (105,250.00) |
| April 19 | (31,500.00) |
| May 18 | (12,250.00) |
| August 31 | 14,425.00 |
| November 18 | 9,950.00 |
| February 29 | 126,885.71 |
| Portfolio MWR % | 1.71% |

But Tandy would also like to know whether his portfolio underperformed or outperformed the benchmark on a money-weighted basis.

In order to calculate the PME and answer Tandy's question, Canard has to determine the benchmark's pro forma ending value. Figure 2 showed how this can be done using S&P 500 index levels on the date of each cash flow. Figure 4 substitutes the pro forma ending value for the portfolio's actual ending value. Applying the XIRR function to the cash flows and calendar dates, Rivanna finds that the PME is 1.54%.

**Figure 4.** Public Market Equivalent

| Date | Cash Flow To (From) Tandy |
|---|---|
| February 28 | (105,250.00) |
| April 19 | (31,500.00) |
| May 18 | (12,250.00) |
| August 31 | 14,425.00 |
| November 18 | 9,950.00 |
| February 29 | 126,659.23 |
| PME  MWR % | 1.54% |

On a money-weighted basis, then, Tandy's portfolio outperformed the benchmark by 17 basis points. Go figure.

## Performance and Risk
March 24, 2012

One of the main topics of discussion at FTF's 5th Annual Performance Measurement Conference, held in New York last week, was the incipient convergence of investment performance measurement and financial risk management.

The two disciplines are conceptually linked; Steve Shefras of BI-SAM memorably said that, rather than being two sides of the same coin, risk and performance are comparable to the 'single' side of a Möbius band. Moreover, there are practical benefits to be gained from fostering sound working relationships between an investment organization's risk management and performance measurement groups. It seems to me, however, that the performance measurement community is substantially the more interested in pursuing these philosophical and organizational links. Risk professionals may be entirely comfortable with the metaphor of heads and tails, each vaguely aware of but invisible to the other, both looking in opposite directions.

The financial risk manager's job is to identify, evaluate, monitor, and control—that is, accept, avoid, share, or mitigate—the firm's exposures to market, credit, and, to some extent, operational events. The performance analyst's job is to assess and explain investment results in view of the intentional and unintentional risks that were taken in achieving them. The risk manager informs and influences investment decision-making, while the performance analyst appraises the impact of decisions on outcomes. In short, while both work for the same firm and concern themselves with the same investment strategies, the risk manager's orientation is prospective, and the performance analyst's, retrospective.

Risk and performance professionals' skill sets are similar but not congruent. It is fair to say that the capable risk manager's grasp of quantitative techniques, especially those associated with mathematical modeling and statistical analysis, typically exceeds that of the competent performance analyst. The latter is more likely to understand how clients select and monitor investment managers, to know performance presentation standards, and to appreciate the nuances of rate-of-return calculations, portfolio characteristics analysis, and attribution methodologies. Performance analysts may also be more practiced in explaining analytical approaches and conclusions to clients and other non-specialists.

Many performance measurement systems offer a battery of descriptive statistics and *ex post* risk measures. (Selecting which to present, and visualizing how to display them, is part of what makes client reporting an art.) However, sustained *ex post* risk analysis goes far beyond calculating a few simple portfolio and benchmark ratios; it includes, among other possibilities, estimating partial moments, historical value-at-risk, and regression-based values such as bull and bear beta. In addition to evaluating performance, this information can be useful in reconsidering risk management policies and strategies and re-specifying risk models. The performance measurement function routinely provides helpful feedback to portfolio managers, and, with further development, it can serve risk managers as well.

In many investment organizations, achieving this potential will require leadership and some measure of re-acculturation. It may also necessitate staff development along with manageable system and process changes. In the interest of effective firm management, though, it seems well worth the effort.

## Materiality
April 24, 2012

Few concepts in financial reporting and investment management are as fundamental, pervasive, and vague as the concept—perhaps I should say the "notion"—of materiality.

Financial accountants are cautioned against material misrepresentations in management's estimates, and auditors, trained in the exercise of professional skepticism, are on the alert for material misstatements of financial position due to error or fraud. Investment professionals are ethically obligated to disclose material changes in the processes they use to analyze investments, select securities, and construct portfolios,[1] and they are legally as well as ethically obligated not to act on material nonpublic information. Performance analysts are expected to correct material errors in the presentation of investment results. Last year the SEC "brought actions against four hedge fund advisers identified through the aberrational performance inquiry for inflating returns, overvaluing assets and other actions that materially misled and harmed investors."[2]

In short, the concept of materiality is ubiquitous in the field of finance. What does materiality mean, and how do accountants, auditors, and analysts decide whether information is material?

It is generally agreed that information is material if it would affect a capable[3] person's economic or financial decisions. The Financial

---

[1] CFA Institute, *Code of Ethics and Standards of Professional Conduct*, 2010, Standard V.B.1. Accessed August 8, 2012.
http://www.cfapubs.org/doi/pdf/10.2469/ccb.v2010.n14.1
[2] SEC Chairman Mary L. Shapiro, "Remarks at the SIFMA C&L Conference," March 20, 2012. Accessed August 8, 2012.
http://www.sec.gov/news/speech/2012/spch032012mls.htm
[3] "The evaluation of whether a misstatement could influence economic decisions of users, and therefore be material, involves consideration of the characteristics of those users." The AICPA's AU Section 312 explains the user characteristics to be assumed when assessing materiality, e.g., they are assumed to "recognize the uncertainties inherent in the measurement of amounts based on the use of estimates, judgment, and the consideration of future events." American Institute of Certified Public Accountants, *AU Section 312, Audit Risk and Materiality in Conducting an Audit*, Paragraph .06. Accessed August 8, 2012.
http://www.aicpa.org/research/standards/auditattest/downloadabledocuments

Accounting Standards Board sees materiality as an aspect of relevance,[4] one of two fundamental qualitative characteristics of useful financial information, and states, "Information is material if omitting it or misstating it could influence decisions that users make on the basis of the financial information of a specific reporting entity. In other words, materiality is an entity-specific aspect of relevance based on the nature or magnitude or both of the items to which the information relates in the context of an individual entity's financial report."[5]

CFA Institute mentions the impact of material information on security prices as well as on investment decision-making: "Information is 'material' if its disclosure would probably have an impact on the price of a security or if reasonable investors would want to know the information before making an investment decision. In other words, information is material if it would significantly alter the total mix of information currently available about a security in such a way that the price of the security would be affected."[6]

And the *GIPS Guidance Statement on Error Correction* states, "Whether an error might affect a prospective client's decision to invest is a key determinant of materiality and the appropriate action necessary to resolve the issue."[7]

But this just kicks the can down the road. How does one determine whether the information in question would affect a reasonable user's or client's financial decision? As the FASB indicated above, two factors are

---

/au-00312.pdf

[4] Information is relevant if it can make a difference in users' financial decisions, and it is capable of making a difference if it has predictive or confirmatory value. Financial Accounting Standards Board, *Statement of Financial Accounting Concepts No. 8* (September 2010). Accessed August 8, 2012.
http://www.fasb.org/cs/BlobServer?blobcol=urldata&blobtable=MungoBlobs&blobkey=id&blobwhere=1175822892635&blobheader=application%2Fpdf

[5] *Ibid.* The other fundamental qualitative characteristic of useful financial information is faithful representation.

[6] CFA Institute, *Standards of Practice Handbook,* 10th ed. (2010), Standard II-A, Material Nonpublic Information, 49. Accessed August 8, 2012.
http://www.cfapubs.org/doi/pdf/10.2469/ccb.v2010.n2.1

[7] Global Investment Performance Standards, Guidance Statement on Error Correction (2010), 4. Accessed August 8, 2012.
http://www.gipsstandards.org/standards/guidance/develop/pdf/gs_error_correction_clean.pdf

germane to this determination: the nature of the information and, where applicable, the magnitude of the item.

- Evaluating the nature of the information in question presupposes an understanding of the business as well as the pertinent accounting and analytical standards and techniques. A software company's failure to disclose that its ownership of critical intellectual property has been credibly contested would probably constitute a material omission of a significant event. A misstatement in an oil company's depletion expense or movements in net proven reserves is more likely to be material than an error in its interest income account. In performance measurement and client reporting, a benchmark change is more meaningful than the composite creation date.

- Establishing a materiality threshold also requires an appreciation of the setting, along with an informed sense of the appropriate scale. An auditor's "tolerable misstatement"[8] may be higher at the parent company than the subsidiary level. A valuation error that distorts a rate of return by 25 basis points is probably more significant in a fixed-income than an equity portfolio. The GIPS Guidance Statement cited above suggests that firms additionally consider whether an error is material relative to the benchmark.

We can't predetermine what will be material in a particular situation any more than we can establish a uniform threshold that would apply in all cases. In the end, deciding whether the nature and size of an item makes it material is a context-sensitive question of professional judgment, and a professional judgment is most likely to be valid if the professional is competent, independent, and objective. These are ethical qualities. Materiality is a financial concept grounded in ethics.

---

[8] AU Section 312, *op. cit.*, paragraphs .34-.36. See also AU Section 350, Audit Sampling. Accessed August 8, 2012.
http://www.aicpa.org/research/standards/auditattest/downloadabledocuments/au-00350.pdf.

# Implementing the GIPS® Standards for Alternative Investments

July 8, 2012

At least some investment measurement performance professionals will be spared the risk of overexposure to ultraviolet rays this summer because the *GIPS Guidance Statement on Alternative Investment Strategies and Structures*[1] becomes effective on October 1st. Firms that manage alternative investments have always been able to comply with the GIPS standards; the 24-page Guidance Statement principally explains how existing requirements are to be applied. Nonetheless, bringing alternative investment products such as hedge funds and funds of funds into compliance is not a trivial matter. This essay is no substitute for a careful reading of the Guidance Statement, but it may serve to point out some of the complexities.

Bearing in mind the principles of "fair representation and full disclosure" and "substance over form," GIPS-compliant firms with alternative investment products must consider the scope and applicability of the new Guidance Statement. Specifically meriting attention are the issues of composite definition, valuation policies, benchmarks, the input data and calculation methodologies employed by the firm's administrators or custodians, the treatment of investment management fees and other expenses, the inclusion or exclusion of side pockets, and the return impact of leverage and derivatives. Given the complexity of many alternative investment strategies and vehicles, it may also take considerable effort to write composite descriptions and other disclosures that the legal department can approve yet prospective clients can understand.

The scope of the Guidance Statement is wide; indeed, most unusually, a Notice appears on the title page: "This Guidance Statement applies to all firms claiming compliance with the GIPS standards and contains guidance that is relevant to firms that may not consider themselves as 'alternative' investment managers." Beyond private equity and real estate, which are already subject to specific requirements, alternatives as contemplated by the Guidance Statement include funds of funds whose

---

[1] Global Investment Performance Standards, *Guidance Statement on Alternative Investment Strategies and Structures*, 2012. Accessed August 9, 2012.
http://www.gipsstandards.org/standards/guidance/develop/pdf/gs_alternative_investment_strategies_and_structures.pdf

underlying investments may be traditional and strategies whose potential return characteristics are significantly modified by the use of derivative instruments such as currency and interest rate futures (thus, portfolios with overlays). In the customary quasi-legal style of such pronouncements, the Guidance Statement says, "if nothing is stated regarding any non-applicability of the GIPS standards to a particular asset class or portfolio type, the GIPS standards are deemed to be applicable."

Some issues may be rather easily resolved. For example, in line with hedge fund industry practice, it is permissible to base rates of return on changes in net asset value (NAV) as long as the firm discloses that returns are presented net of all fees and expenses, including investment management fees, custodial and administrative fees, external legal and accounting expenses, and the like.[2] Similarly, the industry typically precludes intraperiod cash flows by limiting contributions and withdrawals or distributions to specified period-ends that coincide with valuation dates. Other issues, however, are more challenging. They notably include the use of estimated and stale valuations, side pockets, and leverage and derivatives.

*Historical and estimated valuations.* Rather than waiting for extended periods—sometimes months—before final valuations of illiquid or hard-to-value assets are available, many hedge funds managers issue performance presentations and client reports reflecting preliminary estimates or the most recent historical values. Timely reporting is vitally important; neither clients nor senior management will tolerate prolonged delays (nor should they). Nonetheless, using outdated or estimated valuations may be problematic. Here are the major considerations:

- For periods beginning on or after 1 January 2011, portfolios must be valued in accordance with the definition of fair value and the GIPS Valuation Principles.

---

[2] Among other fee-related requirements, the GIPS standards state that, when presenting net-of-fees returns, firms must disclose if any other fees are deducted in addition to investment management fees and trading expenses. *Global Investment Performance Standards* (2010), Provision 4.A.6.a. Accessed August 9, 2012.
http://www.cfapubs.org/doi/pdf/10.2469/ccb.v2010.n5.1 The *Guidance Statement on Alternative Investment Strategies and Structures* addresses the treatment of fees in multi-level configurations such as fund-of-funds and master-feeder structures.

- In the interest of independence and objectivity, if assets are valued internally, firms should ensure that valuations are determined by a unit outside the portfolio managers' chain of command.

- If the firm uses the administrator's estimates, then the firm should confirm, or reconfirm, that the administrator's valuation process is reliable. Outsourcing the valuation function or other services does not absolve firms from responsibility for the validity of performance presentations. Although administrators may not welcome the intrusion, I would suggest that managers aggressively seek to understand the valuation process.

- The firm must assess the effect of the differences between final values and historical or estimated values on total firm assets, composite assets, and performance. Furthermore, in the event the differences are material, the firm must determine whether the composite should be adjusted retroactively or prospectively; if retroactively, the firm's error correction policy should be consulted. If the differences are consistently material, then the firm must reconsider the suitability of stale or estimated values.

*Segregated assets.* For the purpose of this discussion, let us assume that we are dealing with a single-fund composite. The basic decision is whether a side pocket is to be classified as discretionary, and so included in the composite, or non-discretionary and therefore excluded. Regardless of its classification, the firm must disclose in a compliant presentation that there is a side pocket.

- Although the Guidance Statement mentions the firm's definition of discretion, it states that a side pocket can be classified as non-discretionary only if all the following conditions are satisfied: the side pocket is segregated as a separate sub-portfolio in the firm's portfolio management system or at the custodial bank; the assets held in the side pocket are not considered in the fund's asset allocation and portfolio investment process; there are no investment decisions other than monitoring and liquidating the side-pocketed assets; and reduced investment management fees, or none, are charged on the assets in question.

- If the side pocket is deemed discretionary, then the firm must present returns both including it (for the historical record) and excluding it (for the information of prospective clients who will not participate in side pocket performance).

*Leverage.* The Guidance Statement includes pertinent Questions & Answers on leverage, among other things. (Recall that firms claiming compliance must satisfy all requirements of the GIPS standards, including any updates, Guidance Statements, interpretations, Questions & Answers, and clarification published by CFA Institute and the GIPS Executive Committee.) The key ruling is that unleveraged or de-leveraged returns for leveraged funds or portfolios cannot be included in compliant presentations; because they are hypothetical, they can only be shown as supplemental information. However, if the use of derivatives is required by the client (who might specify, for instance, that a portfolio is to be 50% hedged against foreign exchange risk), the firm is permitted to classify the restricted portion as non-discretionary and remove it from the portfolio.

Finally, a word of caution to close this over-long piece. As the foregoing discussion may already have made clear, hedge fund managers who wish to implement the GIPS standards would be well advised to hire an expert—optimally a CIPM certificant—and/or retain a qualified consultant who is conversant, not only with the *Guidance Statement on Alternative Investment Strategies and Structures*, but with the Standards in their entirety. Achieving compliance is extremely beneficial to the firm as well as its existing and prospective clients, but it calls for expert guidance and extensive specialized knowledge.

# Average Invested Capital
August 31, 2012

Because a portfolio's time-weighted rate of return depends upon the sequence of subperiod returns, the average amount invested over the entire measurement period is not a particularly informative value. However, the internal rate of return (IRR) methodology solves for a single reinvestment rate that is invariant across the entire measurement period, rendering the idea of an average level of investment more meaningful. Moreover, the concept of average invested capital invested is potentially useful in money-weighted attribution analysis. My very limited purpose here is to explain how average invested capital is calculated by means of a familiar example, one originally devised for the piece called "Money-Weighted Benchmark Returns" (see above).

Napper Tandy opened an account at Rivanna Capital Management with an initial deposit of $105,250 on February 28, 2011. His assets were to be invested immediately in U.S. large-cap stocks, and the portfolio was benchmarked against the S&P 500® index. Tandy contributed additional amounts of $31,500 on April 19th and $12,250 on May 18th. He withdrew $14,425 on August 31st and $9,950 on November 18th. His account was valued at $126,885.71 on February 29, 2012. These cash flows are summarized in **Figure 1**.

**Figure 1.** Portfolio Cash Flows

| Date | Cash Flow |
| --- | --- |
| 28-Feb-2011 (BMV) | (105,250) |
| 19-Apr-2011 | (31,500) |
| 18-May-2011 | (12,250) |
| 31-Aug-2011 | 14,425 |
| 18-Nov-2011 | 9,950 |
| 29-Feb-2012 (EMV) | 126,885.71 |

BMV and EMV are beginning and ending market value, respectively. For the 12-month period, Tandy's portfolio earned a time-weighted return (TWR) of 3.19% and a money-weighted return (MWR) of 1.71%

Excluding the ending market value, shown as the final cash flow in Figure 1, Tandy's investment varied between the initial amount of $105,250 and a high amount of $149,000 during the year. The daily-weighted average amount invested was $132,178.83. **Figure 2** displays the gross and average amounts invested.

**Figure 2.** Napper Tandy Portfolio

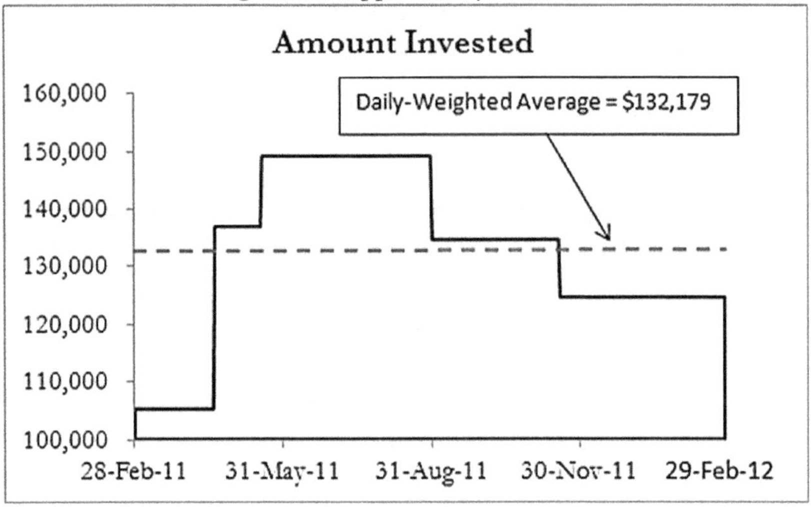

In the world of money-weighted returns, the so-called average capital invested equals the value of all cash flows except the ending market value, discounted at the internal rate of return. This is a sensitive calculation; in order to minimize rounding error, we will expand Tandy's MWR to 1.71165%[1] for the full year or 0.00464% per day. As detailed in **Figure 3**, the average capital invested equals $124,750.42.

**Figure 3.** Calculating Average Capital Invested

| Date | Cash Flow | Days Out | Present Value Factor | Present Value |
|---|---|---|---|---|
| 28-Feb-2011 | 105,250 | 1 | 1 | 105,250.00 |
| 19-Apr-2011 | 31,500 | 50 | 0.997684153 | 31,427.05 |
| 18-May-2011 | 12,250 | 79 | 0.996343419 | 12,205.21 |
| 31-Aug-2011 | (14,425) | 184 | 0.991504094 | (14,302.45) |
| 18-Nov-2011 | (9,950) | 263 | 0.987878579 | (9,829.39) |
| Average Capital Invested | | | | 124,750.42 |

---

[1] The XIRR function in Excel® produces an imprecise result (1.70693%) because it assumes a 365-day year. This presupposition is correct three quarters of the time, but, obviously, the year ended on February 29th had 366 days.

The formula for the present value factor is
$$PVF = \frac{1}{(1 + IRR_d)^{n/366}}$$
where $IRR_d$ is the daily internal rate of return and $n$ is the number of days out from the beginning of the period for each cash flow.

Average invested capital, as calculated above, is the *ex post* present value of the initial investment plus net interim cash flows. In other words, it is the present value *as of* the beginning of the measurement period, taking into account cash flows occurring throughout the period and using a discount rate that cannot be computed until the period ends. It is not a present value in the usual sense, not, that is, estimated to support prospective investment decision-making. It might rather be described as an imputed present value or a reconstruction of what the present value would have had to be in order to account for the results achieved.

Stefan Illmer suggests another approach for determining the average capital invested.[2] Given that the profit or loss on a portfolio is the ending market value minus the beginning market value minus the present value of interim cash flows, the average capital invested equals the profit or loss divided by the IRR. For Napper Tandy's portfolio, for instance, the profit is 126,885.71 – 124,750.42 = 2,135.29, and the average capital invested is 2,135.29/0.0171165 = 124,750.38.

There is, however, a certain circularity here, as the profit or loss is, in effect, defined as the ending market value less the average invested capital. In addition, the client, Tandy, undoubtedly sees his profit as the undiscounted amount of $2,260.71. Illmer's approach merely, albeit instructively, demonstrates the relationship between percentage and (discounted) monetary results.

In the paper cited, Illmer uses the profit or loss and the average invested capital, among other factors, in developing a money-weighted attribution methodology. He notes, however, that "the average invested capital of the total portfolio does not have to be equal to the sum of the average invested capitals of all asset classes." This may be a fatal flaw, and I don't have an intuitively satisfying explanation for it. Illmer remarks in a footnote, "This property is difficult to follow but is correct as it is based on the underlying reinvestment assumption of the IRR methodology." I

---

[2] Stefan Illmer, "Decomposing the Money-Weighted Rate of Return—An Update," *Journal of Performance Measurement*, Vol. 14, No. 1 (Fall 2009), 22-29.

unreservedly agree with the first part of that statement, right smack up to the word "but."

# About the Author

**Philip Lawton** has over 35 years of experience as an investment professional, chiefly at large banks and insurance companies. He was also the founding head of the Certificate in Investment Performance Measurement (CIPM®) program at CFA Institute. His areas of interest include business and investment strategy, leadership and ethics, regulatory compliance, financial and operational risk management, investment performance measurement, and managerial accounting.

Lawton earned the baccalaureate, licentiate, and doctorate degrees in Philosophy in the French-speaking section of the Catholic University of Louvain, Belgium, and an MBA degree with a concentration in Finance at Northeastern University. In addition to the professional designations of Certified Management Accountant (CMA) and Chartered Financial Analyst (CFA), he is Certified in Investment Performance Measurement (CIPM) and Certified in Strategy and Competitive Analysis (CSCA).

Lawton is the co-author of *The Top Ten Operational Risks: A Survival Guide for Investment Management Firms and Hedge Funds* (Stone House Consulting, 2010); the co-editor of *Investment Performance Measurement: Evaluating and Presenting Results* (Wiley, 2009); and the author of numerous articles and scholarly papers in philosophy and finance. He lives in Albemarle County, Virginia with his wife, née Dena Lange, and their dog, Chérie.

# About the Artist

**John Rubino** was born in New York City in 1952. His mother, a gifted sculptor and painter in her own right, shared her love of the arts with him from the time of his earliest memories. Learning to weld at age 10, he spent his free time building and sculpting while his friends played ball. At age 15, he showed his first works at Mari Galleries in New York.

After high school he spent a year at The Academy of Fine Arts in Florence (Italy). This was a definitive time for him, one that continues to influence his thinking. Following this experience, he enrolled at the University of Miami (Florida), and graduated with honors. Rubino is a N.C.B.D.C. Certified Professional Building Designer.

Throughout his career, sculptural form has predominated as Rubino's main interest, which he has explored through the mediums of jewelry, abstract and figurative sculpture, monumental sculpture, architectural design and functional structural sculpture. Rubino has designed, engineered and produced many of the custom tools and machines he uses in his specialized fabrication process.

In addition to Structural Sculpture, Rubino's current work involves portraits, expressive figures and abstract works. Pieces range in size from a few inches tall to larger than life or monumental. Most of Rubino's work is in steel, while some of his sculptures are in bronze. He is currently accepting commissions for new work.

+1.434.409.0532
john@rubinosculpture.com
www.rubinosculpture.com

Download Folio:
http://www.rubinosculpture.com/RubinoSculptureFolio.pdf

# Index of Names

www.ingramcontent.com/pod-product-compliance
Lightning Source LLC
Chambersburg PA
CBHW051305220526
45468CB00004B/1218